This b
latest
anoth
furthe,
made

A
BEARSKIN'S
CRIMEA

A BEARSKIN'S CRIMEA

Colonel Henry Percy VC
and his brother officers

Algernon Percy

LEO COOPER

First published in Great Britain in 2005 by
Leo Cooper
an imprint of
Pen & Sword Books Ltd
47 Church Street
Barnsley
South Yorkshire
S70 2AS

Copyright © Algernon Percy 2005

ISBN 1 84415 309 6

Typeset in 11/13 Sabon by
Phoenix Typesetting, Auldgirth, Dumfriesshire

Printed and bound in England by
CPI UK

Pen & Sword Books Ltd incorporates the imprints of Pen & Sword
Aviation, Pen & Sword Maritime, Pen & Sword Military, Wharncliffe
Local History, Pen & Sword Select, Pen & Sword Military Classics and
Leo Cooper.

For a complete list of Pen & Sword titles please contact
PEN & SWORD BOOKS LIMITED
47 Church Street, Barnsley, South Yorkshire, S70 2AS, England
E-mail: enquiries@pen-and-sword.co.uk
Website: www.pen-and-sword.co.uk

DEDICATED
TO THE MEMORY OF GEORGE,
9TH DUKE OF NORTHUMBERLAND,
LIEUTENANT, GRENADIER GUARDS.
KILLED IN ACTION, FLANDERS,
21 MAY 1940

Contents

Foreword by Patrick Mercer OBE, MP   ix

Acknowledgements   xi

Prologue   xiv

Introduction   xix

Maps   xxx

Chapter 1   Alma   1

Chapter 2   Balaklava   24

Chapter 3   Inkerman   48

Chapter 4   Aftermath   70

Chapter 5   Winter Siege   97

Chapter 6   Nurses and Hospitals   122

Chapter 7   1855: New Resolution   146

Chapter 8   Pyrrhic Victory   172

Epilogue   194

Appendix I: Postscript on the British Italian Legion   211

Appendix II: *The Gallant Grenadier*, by Harry Turner Esq.   217

References   223

Bibliography   230

Index   234

Foreword

by

Patrick Mercer OBE, MP

More than any other battlefield that I have visited, Inkerman remains unchanged. The broken hillside, gullies, low brush and, often, foggy weather makes it almost identical to the field over which Henry Percy charged in November 1854. The epicentre, though, of the battle was the once famous Sandbag Battery. It was here that Henry Percy fought alongside his Grenadiers and was wounded again whilst still recovering from the bullet through his sword arm that he received on 20 September at the Alma.

If you force your way through the thick, young fir you can still find the remains of the Battery. It is now a low earth bank with a couple of embrasures just evident, but if you scuff your boot along the ground buttons, buckles and even bits of broken bayonet are still there. Look a little further and human bones peep out of the grass. Just here Russians and Britons fought a medieval combat. The tide of killing swept back and forth throughout the day and in the middle of this mêlée was Percy.

I can't recommend this book too highly. Percy emerges as, above all else, a principled, determined young man who cared deeply for his soldiers and the honour of his Regiment. His courage was justly rewarded with one of the first Victoria Crosses, but his letters put flesh on his bones. Irascible, intolerant – certainly, but Percy leaps from these pages as a real Victorian who was able to brush off physical pain, hardship and danger. The incompetence of his leaders, however, is another matter. This hurts him more surely than any Muscovite blade.

In May 1940 another Percy charged another enemy on the other side of the continent. They may have been separated by time and geography, but the two young men could have been almost one. George, 9th Duke of Northumberland, died at the head of his platoon of Grenadiers in the desperate fighting before Dunkirk. At the time it was mooted that he would be awarded the Victoria Cross, but, in the event, one of his men, a young Nottinghamshire soldier, Lance Corporal Nicholls, gained the award. Whether George's courage was rewarded is irrelevant for I have no doubt that his forbear Henry was looking down with a quiet smile of satisfaction and family pride.

This book gives the real feel of the Crimea from the eyes of regimental officer. He knew little of the politics, the stratgey or the diplomacy. But he knew plenty about the fighting and the men of both sides who had to do it. I have learnt a huge amount from his splendid book.

Acknowledgements

First and foremost I must thank those who have provided me with my primary sources: most importantly the Duke of Northumberland for giving me unfettered access to Henry Percy's papers. In addition, the Earl of Leven and Melville, Lord Balgonie, Viscount Ridley, Sir Charles Fergusson Bt., Egerton Skipwith and Brioni Armitage have been as generous in their hospitality as they have been enthusiastic about allowing me to inspect their family artefacts. I am very grateful also to Clare Baxter and Colin Shrimpton of the archives department at Alnwick Castle, and I am indebted to Major General Bernard Gordon Lennox, Lieutenant Colonel Conway Seymour, the late Captain Mason and Majors Eastwood and Woodfield of the Grenadier Guards. Joan Soole, who helps the Grenadiers with their archives, has been incredibly tolerant of what must have seemed an endless quest by me to leave no stone unturned. Captain David Horn, curator of the Guards Museum, has also been most helpful. My thanks too to Alastair Massie of the National Army Museum for allowing me to include extracts from Cameron's and Hood's papers, and the staff there who have helped me – particularly Joanna Quill in their picture Library. I am also very grateful to the Countess of Derby and her father, Lord Braybrooke, for facilitating my enquiries into their forebears, the Neville brothers. In addition, Gareth Hughes of English Heritage, Kira Charatan of Cadogan Estates and Michael Springman have been very accommodating, as have been Staffordshire and Bedfordshire County Councils. My cousin Diana de Cabarrus did a fine job in assisting me ferret around in the National Newspaper Archives and the British Library for material on our mutual forbear. My step-sister, Jane Ridley, kindly corroborated the tentative information I had about Henry Percy's meetings with Queen Victoria and the Prince of Wales.

I am grateful to Christopher Hibbert for granting me permission to reproduce a passage from *The Destruction of Lord Raglan* (Longman 1961), and to Constable & Robinson Ltd for permission to quote from Hugh Small's *Florence Nightingale: Avenging Angel* (Constable 1998).

The illustrations for this book have come from a variety of sources. Plate 8 is reproduced with the kind permission of Lord Braybrooke and English Heritage. Plates 2, 11, 13, 14, 15, 16, 17, 18, 19, 21, 24, 30, 32, 33, 34 and 35 are reproduced by permission of the National Army Museum and plates 9, 12, 23, 29 and 31 are from the Gernsheim Collection, Harry Ransom Humanities Research Centre, the University of Texas at Austin. The picture on the front cover is by courtesy of the Grenadier Guards. It hangs in the conference room at Horse Guards and proved to be extremely difficult to photograph. Without the assistance of the photographer, Sergeant Michael Harvey, RLC, I would not have been able to reproduce it.

The original impetus for this book came from two visits to the Crimea in 2003. The first could not have happened without Giles Howson, who was then living in Kiev and who not only provided me with a reason for going to the Ukraine in the first place, but made my somewhat amateur first trip to the Crimea possible. Sir Julian Paget's advice and maps made the expedition all the more worthwhile, and without my companions, Charlotte Eagar and William and Natasha Ramsay, I might never have made it back! My second visit was entirely at the behest of Patrick Mercer, and organized by Ian Fletcher. With them I met Harry Turner, who has generously allowed me to reprint the poem 'The Gallant Grenadier' from his book, *Wrapped in Whirlwinds: Poems of the Crimean War* (Spellmount, 2005).

In my attempt to turn all this material into a publishable book, I have surely had more assistance than most authors can dream of. Colonel Oliver Lindsay, editor of *The Guards Magazine*, made some enormously helpful suggestions as regards publication. My friend Emma Kirby, having read my efforts at various stages, freely used her experience as a successful literary agent not only to point me down the right track, but to lead me all along the way. Matt Ridley has proved to be a good sounding-board. I am grateful to Brigadier Henry Wilson and Tom Hartman of Pen & Sword Books for being so receptive to my ideas.

Finally, I would like to thank my friends and family for their encouragement and support over the last year, with special mentions for Frances Osborne, Rachel Peppiatt, Harry and Alice Bott; my aunt, Elizabeth, Duchess of Hamilton (Henry Percy's closest living relative), Ralph and Jane, my cousin Katie and my brother Josceline.

Prologue

In the spring of 2003 I visited a friend who was at that time working for a defence company in Kiev. One might not immediately make the connection between this city and a peninsula on the Black Sea some four hundred miles further south, for the Crimea is more commonly associated with Russia than with the Ukraine. 80% of its population are ethnic Russian and the coastline around Yalta has always been famous as the holiday riviera of Moscow apparatchiks, under Tsars and Commissars alike. But under Stalin's policy of 'divide and rule', the Crimea was transferred to the Ukraine, and the Tartars, a Turkic people who had occupied the area since the thirteenth century but found themselves subject to an inexorable process of Russification when their new political masters arrived in 1783, were deported *en masse*.

My visit to the Crimea was largely opportunistic: it was clearly not every Englishman's top holiday destination, but I knew that it was an interesting and attractive region. I was also vaguely aware that a relative of mine had won the Victoria Cross in the Crimean War, and so resolved to go and have a look at *The Seat of War in the East*.*

Giles, my super-efficient ex-army officer friend, who speaks fluent Russian and Ukrainian, kindly arranged for me and my three companions to have at our disposal in Sebastopol 'staff' on the scale I that imagine Lord Raglan had. Giles was unable to accom-

* The title of William Simpson's book of lithographs, published by Colnaghi and Sons in 1855.

pany us, but he furnished us with an interpreter, a guide, a local historian and a driver. Having explained that we were interested in the Crimean War of 1854–56, but only wished to spend a day and a half in the area around Sebastopol - for we also wanted to visit the Woronzoff and Livadia palaces near Yalta, as well as the Massandra vineyards - we were taken on our first morning to the site of the Grenadier Guards' camp, four or five miles south of Sebastopol.

We trundled past small wooden dachas down a dirt track across the barren and stony soil that is typical of that region, until we reached what looked like yet another random scattering of rubbish in the middle of the countryside, sadly so common all around Sebastopol. It was indeed a refuse tip, though this particular one dated from the mid-1850s and was where the British Guards dumped their old bottles: mostly thick, dark-coloured and almost opaque remnants of porter bottles, with a few of the officers' more delicate wine bottles among them. There were hundreds of pieces of glass scattered about, and if one dug a little with bare hands one could find items almost completely intact. Here and there, in little clumps over a wider area, crocuses sprouted up, which we were told by Pasha, our historian, were planted by the British army officers outside their tents.

From that moment on, and before we had been anywhere near a battlefield, I was captivated by the idea of finding more evidence of the 1854–56 war and in discovering my forebear's part in it. Henry Percy was a younger son, and never married nor had any children; the memory of this distinguished soldier, whose portrait at Alnwick Castle shows him in general's uniform wearing the medals of the VC, KCB, Légion d'Honneur, etc., quickly faded with the passage of living memory at some point in the first half of the twentieth century. As far as his family in 2003 were concerned, he was simply one of the 1,354 names on the Victoria Cross register and the only hard evidence that he ever existed appeared to be the medal itself and the sword that he carried at the battle of Inkerman, which is displayed in the hall at Alnwick. As one of his nephews' great-grandsons, I resolved to put this right; his letters home from the Crimea and the correspondence he received from his family had not been looked at since my great-grandfather went through them cursorily and placed them in rough chronological order in 1904. No historian had ever seen them, but I found buried among them some treasures, such as a letter from Colonel Reynardson, commanding officer of the 3rd Battalion of the Grenadier Guards in the Crimea, describing the action at Inkerman, which had barely seen the light of day since it was passed on by the recipient at Horse Guards to Prince Albert, Colonel of the Regiment, and thence on to Henry's father, Lord Beverley, for his perusal.

A couple of months after returning from the Crimea in early April 2003, I dined with Patrick Mercer, the leading authority on the battle of Inkerman. By coincidence, he had been out in the Crimea the week after I had and encountered a Russian who told him that some lunatic Englishman had been seen wandering about the battlefield of Inkerman a few days previously, claiming to be descended from a holder of the Victoria Cross! To Patrick Mercer's great credit, on hearing the name Percy, he was immediately able to put this Russian's story into context, despite the fact that Henry Percy was only a company commander and played a relatively small part in the fortunes of a day that involved upwards of 60,000 men on the field of Inkerman.

Patrick kindly asked me to accompany him on an expedition to the Crimea which took place later that summer, at which time he took me to the site of the Sandbag Battery at Inkerman, scene of the heaviest fighting, and where Henry Percy displayed the gallantry which earned him his VC. When he originally traced its location in the late 1990s, he may have been the first Englishman to stand on that spot since the veterans themselves visited it in 1904. He must surely have been the first since the 1917 Revolution, a privilege for which he earned a spell in Sebastopol gaol, because the site is in a restricted military zone. In 2003 it was still necessary to take care to evade the plain-clothes military police who liked to trail our movements around Sebastopol and, once we had skulked into the thicket unseen, only a complicated mental rote involving compass bearings, step-counting and marked trees could take us to the small glade where so much blood had been spilt a century and a half before.

The genesis of this book lies in my first archaeological encounter at the Guards' camp, and the resultant more poignant, even grue-some, discoveries made with Patrick Mercer at the Sandbag Battery later that year; and through the good fortune of having access to Henry Percy's letters I hope that I have been able to convey a sense of the astonishing bravery and fortitude which he and his brother officers of the Grenadier Guards displayed, and their families endured, during the war with Russia, 1854–56.

Introduction

After leaving Eton the Hon Henry Hugh Manvers Percy secured an Ensigncy in the Grenadier Guards, a month before his nineteenth birthday in July 1836. The army was a natural occupation for a younger son of the 2nd Earl of Beverley and the Percies had long been a military family. Henry's eldest brother, Algernon, Lord Lovaine, was already a Lieutenant in the Grenadiers. Uncles William and Josceline served with distinction in the Royal Navy, both becoming Admirals. Uncle Francis had been a Captain in the 23rd Regiment of Foot (Royal Welch Fusiliers) during the Peninsular War, where he died in the retreat before Corunna in 1809. But of all his relatives, Henry was most anxious to follow in the footsteps of his Uncle Henry, who had served as General Sir John Moore's Aide de Camp (ADC) in the Peninsula* and then as one of the Duke of Wellington's ADCs. As a child, the young Henry had often seen the bloodstained coat worn by his uncle at Waterloo, which was kept at the family house in London, No. 8 Portman Square, and with it the lady's velvet sachet given to the ADC as a keepsake seventy-two hours previously at the Duchess of Richmond's ball, in which Uncle Henry had brought back to London Wellington's famous despatch announcing Napoleon's defeat. The young Henry was greatly interested in, and proud of, his family's history and later it would be entirely at his suggestion

---

*Captain the Hon Henry Percy, 14th (the Duchess of York's Own) Regiment of (Light) Dragoons, was standing beside Moore when he was mortally wounded at Corunna, and comforted him during his last minutes that night.

that his friend from Crimean days, Edward Barrington de Fonblanque, wrote the *Annals of the House of Percy*, published in 1887.

Although Henry's father was heir to his childless first cousin, Algernon, 4th Duke of Northumberland, this side of the family was a junior branch. The 1st Lord Beverley had been a younger son of the 1st Duke of Northumberland and made his own way in life, becoming a minister in Pitt's Government and then a prisoner in France (where he remained for many years, serving his country by refusing Napoleon's offer to exchange him for two French generals).[1]* They lived a great deal more modestly than their cousin, whose estates in the north extended to 180,000 acres and who had no difficulty in financing from his prodigious coal-related revenues expensive projects at Alnwick Castle and his two great houses in London, Northumberland House in Trafalgar Square and Syon House in Brentford.

Both Lord Lovaine and his brother Henry had purchased their Ensigncies in the Grenadiers. Until the Cardwell reforms of the 1870s recruitment to the army operated on an arcane system dating back to the reign of Charles II, largely requiring officers to purchase their first commissions, with further payments for each step up in rank to Lieutenant Colonel, beyond which promotion incurred no cost. In peacetime about two-thirds of commissions were obtained in this way, the remainder being given out, for example to successful Sandhurst cadets or non-commissioned officers as a reward for long or distinguished service. In wartime the situation was inevitably more fluid and in 1855, at the height of the Crimean War, only twenty-seven per cent of commissions were obtained through purchase.[2]

Normally, however, a fee had to be paid with each step up in rank: the face value of this could be substantial and, depending on the circumstances, the market often dictated that an unofficial premium had to be paid to the seller. The cost of a commission was highest in the three Guards regiments (the Grenadiers, the Coldstream and the Scots Fusiliers), which were at the top of the infantry's hierarchy and took precedence over the Line regiments.

* See Reference Notes, p. 223

According to the Regulations, the cumulative cost of a Lieutenant Colonelcy in a Guards regiment at this time was £9,000, as compared with £4,500 for an officer of the Line; however, a Royal Commission established in 1856 to look at the Purchase System found that, in practice, commissions were often changing hands for twice the regulation amount. For example, the actual cost of a Lieutenant Colonelcy in the Guards was typically more like £13,000,[3] equivalent to nearly £1,000,000 in today's money. Although this would not all have been paid in one lump sum, as it would take many years to graduate all the steps up to Lieutenant Colonel and most officers would put money aside long in advance of their next promotion, it was by any standards an enormous outlay. Furthermore, not only did Guards officers typically have to pay much more for their commissions than did officers in regiments of the Line, but they also received a lower allowance for their board and lodging expenses.[4] In view of all this, it is not surprising that the officer class in the Guards regiments contained an unusually high proportion of aristocratic and wealthy families.

Though it may seem extraordinary, the sale of commissions was in fact a convenient way to finance the army, for an officer's pay, once he had financed the cost of his uniform, board, lodging etc., and taken into account the interest on his capital outlay, amounted to virtually nothing. Shortly after the Crimean War, E. B. de Fonblanque* published an analysis of the Purchase System showing that the capital outlay attendant upon each step-up in rank increased at a faster rate than the incremental rise in salary, such that a Lieutenant Colonel effectively had to pay a significant annual sum 'for the privilege of serving Her Majesty'.[5] Until June 1854 colonels of regiments were also responsible for providing their men's uniforms; at the extreme, Lord Cardigan was said to spend £10,000 per annum (about £750,000 in today's money) on extravagant outfits for his regiment. The Purchase System also encouraged good behaviour, for an officer who was cashiered could lose his commission and its attendant capital, and it

---

* Edward Barrington de Fonblanque (1821–1895), civil servant and diplomat. He was a prolific author – on subjects as diverse as history (including *The Annals of the House of Percy*), biography, Japan and a children's fairy story.

encouraged an officer's pride in his command, as commissions in poorly regarded regiments were less easy to sell. Nor did the system mean that affluent young men could secure themselves seniority in rank simply by writing a cheque. Certainly, it helped to be rich if one wanted to get on in the army, but promotion was still chiefly dependent on length of service and in peacetime officers climbed their way up the ladder slowly. The possibility of a step up in rank depended upon availability and in a desirable regiment vacancies were few and far between.

Lord Lovaine (who *Vanity Fair*[6] uncharitably said, 'offered his party a support that was always quite certain, yet never very valuable') defended the Purchase System vigorously as a Tory backbencher when it was debated in the House of Commons in March 1855.* He made the point that the system of promotions in England could not be compared with that prevailing in continental armies, which were largely run on the basis of conscription. Despite the fact that French army officers nominally gained their commissions through merit rather than purchase, he observed, there was as much, if not more, disquiet within the French ranks about the injustices of promotion through political favouritism etc. as there was in the British Army. He went on to say that 'the officers in the Crimea to whom blame has been attributed were those who did not obtain promotion by the system of purchase, for they were the officers of the Medical and Commissariat Departments. "Oh," it was said, "no wonder the Commissariat has broken down, for the Government make the appointments, and they trust to their own nominees." But would not the same complaint be made with respect to the army generally, if all the promotions were in the hands of the Government?'[7]

Lovaine blamed the failings of the Commissariat on its 'being almost annihilated by the parsimonious economies of late years, and that when officers were required for the Crimea, only one old man could be found who was at all acquainted with the routine duties of the service, the details of which were necessarily entrusted to new and inexperienced hands.'[8] He was making an important point, which is perhaps easier to understand when one considers

* Lord Lovaine, as 6th Duke of Northumberland, eventually served in Mr Disraeli's cabinet as Lord Privy Seal 1878–80.

that the Commissariat, which took charge of supplies, and in theory transport for the army, was not controlled by the military at all, as it was a department of the Treasury. Nor was the Medical Department controlled by the army. As Fonblanque, who had himself been a Commissariat officer in the Crimea, observed in 1858:

> There is no distinct definition of duties, division of labour, or concentration of energy . . . . During the late war, it was no uncommon thing to find several financial agents, each accountable to a distinct head, bidding against one another in the money market, or competing for supplies destined for the same object. . . . Unity of action became impossible – no man knew where his duties commenced, or his responsibilities ceased – contradicting orders – conflicting interests – official jealousies, increased a confusion which concentrated in the headquarters of our army, rendered Balaklava and Chaos convertible terms, and formed a chapter in the history of the war which may instruct, but can never edify future generations.[9]

So, having committed himself to the service of this peculiar institution, in 1838 Percy was sent with his Regiment to deal with the insurrection in Canada. Although this had subsided by the time he arrived and he never saw action, the four years he spent there gave him a good grounding in the trials of poor accommodation and severe weather. The period from the Grenadiers' return from Canada in 1842 until the outbreak of the Crimean War in 1854 was uneventful for the Regiment, but Henry Percy remained a dedicated soldier, as well as an ambitious officer. In the early 1850s he and a brother officer, Colonel F. W. Hamilton, were responsible for selecting the Aldershot Heath and its surrounding area as the new training ground for the army. He was interested in the art of musketry and wrote a book called *Brigade Movements*, copies of which were well received by assorted Generals, right up to Prince Albert. However, in 1854, he was still only 'Captain and Lieutenant Colonel'. Regimental officers in the Guards who had purchased their commissions held an army rank a step ahead of their regimental rank; this was perhaps some compensation for the fact that advancement within the Guards was apt to be slower than it was in many other regiments, because these commissions were tightly held. So although Percy had done eighteen years' service, he was really only in the position of a company commander (i.e. in charge of a hundred or so men). Lovaine argued that without senior officers being able to sell their commissions, younger men would have even fewer opportunities of securing advancement. Whatever the rights and wrongs of the Purchase System, it was still thoroughly frustrating for an up and coming career officer to have to wait so long for promotion.

Not caring greatly for London society, Henry preferred to spend his spare time travelling alone and pursuing his interest in languages. In the 1840s he found the time to tour all over Europe and the Middle East, where he became competent in Turkish and Arabic, in addition to the major European languages. As a rather cantankerous general in later life, one of his pet subjects was the importance of learning languages from an early age. He advocated that a system of examinations should be instituted specifically for the military, so that soldiers would be encouraged to gain additional qualifications, and study 'any language they fancy, for it may turn out to be useful, and they should get credit for it'. Even knowledge of the most unlikely language, he said, could prove invaluable to the country.

By 1854, in spite of the long peace, he was no stranger to the physical discomfort that would come with an extended campaign overseas. He was apt to gloss over the perpetual cold and wet in his letters home from the Crimea, often brushing off his own personal discomfort with a wry comment, such as, 'I have got so accustomed to living in a tent that when I come home I shall pitch one in Portman Square. I shall not be able to breathe in a house!' Being essentially a loner, however, lack of personal space was more of a trial: 'I don't mind bivouacking, but I don't like being five or six in a tent at all.'

He counted among his friends a wide variety of people from various nationalities, but was not 'clubbable' in any way and had no time for pompous and dandyish cavalry officers, regarding with disdain those who he felt had been promoted because of their aristocratic or Whig connections. Indeed, he was apt to be somewhat fractious with his fellow men, as the following extract from a letter home written in May 1854 by a subaltern in his company, William Cameron, shows:

I had a row with my Capt. and Lt Col. of my Company the other day. He's always quarrelling . . . . I am sorry, however, as we have always been friends and he is one of the cleverest officers out here. He is eligible for any appointment but makes himself so generally disagreeable that his relations, though the highest in the land, are not much inclined to do anything for him. He had a narrow escape from being the Duke of Northumberland,* only his brother most unexpectedly married the other day. I mentioned his name (Percy) I think in my last letter.[10]

He could indeed make himself disagreeable, but, as this letter implies, he earned forgiveness and understanding from his friends and they gained his loyalty in return. Furthermore, although his no-nonsense attitude may have been at times intimidating, it did command respect. A few years after the Crimean War the Queen and the Prince Consort paid a visit to the Grenadiers on a field day in Ireland. Percy was by this time in command of the 1st Battalion and had been given special charge of the Prince of Wales, who was a junior officer in the Regiment. Queen Victoria and Prince Albert were thoroughly impressed with the Colonel's treatment of their eldest son; he was the only man in the whole of the army to treat the Prince of Wales just like any other officer and give him proper jobs to do – 'and yet Bertie likes him very much', Prince Albert recorded in his diary.[11]

He may not always have got on well with his fellow officers, but he was kind to his men. Their respect for him showed itself at the battles of the Alma and Inkerman, when on three separate very difficult occasions they followed him into the teeth of adversity. He was meticulous about writing to the families of those who had been killed and generous to the widows and orphans of the men in his company; he was a significant benefactor to charities in later life.

It is obviously dangerous to try to characterize someone four generations back whom one never met, yet one does get a sense from his letters that all the bravado hides a certain vulnerability. At times supreme self-confidence is combined with a mental anguish verging on paranoia. His dealings with women were very

* Cameron is exaggerating: by 1854 Henry was only seventh in line to the Dukedom, having two elder brothers, both of whom already had sons.

much at arm's length and he never married. Notwithstanding this, he may not have been as immune to sentimentality in that department as he would perhaps have had the wider world believe. Ironically, on his journey out to the East, when Great Britain's declaration of war with Russia was only days away, he stayed in Paris with a friend who had married a Russian princess. Henry's letters home to his family were apt to be, whatever the subject matter, thoroughly unsentimental and he was teased even by his own family for this trait; the only time he displays any weakness for the fairer sex is on writing to his father with a description of this Russian lady:

> I put up at Paris in the house of a friend who married a Russian Princess Lobanoff-Rostoff – a little clever piquante woman, very agreeable, pleasant and convivial and with whom I got on easily. She was very Russian, of course, and talked so much more clearly, sensibly and moderately than anyone else I have heard on the business that I could not help telling her on my departure that it was lucky I could not stop, as they thought I was going to do, three days, as she would have *ébranlé mes* convictions a little. She was very nice, and as my friend was once a brother officer of mine, put herself quite on a footing of camaraderie and good humour. Everybody but me seems to marry a nice wife without having more physical, or apparently more moral advantages than me. *C'est désesperant.*
>
> She has to renounce Russia and to sell her property within a year for having married an Englishman – a piece of absurdity I think – for after all, an admixture of English blood could not damage the Tartar. She thought the Emperor dreadfully ill-used by us and France.

Percy's letters home from the Crimea are different in tone from those of his contemporaries who have had their letters and memoirs published during the course of the last 150 years. In truth, he does not write as well as many other officers did and his correspondence, although voluminous, tends to be quite disjointed. The usual complaints are, of course, expressed: the progress of the war, the failings of the generals, the sufferings of the men, the lack of supplies, the appalling medical arrangements, the lack of promotion for regimental officers etc., etc. But there are few blow-by-blow accounts of action and there is little detailed description of day-to-day conditions, although there are some gems of observation, sometimes in dry, almost black humour. There is never any longing for a spell of leave: the over-riding concern of all his correspondence is for a more effective prosecution of the war effort. Indeed, when he was invalided home in January 1855, he could not wait to get back to the Crimea and almost bribed the doctors to give him the 'all clear' to return to the front. Even when peace was in the offing during the winter of 1855–56, and after all the suffering, of which he had certainly had his fair share, Henry, unlike many of his contemporaries, wanted the war to continue. He could not bear the thought of a peace bought about by stalemate: unfinished business meant wasted lives.

He was not really interested in politics, despite the fact that his two elder brothers were MPs, as was his father before he succeeded to the Earldom. Nonetheless, he was a Tory by nature and, as regards foreign policy, a fairly jingoistic one at that. He was a firm believer in a pre-emptive war against Russia and despised the weakness of those who would have peace at any price, to the point of sometimes privately referring to the near-pacifist Prime Minister Lord Aberdeen as 'Aberdeenovitch'. But his attitude to foreigners was no stereotype of the Victorian imperialist and in the 1865 general election he campaigned on the basis that 'the horrors of war . . . [are] most certain to be averted by a prudent abstinence from interference in the internal affairs of other nations'.[12] As a younger man, he may have advocated gunboat diplomacy, but he did not display racial prejudice on the scale of most of his contemporaries, typified by Lord Palmerston, who said in 1850, 'Half-civilised governments, such as those of China, Portugal, Spanish America, all require a dressing down every eight or ten years to keep them in order'.[13] Against the grain, for they were constantly cursed as ignorant and barbarous by their allies throughout the Crimean war, Henry Percy loved the Turkish people. His attitude to the French, too, was not what one might have expected from an English army officer whose commander, Lord Raglan, had lost his arm at Waterloo and in the Crimean War frequently referred inadvertently to his French allies as '*l'ennemi*'. For his part, Henry was particularly fond of the Zouaves, the French North African troops.

The Crimean War broke out between the Ottoman Empire and

Russia on 5 October 1853 following the Russian invasion of Moldavia and Wallachia, then nominally part of the Ottoman Empire (and now part of Romania). The Russian pretext for waging war against Turkey was the supposed necessity of protecting orthodox Christians living in the Ottoman Empire from persecution by their Muslim masters. For two years the argument between Orthodox monks and the Roman Catholic church over the guardianship of the Holy Places in Palestine had been a running sore between Russia and the Catholic church, and the Ottomans were caught in the middle. In reality, however, Tsar Nicholas I was pursuing an unashamedly expansionist policy: that of putting what he called 'the sick man of Europe' – i.e. the Sultan – out of his misery and annexing Constantinople and the Dardanelles, thereby securing an outlet to the Mediterranean for the Black Sea fleet. There was little reason for the Tsar to suppose that he could not succeed in this goal: the Porte had been in decline for years, soured from within by corruption and weakness, and pressed from without by surging nationalism. Russia was continuing where she had left off before: there had been six Russo-Turkish wars since 1710. In 1812 Russia annexed Bessarabia and in 1829 she backed her Greek Orthodox cousins in their bid for independence, thereby securing territorial gains at the expense of the Turkish Empire in the Balkans and the Caucasus.

The Tsar miscalculated terribly in thinking that Britain and France would stand idly by. There was no love lost between Napoleon III and Nicholas: the latter regarded the former as a jumped-up impostor, ruling over a country filled with revolutionaries. Napoleon III, for his part, saw a chance to woo the Catholic church in the dispute over the Holy Places, and was keen to emulate the military glory of his uncle. Great Britain had been at peace since 1815 and Lord Aberdeen, whose abhorrence of warfare stemmed from his presence at the Battle of the Nations at Leipzig in 1813, desperately wanted to keep it that way, in consequence of which the diplomatic chatter between London and St Petersburg led the Tsar to believe that he could push his luck.

The position changed dramatically after 30 November 1853 when a Turkish fleet at the port of Sinope, carrying supplies to the Caucasus front, was demolished by the Russian navy, which had been sent out from Sebastopol, only 100 miles across the Black Sea.

Within the course of an hour, the whole flotilla had been destroyed, including one British-registered transport ship, and the town itself was ablaze. Several thousand Turkish sailors were killed. In as much as this action occurred nearly two months after war had been declared and it was one naval force against another, it was a 'fair' fight; the Russian victory was largely attributable to its novel use of exploding shells.

John Bull, however, fuelled by stories of helpless sailors being gunned in the water, saw the Battle of Sinope as an outrageous massacre of innocent Turks by belligerent Russians. This public clamour, combined with the fact that Great Britain had long been the effective guarantor of Turkey's sovereignty, forced Aberdeen's Whig government to take Britain into the war on 28 March of the following year. France declared war on Russia on the same day. Ultimately, Britain's interests were in preserving the balance of power in Europe (the sub-text being that any aggression on the part of Russia in the East could affect India) and in countering the threat of a resurgent Russian navy in the Mediterranean. It was therefore necessary to despatch a task force to destroy Sebastopol, the Russian naval base in the Crimea.

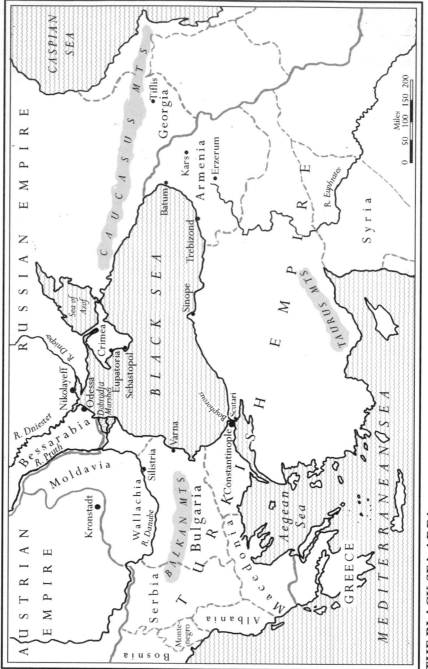

THE BLACK SEA AREA

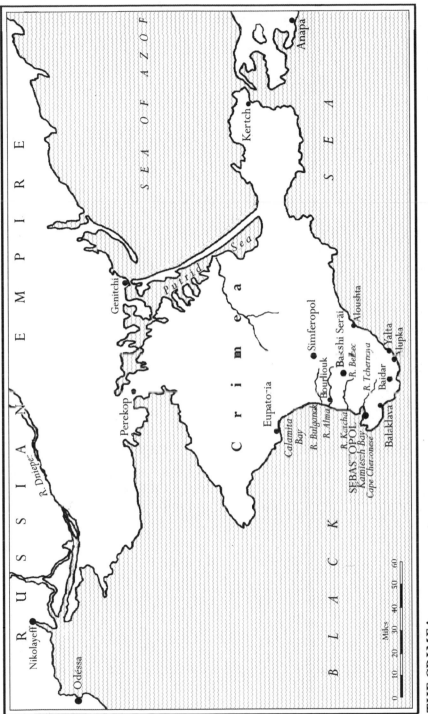

THE CRIMEA

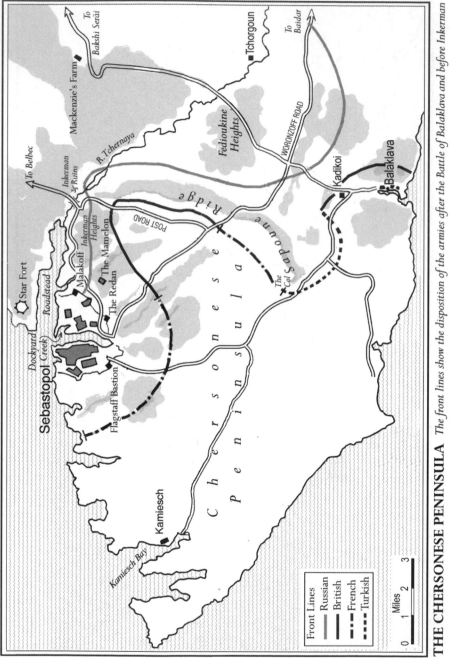

THE CHERSONESE PENINSULA *The front lines show the disposition of the armies after the Battle of Balaklava and before Inkerman*

Front Lines

Russian
British
French
Turkish

Miles
0   1   2   3

To Bakshi Seraï
Mackenzie's Farm
Tchorgoun
To Baidar
R. Tchernaya
Fedioukine Heights
WORONZOFF ROAD
To Belbec
Inkerman & Ruins
Kadikoi
Balaklava
Star Fort
Malakoff
Inkerman Heights
The Mamelon
Sapoune Ridge
POST ROAD
The Col
Dockyard
Roadstead
Sebastopol Creek
The Redan
Flagstaff Bastion
Chersonese Peninsula
Kamiesch
Kamiesch Bay

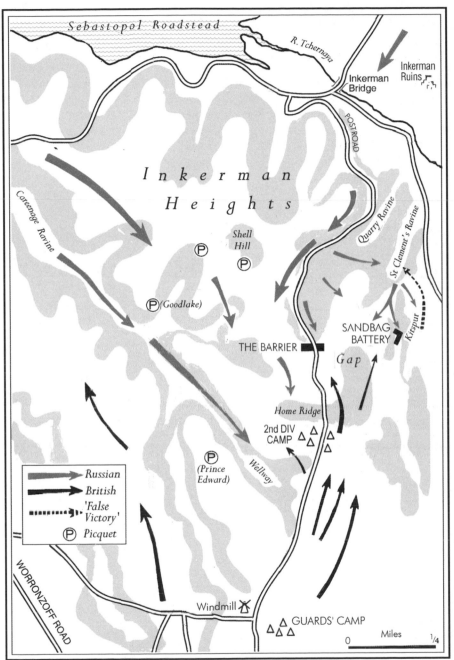

Sebastopol Roadstead

R. Tchernaya

Inkerman Bridge

Inkerman Ruins

Inkerman Heights

POST ROAD

Careenage Ravine

Shell Hill

Quarry Ravine

St Clement's Ravine

Ⓟ

Ⓟ

Ⓟ *(Goodlake)*

Kitspur

SANDBAG BATTERY

THE BARRIER

Gap

Home Ridge

2nd DIV CAMP

△ △
△ △
  △

Ⓟ
(Prince Edward)

Wellway

	Russian
	British
	'False Victory'
Ⓟ	Picquet

WORRONZOFF ROAD

Windmill ⚙

△ GUARDS' CAMP
△ △
△ △

0   Miles   ¼

THE BATTLE OF INKERMAN, 5 NOVEMBER 1854
Early morning, before the arrival of French troops

Chapter 1

Alma

On 22 February 1854, long before dawn, the Guards left their barracks at Horse Guards. As they marched along the Strand at five in the morning to catch their train from Waterloo station, windows opened up and down the street and figures still in their night dresses waved their handkerchiefs. In spite of the hour, thoroughfares all along the route spontaneously filled with crowds and the police had difficulty in restraining the bounding enthusiasm of well-wishers wanting to shake the hands of their departing heroes one last time.[1]

The Grenadiers were seen off at Southampton later that morning by their Colonel, HRH Prince Albert. But behind the impeccable turnout of the Guards, in their red coats and black bearskins, there were early signs of the difficulties that would plague the army for the ensuing two years. For a start, the Grenadiers found that the *Ripon*, a P & O paddle-steamer allotted to them by the various officials organizing this great embarkation, could not possibly take the whole battalion. The adjutant considered that these bureaucrats must have been 'ignorant or unaware of the bulky proportions and special equipment of our men'. Perhaps, not unnaturally, they did not appreciate either that, in the carnival atmosphere, some would be bringing their wives with them – not always with permission – though a few men persuaded their officers that spouses could be employed as regimental laundresses. In the event another small steamer, the *Manilla*, was found to take two companies; it was, however, so slow that the two halves of the battalion did not see each other for three weeks. *Manilla*'s engine was, according to one of the officers who found himself consigned to her, 'only three or four donkey-power, instead of the sixty horse-power she professed to possess, which was little enough at best'.[2]

On the larger ship was Lieutenant Colonel the Hon George Cadogan, Henry Percy's greatest friend among his brother officers in the Grenadiers, who composed a song as they wiled away the time on board; one of its verses was:

> Southampton Docks are reached at last,
> Our stout and gallant band
> Have trod the deck that wafts them from
> Their native British land.
> One more 'Hurrah!' The anchor's up,
> And now our ship so brave,
> As conscious of her gallant freight,
> Stems high the ocean wave.
>> But our Gren-a-dier
>> Feels a-leetle-queer,
>> For he really had no notion
>> Of the ocean's funny motion;
>> But 'Hurrah!' cries he,
>> 'Guardsmen bold are we,
>> And proud, I ween,
>> To serve the Queen
>> By land or sea.'[3]

After a long voyage and a stopover in Malta involving numerous disappointments (such as still not receiving their new Minié rifles), by late April they were steaming up the Aegean sea in the SS *Golden Fleece*, the Old Etonians among them, including Henry Percy, George Higginson, George Cadogan and Henry Neville, mobbing each other as to how many times each was 'reported' for not knowing the ancient and modern names of the islands they passed.

Six weeks encamped at Scutari, on the eastern side of the Bosphorus from Constantinople, saw the Miniés arrive, but little else, so there was much moaning and groaning about the in-efficiencies of the Commissariat. In target practice the Miniés were found to be highly efficient rifles, but they were still muzzle-loaders and Henry Percy noted that they weren't as good in rapid fire as the old-fashioned muskets because the cartridges' grease lubricant tended to dry out, which made reloading rather an effort.

In mid-June the situation in the Balkans required the British Army to join its French allies at Varna in Bulgaria. From then on conditions deteriorated rapidly. Varna was stiflingly hot: in July Henry recorded the thermometer reaching 109° in the shade and the authorities had not thought sufficiently about securing an adequate supply of clean water. Accordingly, cholera was beginning to affect both armies; the French suffered more than the British, especially after they sent a force of 10,000 men to the Dobrudja marshes in pursuit of the Russians, who had withdrawn from the occupied territories of Moldavia and Wallachia, their siege of the Turkish army at Silistria having failed towards the end of June. During the month of August the Grenadiers were losing about one man a day to cholera, fever and dysentery; the company officers, who understood that cholera was not contagious, made every effort to nurse their men as best they could, but four Grenadier officers were invalided home before they got to the Crimea. Ominously also, no one was able to secure enough horses for the cavalry, let alone pack animals to enable the Commissariat to supply an invasion force.

The two months in Varna represented a deeply trying period for the army, all the frustrations attendant upon an expeditionary force on campaign 1,400 miles from home being coupled with no apparent prospect of action against the enemy. There were few amusements to occupy this dreary time, but the soldiers fraternized merrily enough with their French counterparts. Some of the officers organized quail and hare shoots on the grassy plains. One party went out in search of some specimens for Captain Tipping's collection and were delighted when they bagged a brace of bee-eaters and a hoopoe.[4] At least they no longer had the temptations of Constantinople to resist: Captain William Cameron was glad to get away from the city because the luxuries favoured by his three messmates, Lord Balgonie, Sir Charles Russell and the Hon Henry Percy, were expensive and he had found it hard to keep up with them when they were at Scutari. Even so, while the market place at Varna was a fairly spartan affair, largely consisting of tempo-rary shops set up by the French, there was still enough to tempt the

3

occasional visit. Lieutenant Sir James Fergusson recorded going on one such foraging expedition with Percy: they each managed to have a bath and procure some cigars from the steamer *Hydaspes* – two comforts which were then somewhat negated by their being thoroughly drenched by a thunderstorm before they got back to camp.[5]

There was plenty of time also for social calls to the camps of other regiments. Henry Neville's brother, Grey, was in the cavalry's Heavy Brigade, and found time to visit his sibling on a number of occasions, in the knowledge that his brother's company commander, Henry Percy, was an old family friend.

Some temporary relief from the listlessness of that summer near Varna came to Colonel F.W. Hamilton and Lieutenant Colonel Percy when they were granted a week's leave by Lord Raglan, Commander-in-Chief of the British expeditionary force. A few officers could be spared from each Brigade as transports were not ready for the conveyance of the armies to their next destination and the enemy appeared to have disappeared from the banks of the Danube. The two Grenadiers decided to explore the interior of Bulgaria and see if they could gather more information about the movement of the Russian army across the Danube. Apart from a couple of half-hearted volleys fired at them from across the river, their sortie was uneventful and they finished up at Silistria; here the two men examined the Turkish defences and acquired much practical information about the country.[6]

While Percy was away there were some changes going on in his company. Cameron, the junior subaltern, clearly wasn't fitting in, so he was transferred to another company. This left a coveted vacancy, as the 8th Company was a light company, whose training emphasized skirmishing and marksmanship, and in the event of hostilities could form part of a special light battalion, of which Percy would be second-in-command. Sir James Fergusson was an ambitious and able young officer; back in Malta he had recorded in his journal how he found his existing company rather frustrating: 'the company are dirty and not very smart, and I cannot do as much as I could if I were captain to improve it. I do not care much for any of my brother company officers, which is a bore, as I have to be so much with them.' At Varna Sir James, who was only 22, had a private chat with the adjutant, Captain

Higginson, about his career, which he believed was being hindered by the attitude of senior officers, some of whom he felt had 'slighted' him. The kindly adjutant reassured him that all junior officers feel like that on occasion and that he shouldn't worry: his turn would come.

It duly did, and on 20 July Fergusson reported in his journal:

I went on fatigue early with 100 men to build the Engineer's store at the wharf by the lake. It was slow work enough and the men worked lazily. When I got home at 12 o'clock the C.O. [Colonel Hood] sent for me and offered me the vacant place in the 8th Company, Percy having got rid of Cameron, and Munro who was to be appointed, being to go home on sick leave. I asked leave to consider it for an hour, which he granted, as I did not feel sure about all the arrangements. On the one hand I felt a delicacy in speaking to Cox about leaving him, and I had to see if Russell and Balgonie would take me into their mess. While I was thinking how I should break it to him, Cox came to my tent, and told me he knew of it, and advised me not to be prevented by personal feelings from taking it, if I thought it for my advantage. I went to Col. Hood and asked his advice, and he gave it most strongly for taking it; saying very handsomely that he thought it due to me to offer it to me for my attention to my duty and activity in doing adjutant's duty etc., and that if there was active service the Light Battalion, into which the light companies of the Brigade are formed, would have the most of it, mentioning the case of Hougoumont, which was held by the light companies of the Guards. I could not hesitate after this, and thanked him for it. Russell and Balgonie are quite happy to have me, and Cameron being appointed to the 1st Company, we shall just change messes.[7]

Percy's company now found stability, and as long as they continued on active service, Henry Neville and Jim Fergusson remained with him as his two Lieutenants.

Aug 18th
About 6 miles from Varna

My dear Father,

Here we are encamped on the hills opposite Varna on the South side of the bay, with a fine view of the sea and a fresh breeze but little water – a great inconvenience where one perspires freely. The air in the plain of Varna is terribly hot. We passed one night there;

indeed the whole place is *empesté* by the dead cattle and horses which the Turks leave always to be gradually sublimed . . . .

We are getting better: cholera has ceased with <u>us</u>, but came out in the Coldstreams and Scots Fusilier Guards. The story is that they had been previously exempt, nearly. We have lost 30. The 93rd and 79th are very bad, and the Light Division were reported unfit to march, their men were so weakened – but the mere idea of Sebastopol will brush them up. Our embarkation is delayed, if not I fear postponed altogether by the cholera which has appeared in the fleet. HMS *Britannia* lost 50 in one day. The French are worse. Excuse my writing – my knee is not a good table. A 1,000 thanks for the cushions – they have not come yet.

Your most affectionate son,

H. Percy

P.S. It will be horrible if we don't go to Sebastopol . . . . I forgot to tell you that Varna was more than half burnt down the other day – nobody's doing. The Commissariat stores were burnt with all the barley, consequently our horses are almost starving. It would have been easy to dispatch a steamer to Constantinople to get some, but they don't seem to care about it much in the Commissariat. Having marched us up here they have discovered we have hardly enough water for the number of men.

The withdrawal of Russia from the Danubian principalities did not, as might have been expected, end the war. The view in London and Paris was that a huge expeditionary force had been sent out to assist the Turks in avenging the massacre at Sinope; it had taken nearly six months to get a total force of about 60,000 French, English and Turks to the Danube theatre of war. They were not going to go home without finishing the job and ensuring that Russian power in the east was curtailed for good. In any case, by August the war was well under way in other theatres: the Russians were attacking the Turks in the Caucasus; the British Navy had captured Bomarsund in the Baltic Sea, bombarded Kola on the Barents Sea and launched an abortive expedition to Petropaulovsk in the Far East. So, although the allied army in the Balkans had experienced something of a 'phoney war' for several months, there was no going back. They were certainly going to attack either Odessa or Sebastopol, or both; and whilst plans were vague, they knew they would embark sooner rather than later, as any strike against the Russian mainland would have to take place well in advance of the winter.

Aug 22nd
Near Varna

My dear Father,

Lord Raglan is very well and very civil and good humoured. I see him sometimes and like him very much. He is so accessible and amiable. The French officers are very fond of him. He follows the Duke's principle of dead silence upon his plans. Everything Lord Raglan does for the troops is marked with the greatest tenderness and consideration, but is generally annulled by the inefficiency or pomposity of his subordinates.

We are to have the first coats which the Queen writes to Prince Edward* are both comfortable, and she says 'you will find becoming'. If she has tried her hand at it, I dare say they will be: a woman is sure to have good taste – not so, the Prince. If they are comfortable, well, the look is nothing. We find our dress hideous and most uncomfortable, and they seldom allow us to wear our blue coats, our only comfortable dress.

The conduct of the soldiers still continues in the highest degree. Exemplary – hardly ever a trivial offence. I suppose there never was so well behaved an army turned out. We are not very well off here for water. The luxuries of eggs, milk etc. are nearly unobtainable. In other respects there is nothing to complain of. The French have set up shops where one may get minor luxuries.

I hope you are quite well. My love to everybody. Tell Isabel† I got her letter and will answer when I get more matter. I am glad the dresses gave satisfaction. Being now able to jabber Turkish with ease, I am going to learn Russian.

Believe me, my dear Father, your most affectionate
H. Percy

The reference to Lord Raglan reflects the prevailing view among all the troops at the beginning of the campaign. With hindsight, he was probably not the most suitable candidate to command a potentially long and arduous expedition to a far-away country. At the age of sixty-six, and having lost an arm at Waterloo, he was

---

* HH Prince Edward of Saxe-Weimar was a Captain in the Grenadiers.
† Henry's first cousin, Isabel Greatheed-Bertie-Percy (1834–1891).

hardly a man in his physical prime. Moreover, while he had justifiably been the Duke of Wellington's clear favourite and his indispensable right-hand man in old age, Lord Raglan had essentially been confined to a desk job for the last thirty-nine years. Nevertheless, he was a diligent and thorough worker, whose kindly manner and impeccable politeness made him universally popular with men and officers alike; throughout the war he would continue to display total loyalty to his immediate subordinates in the face of insistent pressure to the contrary. He hated publicity and his modesty was apt to make him painfully embarrassed by public praise or adulation, and on active service he much preferred to wear drab civilian clothes, often wandering about the camps virtually incognito. The geographic separation from his political masters at home and the uneasy relationship that Britain had with her French and Turkish allies meant the burden placed upon his shoulders was not an easy one to bear.

In any event, after a lot of, in Henry's words, 'shilly-shallying', the Guards received the order to embark on 29 August. They boarded HMS *Simoom*, a large troopship, built to a modern design – iron-hulled and powered by a coal-fired steam engine driving a screw propeller. She had originally been a man-of-war, but until proper armour plating was developed in 1860, metal ships were considered unsuitable for naval warfare, because wrought iron shattered into splinters when hit by shot or shell. Even as a troopship, though, *Simoom* could still be troublesome. Sir James Fergusson had previous experience of her on his original voyage out from England, when he found himself travelling with the Scots Fusilier Guards, and 'in the worst berth of the ship, close to the engine . . . . The engines are so weak that they are constantly going wrong . . . . They are totally incapable of propelling this ship against the wind, and whenever the wind is strong enough to drive her more than 10 knots, she overstrains her screw, and they are obliged to stop it.'[8]

The party that boarded this vessel numbered 1,300 men, but the *Simoom* was only designed to carry 1,000,[9] so conditions were crowded even when 200 were removed to another ship; several men went down with cholera shortly after they came on board, including the *Simoom*'s Captain.[10] They spent more than a week moored in Varna Bay before they got under way because it took longer than expected to load all the ships, the invasion force amounting to more than 350 vessels and 60,000 men in the first wave. A number of cholera victims were buried at sea and by the time they finally got under way, Varna Bay was putrid with bodies which had become so bloated with gas that they floated to the surface in spite of the 32lb cannon balls that had been attached to their burial sacks.

The Guards spent a total of seventeen days on board ship (only three of which were actually crossing the Black Sea) in over-crowded conditions and without any fresh provisions – just salt pork and biscuit. Yet, as Captain George Higginson put it, 'the novelty of the scene and the prospect of adventure acted favourably on the men's spirits and physical condition.'

HMS *Simoom*, Black Sea
Sep. 8th '54

My dear Father,

I write from the middle of the Black Sea where we are now. We are to land near Eupatoria, about 20 miles from Sebastopol. We are to carry 3 days provisions, officers and all, and nothing but what we take on our backs. No horses will be landed. The French land nearer to Sebastopol than us. Our ship is a man of war troopship. Nasty enough.

I have nothing further to say except to say you will remember and give my love to everyone. I suppose the day after tomorrow we shall be at our destination. I fancy we shall not be opposed when we land as it is a smooth beach entirely covered by the guns from the ships. Nobody seems to know what force the Russians have. Whatever it is, it can't be their best.

Believe me, my dear Father, your most affectionate son,
H. Percy

P.S. The sickness seems much abated but the troops have suffered less in proportion than the Navy and incredibly less than the French. Either the latter's habits or constitutions are more favourable to cholera and influenza than that of the English.

They first sighted the Crimea on 12 September and sailed up the coast away from Sebastopol, towards the village of Eupatoria. Although it seems incredible, the invasion force had done very little reconnaissance and the decision where to land was practically taken on the spur of the moment. They did, however, find a flat sandy beach at Calamita Bay, about 25 miles north of Sebastopol, where they were able get ashore in a flat calm sea and with no Russian army in sight, other than two or three Cossack horsemen who briefly surveyed the invasion from the cliff which overlooked the scene.

There followed a hard march in the heat of the day across four miles of unenclosed smooth grassy plain, each officer wearing a bearskin hat, double-breasted coatee with heavy gold filigree epaulettes but no pockets, and grey trousers. He was additionally burdened with a great coat, a haversack containing three days' provisions, a revolver in a leather case, a flask on the right hip and a sword on the left – the last attached to a white leather belt.[11] The coatee, which was a small tight-fitting scarlet tailcoat, certainly looked as a redcoat should, but by the 1850s was considered out of date and impractical. 'One's uniform kills one,' Henry wrote after this first march, 'it is comfortless and painful.' No wonder he had been so anxious to try Queen Victoria's new design of coat.

The men were also badly off for, unbeknown to their officers, the medical staff, with a view to lightening the soldiers' loads in the heat, had advised Lord Raglan to issue an order for the men's knapsacks to be left on board ship. They were instead instructed to form a roll or pack out of a heavy blanket, on the top of which a great coat and mess-tin carrying three days' rations and water was to be placed. This made for a deeply uncomfortable contrivance. As it turned out, too, they did not get their knapsacks restored to them for some weeks, by which time many of them were, inexplicably, almost empty.[12]

In spite of the long weeks of preparation and a fortnight on board ship, the first night on hostile soil was spent without any tents or personal comforts, all of which had been packed right at the bottom of the ships' holds. It rained incessantly and they could only try to sleep on the ground, barely covered by their coats. The resultant quagmire the following day made it more difficult to land supplies. There appeared to be no wood whatever in the region for lighting fires. How Henry Percy must have rued the day back in June when, in the blistering heat at Varna, he sold a small tent that he had privately brought out from England to Grey Neville. Army-issue tents did eventually appear on the 16th, but there were not nearly enough and officers who were used to having a tent to them-selves, or perhaps sharing with one other, found themselves crammed in with six or seven of their comrades. That night a false alarm was sounded in the small hours. Everybody awoke in their tents to a great clamour, the only audible word being 'Cossacks!'. In Henry Neville's tent there was a tremendous scrimmage, with everybody scrambling for the tent door at the same time, franti-cally tearing out its hooks, only for half of them to rush back in again to get their weapons. In this absurd manner more than one bleary-eyed subaltern flew off in the direction of the alarm post in his shirtsleeves and without boots, brandishing a revolver and a drawn sword.[13] Most of the men fell in as if it had been a parade ordered the day before.[14]

Nobody need have worried about their torn door fasteners, as the tents were sent back to the ships the following day when the invasion force moved off, for the Commissariat Department had only been able to supply enough transport to take care of the ammunition. The acute want of horses was already proving to be a serious problem. Even the ambulance wagons had to be left behind in Bulgaria. Fortunately the local Muslim population, the Tartars, who, according to Henry, spoke 'bad Turkish', were friendly enough and quite willing to sell the allied force provisions. Higginson managed to buy a couple of sheep for five shillings, which he brought back to their rudimentary camp, much to the delight of his company. There were also a few scrawny ponies available, one of which Percy got hold of, though it hardly seemed to improve his mood: one day Fergusson wrote that he had a 'bit of a shindy with Percy . . . who ever since we landed had increased in ill-temper and fussiness. So, as I was rather slow with my baggage, which his pony was to carry, he declared I should carry it myself.' The subaltern had the last laugh, though, when he persuaded another officer, Bradford, to carry his pack on his horse (the purchase of which Fergusson had negotiated the evening before).[15]

There still being no sign of any major Russian force coming to attack the bridgehead, it was decided on the 18th to march south for Sebastopol. The British had the worse lot as they took the left of the line, so they were further inland than their French allies, exposed on their flank and miles from their transport ships. In the sweltering heat and damp conditions, cholera took its toll once more: men would suddenly grasp at their stomachs, paralysed by an excruciating cramp as if they had just ingested poison and cry out piteously for water. More often than not they were dead within a few hours.

They soon reached the valley of the Alma, which meanders east-west across the rolling Crimean countryside, flanked on its south side by hills rising higher and higher as the river takes its course down the valley, until the estuary itself is overlooked by cliffs. On the 19th they encamped within sight of this high ground, but still the Russians showed no sign of wanting to outflank them. There had been earlier in the day a small stand-off between the English and Russian cavalry at the River Bulganak, but the only action was brief exchange of artillery fire. However, by dawn on the morning of the 20th the army was ready and under arms in anticipation of finally seeing action that day, for the enemy had decided to make a stand on the high ground, fortifying it with gun emplacements to command the bridge where the road crossed the Alma about two and a half miles from the sea. It was a formidable sight. The Russian front line was visible on the brow of the hill the other side of the Alma, extending to two or three miles in length, with batteries of artillery placed on strategic knolls. The most impressive of these stood on the Kourgané Hill, and the breast-work there, which became known as the Great Redoubt, enclosed twelve guns, firing round shot (solid cannon balls), exploding shells and grapeshot.

It was decided to make a full frontal assault, the British on the left and the French and Turks on the right, near the sea. It would be difficult to improve on the account that Captain Alfred Tipping, Grenadier Guards, made in his diary of the march towards the River Alma:

In this order we marched for a considerable time, and the heat being overpowering, we made frequent halts, and it was not till eleven o'clock, that we came in view of the village of Alma, and the heights overlooking it. We could plainly see thousands of bayonets glistening in the sun's rays, on the top of the hill, and crowning some rising ground, on the highest point of which, an unfinished building was evidently surrounded by a mass of troops. We were now

12

ordered to halt, to sit down and dine upon whatever we might have provided for ourselves in our haversacks, and I do not think the appetites of any of us proved the less keen, from the fact of being overlooked by our 'Friends' on the opposite side of the river.

A hare jumped from amongst us, and a little Bull Terrier (belonging to a man in my company, and who had brought it out from England), after a chase consisting of a number of dodges between, and in and out of the men's legs, succeeded in catching it, and the prize was accordingly pocketed for consumption whenever 'the toils of War' should be ended, an event rather beyond the limits of human foresight to determine.

The Assistant Adjutant General had come up, and informed us that we had forty battalions of Russians opposite to us, in a strong position. This number could be plainly seen, and had been ascertained by those sent forward to make the needful reconnaissance.

After halting for about half an hour, we again marched forward, and now perceived smoke and flame issuing from the village [of Bourliouk] in such dense masses, and from so many quarters at the same time, that no doubt could exist as to its having been fired by the enemy for some crafty purpose.

We had not advanced far in a forward direction when the rifles who were in skirmishing order in our front began to be assailed by heavy round shot, fired by a battery on the heights, upwards of a mile distant. The farther we proceeded, the heavier became the roar of the cannon, and now the great ponderous round shot came bounding along the ground like cricket balls. As the men saw them approaching, they opened the ranks, and the balls went hissing past in their resistless force. The little Terrier I have mentioned, whose blood was up from its late success, chased the first few of these missiles, which passed through us, following them at full speed for twenty or thirty yards, but finding that the round shot were rather quicker in their movements than his former victim had been, he soon gave up the pursuit. I actually saw him trying to intercept, and cut in upon a spent shot, which came rolling through our ranks, at an apparently sluggish pace, but quite sufficient to have taken one's leg off, but even this was too fast for him, so following the example of many sensible young ladies, he gave up 'balls', finding the results not equal to the expectations.

We now began to walk over the recently slain bodies of the poor fellows, who had been eating their last meal but half an hour before and looking forward with glee to the forthcoming conflict. The colour has scarcely left their cheeks, but they were generally fearful sights, as from our distance from the batteries they were of course killed either by round shot or shells, which always mutilate frightfully.

Having advanced rather too fast, we now received orders to lie down, so as to give time for the other divisions to form line – the recumbent position affording a better chance of escape than that of standing upright, and while we remained thus prostrate, the shells came rushing through the air – some of them burst just before us, some over our heads, and others in rear, and it was about this time that poor Cust* was struck, and his leg carried completely away, a loss which he survived, but a very short time.

When in line with the others, we again proceeded, and the smaller the space we placed between ourselves and the batteries, towards the teeth of which we were now marching, the hotter the fire.

We were now within reach of their Riflemen, who commenced making sad havoc in our ranks. Every now and then, a rattle close at hand induced one to turn to right or left, as it might happen, and then one saw some poor fellow rolling over, his bayonet and musket clanking as they fell to the ground.

Another hundred yards brought us to the vineyard,† which was bounded on one side by a low wall, and on the other by the river. We saw a line of red coats lying under the wall, and thought of course they were all wounded men, who had dragged themselves there, as a partial shelter from the pelting storm of bullets. However, I was sorry to see some few amongst them apparently unwounded, and uninjured, except in the nervous system, which I suppose the deafening cannonade had shocked too severely to allow them to advance. One poor fellow with both legs gone raised a feeble cheer as we scrambled over the vineyard wall, and throwing up his shako‡ into the air, shouted out, 'Go it beauty Guards', 'Go in and win', etc. This must have been pretty nearly his last cheer, poor fellow. We scurried through the vineyard, and down to the river, under a perfect hail storm of bullets, and scrambled up the opposite bank.[16]

Along a two-mile front the attacking force crossed the river in a succession of thin red lines. The Alma was relatively easy to ford

---

* Captain Horace Cust, Coldstream Guards, ADC to Brigadier General Bentinck.
† The vines were in fruit and a lot of men took this opportunity to pick grapes as they passed, such that a number of them still had bunches of grapes between their teeth during the fighting that followed.
‡ The Albert Shako was a type of cylindrical service hat, with peaks fore and aft.

and the high bank on the Russian side put the river itself in dead ground. It was no more than waist-deep in most places, but there were a few deep holes which required some men to wade chest-deep, holding their rifles high above their heads. Fergusson reckoned that he saw Henry Neville having to swim a couple of strokes.[17]

The Grenadiers' commanding officer, Colonel the Hon Grosvenor Hood, always a stickler for discipline, wanted to avoid the confusion seen in some regiments when men scrambled up the far bank and then straight on up the hill before all members of their units were across the river. Great swathes of smoke drifting across the battlefield not only shielded the eyes from some of the horrors ahead but made it difficult for the attacking force to discern the correct order, though, as one officer observed, the smoke did not stop lead from finding its target.[18] Hood ordered his Regiment to wait after they had negotiated the water and lie down out of sight of the Russians. On the far bank they lined up against the crest of the incline, all quiet but weapons at the ready, until the order was given for them to go over the top, as one. Henry Percy commanded the 8th Company, the left flank of the Grenadiers, immediately to the right of the Scots Fusilier Guards. The Guards were renowned for preserving formation and one Russian observer later said that he 'did not think it possible for men to be found with such sufficient firmness of morale to be able to attack, in this apparently weak formation, our massive columns.'[19] As seven of the Grenadier officers present had served as adjutants,[20] including Percy, they certainly knew how to keep the line straight. Unhappily, the same could not be said of their neighbouring Fusilier Guards on this occasion: in their enthusiasm, and to their cost, they got too far in front of the line while the rest were still reforming.

The total breadth of the combined British and French lines extended several miles along the river, but it was the fortune of the 8th Company of the Grenadier Guards to be one of those directly in front of the Great Redoubt, albeit they were not in the first line. After they clambered up onto the sloping plain above the Alma they were fully exposed to the enemy again, and much closer this time than when they had previously been directly under fire. The enemy artillery's effect was suddenly that much more devastating and quickly several redcoats stumbled and tumbled back down the bank. Lieutenant Burgoyne, carrying the colours, had barely gone six paces when he was hit in the leg; he could go no further and passed the flag on to Lieutenant R.W. Hamilton (Colonel F.W. Hamilton's nephew). Percy too was hit in the arm by a ball. Both were casualties of grapeshot from the guns they were trying to capture, still now some three or four hundred yards up the hill in front of them. Russian smooth-bore muskets were not much use beyond a hundred yards – as the enormous number of men who were hit by spent rounds could gratefully testify after the battle. Grapeshot, however, had killing power at 400 yards (and the effectiveness of solid cannon balls was measured in thousands of yards). Burgoyne's leg was fractured, but fortunately the ball which struck Percy went straight through the flesh of his upper arm, just missing the bone, carrying pieces of shirt and tunic with it. He stopped briefly to bandage it up with a handkerchief that his young cousin Isabel had given him, but determined to keep formation, refusing to leave the field. Burgoyne was helped back into the dead ground at the riverside by a sergeant.

The Light Division, in the first line, had meanwhile reached the Russian battery and temporarily displaced its defenders. These regiments had incurred heavy casualties, particularly among the officers, who had made themselves extremely visible at the head of their men and consequently been marked by the Russians. The Queen's thirty-five-year-old cousin, HRH the Duke of Cambridge, who commanded the 1st Division, including the Brigade of Guards, incurred some criticism after the battle for not following the second line quickly enough; they did not cross the Alma until the Light Division were several hundred yards ahead of them and almost upon the Russian guns. These regiments did manage to expel the Russians from the Great Redoubt, but they were ultimately repelled due to the lateness of the supporting second line, though this was no fault of the regimental officers – rather a breakdown in communication between Lord Raglan and his general officers, and consequent dithering by the Duke of Cambridge.

The retreat of the Light Division regiments as they were pursued back down the hill by Russian infantry bore down upon the second line's central battalion, the Scots Fusilier Guards, who were supposed to be on Percy's immediate left, but who in their haste had broken formation and got too far forward. They almost reached the Russian guns just as the Royal Welch Fusiliers ahead of them were forced into a rapid retreat from a new and shattering volley of musketry from Russian infantry, who followed up their fusillade by swarming over the parapet, bayonets forward. Several Scots Guardsmen were physically knocked over by the headlong retreat of their Light Division comrades. Yet still came the cry from within the mêlée: 'Forward Guards! Forward Guards!' despite the fact that their adjutant was charging around on his horse, waving his pistol in the air, desperately trying to hold them back. Percy, Neville and Fergusson could clearly see a potential disaster unfolding and Neville shouted across to his fellow subaltern, 'By Jove, it's a bad job – look at the Fusiliers!'

Meanwhile, to their left, Lieutenant Robert Lindsay of the Scots Fusilier Guards was in the vanguard with their colour party. Afterwards he recalled getting to within twenty yards of the redoubt, at which point they were received by such a hail of bullets that his three colour sergeants were cut down and the flagstaff he was holding shattered in his hand.[21] Then they were almost surrounded by Russians. The Duke of Cambridge told Lindsay's father, 'How he escaped has been a marvel to me. I watched your son with the Queen's Colour at Alma – at one moment I thought him gone, the colours fell and he disappeared under them. But presently he came out from below them . . . raised them again and waved them over his head.' Lindsay was later awarded the Victoria Cross; four of the seven VCs awarded either wholly or partly for the Battle of Alma went to the Scots Fusilier Guards.

When they were eventually forced to retire, it was too late for a number of these gallant men to escape being stabbed and slashed in the back as they tried to get back through the congested ranks behind them towards the river and their correct place in the line. This unfortunate episode cost the Fusilier Guards a great many casualties and opened up a huge gap in the ranks of the Brigade, which a new Russian infantry column, the Vladimir, was bearing down on. It would have been a disaster if the Russians, once more in control of the Great Redoubt, had broken through the advancing second line of redcoats. Adding to the confusion, a mounted officer appeared at the Grenadiers' place in the line and gave the order, 'Retire!' A.W. Kinglake, in his eight-volume *Invasion of the Crimea*, wrote:

17

Percy, looking at the Vladimir column, and seeing in an instant what ought and what ought not to be done, inferred, or professed to infer, that the manoeuvre which the conjecture required was the one which the mounted officer must mean. 'Retire!' he said. 'What the devil do they mean? They must mean "dress back."' Percy then, aided by Neville, his senior subaltern, began causing the subdivision to 'dress back' in such a way as to face the Vladimir column; and this it quickly appeared, was exactly what Colonel Hood desired, for he rode up and told Percy to go on with the operation.[22]

The Grenadiers stood fast, letting the remnants of the Light Division pass through their line. Hood later commented that they 'opened out to let them past, and closed up as coolly as if in Hyde Park'. Thus Percy ordered the left wing of his company to fall back and make a right angle from which to fire into the flank of the Russian onslaught. Receiving an organized volley of rifle fire, they soon fell 'like corn before the wind', as he described in one of his letters home. The Russians were 'astonished at the extraordinary firmness with which the red jackets, having crossed the river opened a heavy fire'. Seeing the effect of this withering fusillade on the enemy, which included shooting Prince Gortschakoff's horse from under him, the Grenadiers cheered and fired alternately.[23] As the Russians retreated back up the hill two pieces of heavy artillery managed to place a succession of exploding shells right in amongst them, each volley killing scores, and clearing a space all around.[24] With order restored, the Scots Fusilier Guards re-formed and remnants of the Light Division (including the remaining members of the Royal Welch Fusiliers and the 95th Regiment) were only too keen to fill gaps in the left flank of the Grenadiers' line so that they could join the advance once more.

Colonel Hood, intensely proud of his regiment, wrote after-wards that the leading part which the Grenadiers played in this action represented the 'common-sense manoeuvre of a line against a dense column. I hope due credit will be done to my fine fellows, for it was a proud sight to see them behave so well. What an honour to command such a body of men! . . . In five minutes the Russian column faltered, then turned, then ran.'[25] It was a small victory in the context of a great battle, but certainly no sideshow, for Henry Percy's 8th Company of Grenadiers, together with Lieutenant Colonel Edward Pakenham's 7th Company, went on to storm the Great Redoubt and take the remaining gun once and for all, the others having been carried away by the Russians. The battle was effectively already won, as the French, despite having more precipitous cliffs in front of them, had succeeded in removing the enemy more quickly than the English on their left, largely because they had covering fire from the ships in the bay.

Out of a total strength of 873, the official returns show the Grenadiers having suffered 191 casualties in the action, of which 11 were killed.[26] It is perhaps surprising that more were not lost, given the intensity of fire (which several old Peninsular War veterans said was heavier than anything they had seen,[27] and Lord Raglan maintained was as heavy as it had been at Waterloo[28]), though it should be added that some of the wounded subsequently died at Scutari Hospital. The survivors of the assault all felt that they had had miraculous escapes that day, and most had buttons carried away, chin straps shot off, coats torn, etc. Notwithstanding this, the Grenadiers had on this occasion been relatively fortunate in being behind the Light Division, who had taken the brunt of the Russian guns before they, at least temporarily, put them out of action. Of the Brigade of Guards, the Scots Fusiliers suffered considerably from their having got too far in front after crossing the river, with 29 dead. The high number of wounded relative to killed may be attributable, apart from being before the advent of high explosive, to the very broad front upon which the Battle of the Alma was fought and the modest killing range of the Russian muskets. Percy had been hit three times, but two of these were spent rounds, doing no damage beyond perhaps a nasty bruise. The Russian muskets were highly inaccurate and of limited range. In contrast, the British Minié rifles were sighted up to eight hundred yards and could theoretically kill at a mile; certainly at close quarters a Minié bullet could pass through six or seven men. No wonder that, despite their force of numbers, the densely packed Russian columns were no match for organized rifle fire from a thin red line of British infantry. Even so, total allied casualties were 3,500 killed and wounded; the Russians over 5,000.

Because of the wound to his right arm, Henry was only able to dictate a brief note to his father:

My dear Father,

I am obliged to employ an amanuensis as I was shot through the right arm yesterday in forcing the passage of the Alma. We took an entrenched position & captured one 32 pounder in which operation we lost 114 killed and wounded, but we everywhere and effectively beat the Russians. My wound is not dangerous nor was it sufficient to make me fall to the rear, and as a wound it may be considered a very lucky one as the ball passed <u>straight</u> through without injuring the bone. Six or seven guns at the least, a Russian general and some colours are taken. The Russians fought very well. We advanced under a perfect storm of shrapnel, round shot and musquetry & it was very stirring . . . . The Russian soldiers, of whom there were lots on the field, appear very well clothed, but their head is filthy [sic] and at first sight is indistinguishable from their excrement.

The Minié worked very well. The position was a high flat range of hills commanding a valley through which runs a winding stream with steepish banks, and as the Russians had marked their range beforehand on the plains over which we had to march, you may imagine what it was. I had *hors de combat* out of my company including myself 27, but only one other officer is wounded, of the Grenadiers, but almost all had some part of their clothes marked with shot.

I shan't trouble my kind scribe any more – my love to everybody–
Ever yours most affectionately,
Henry Percy

There is another position to take before getting to Sebastopol but we shall probably take that with the aid of the fleet. It is suspected that the Russians are much weaker than they wish to acknowledge.

Neville, however, was able to give a more detailed account of their Company's action during the course of the next few days:

The firing commenced with the artillery, and was very severe; but they had 32-pounders, which were, of course, heavier than our field pieces. As we advanced, it got very exciting, getting out of the way of the round shot, which came hopping along and doing but little damage. After the artillery had pounded away, the Light Division advanced in line to the stream, which they crossed, but were dreadfully cut up by the fire from the forts; we followed them, and it was certainly the most awful moment of my life – shot, shell and musket-balls falling in every direction; and when one considers the shower of bullets, it seems a miracle how anyone escaped. We advanced to the stream, which we forded, and formed the other side, under a steep bank. On arriving at the top of the bank, the fire was awful, and we were horrified to see the remnants of the Light Division rushing down the hill, followed by the Russians; they passed through us, and then, 'Up Guards,' etc., we stopped the Muscovites, and sent them back up the hill. For a moment, I thought it was all over, as the Scotch Fusiliers, who were on our left, were quite staggered by the tremendous fire; but, luckily, our men behaved admirably; and everybody allows that <u>we</u> retrieved the check which had been received . . . . The evening saw us masters of the position, after about four hours of severe fighting.

Our loss has been severe – 107 casualties; Burgoyne, broken leg; Percy, wounded in the arm, and several others struck and grazed. I am glad to say that we have not many men killed . . . . We, as you see, have been very lucky, and I cannot say how grateful I feel that my life has been preserved. We have gained a great victory, but at a great loss; the amount of our killed and wounded being, as I hear, about 2,000 . . . . They got a licking yesterday that I do not think they will stand. I had no idea that the excitement could be so great; as long as one was quiet, the buzzing of shot and shell made one feel nervous; but when we commenced advancing and firing, one lost all feelings of the kind . . . . I think we shall be engaged again tomorrow, and I trust God may preserve me again, of His infinite goodness; but I assure you, from what I saw yesterday, I never wish to see another battle.[29]

Reflecting many years later, Higginson (who as adjutant to the Battalion was a mounted officer) described how, immediately after the battle was over, he was asked by Colonel Hood to ride back down the hill and cross the Alma, so that he could check the vineyards which they had advanced through at the beginning of the action for casualties:

My errand took me across the battlefield, which presented a scene that not even the sixty years which have since elapsed can obliterate from my memory. As I turned back towards the Russian entrenchment, which was the chief object of our contest, the very atmosphere seemed to be tainted with an inexpressible odour of bloodshed. The unnatural attitude of the dead and the contorted movements of the wounded gave rise to feelings which it needed all one's resolutions to control. Almost the first among the dead whom I recognised was poor little Harry Anstruther, his red coat and shirt thrown back, disclosing the bullet wound which had struck him full in the heart. Only two days before he had found me lying prone on the grass writing a hurried letter to my people at home, and throwing himself down beside me, asked for a slip of paper on which to write a few lines. I have reason to know that the dear little lad expressed in those hurried lines the conviction that he should meet his death in the approaching fight.

Riding on a little further, I met a litter carried by four bearers of the Scots Fusilier Guards, conveying to the ship for embarkation Frank Haygarth [who lost an arm and a leg]. He looked so pale and exhausted from the fearful wounds he had received that as I bent over him and heard his half-whispered 'good-bye, Hig!' I little thought that for many long years afterwards we should talk over events of the campaign in which we had shared the opening scene. Before reaching the river I met another litter, also carrying to the shore a grievously wounded soldier whom I recognised by the cap which lay upon his prostrate form, as a private in the Guards. As he turned his face towards me I saw his lips move, and in the belief that he had some message to convey to his friends at home, I halted the bearers and bent over my saddle to listen. With a faint attempt at a smile he simply said, 'I think, sir, they'll say we did our duty today.' Nothing more! I signalled to the bearers to proceed, and reflected as I rode forward how much true nobility may lie beneath the rough garb of a private soldier.

I crossed the river and, happily, found few of our men, and they past all help, the wounded having found their way to the field hospitals.[30]

Over the following two days all able-bodied men helped recover the wounded and bury the dead, friend and foe. Lieutenant Colonel George Cadogan superintended the embarkation of wounded Grenadiers onto hospital ships, but he was unable to persuade his impetuous friend Percy into doing any such thing, as the great victory at the Alma meant the way was open to Sebastopol and no one wanted to miss out on the final denouement, even if there was a deal of grim work to do in the interim. The aftermath of the battle was recorded by William Howard Russell of *The Times* on 22 September:

The Russian dead were all buried together in pits, and were carried down as they lay. Our parties, on the 21st, and to-day, buried 1,200 men. The British soldiers who fell were buried in pits the same way. The forelocks, and the useful portion of their equipment, were alone preserved. It was a sad sight to see the litters borne from all quarters hour after hour – to watch the working parties as they wandered about the plain turning down the blankets which had been stretched over the wounded to behold if they were yet alive, or were food for the worms, and then adding many a habitant to the yawning pits which lay with insatiable mouths gaping on the hillside – or covering up the poor sufferers destined to pass another night of indescribable agony. The thirst of the wounded seemed intolerable, and our men – all honour to the noble fellows! – went about relieving the wants of the miserable creatures as far as they could . . . .

When I was looking at the wounded men going off to-day, I could not see an English ambulance. Our men were sent to the sea, three miles distant, on jolting arabas* or tedious litters. The French – I am tired of this disgraceful antithesis – had well-appointed covered hospital vans, to hold ten or twelve men, drawn by fine mules, and their wounded were sent in much greater comfort than our poor fellows, so far as I saw.[31]

* Araba: a type of country cart, usually drawn by bullocks, found in Turkey and the Crimea.

Chapter 2

Balaklava

In spite of his wound, Percy stayed with his Regiment. After the Battle of the Alma, there were less than twenty miles of rolling plain and two small rivers, the Katcha and the Belbec (both flowing east to west like the Alma), between the British army and Sebastopol. As the invasion force set off southward, the route was strewn with the abandoned accoutrements of fleeing Russian infantry, thus advertising the enemy's state of demoralization and confusion. If there was to be another battle, the odds would be decidedly better than they had been at Alma and Henry was determined that he should be a part of it.

However, at the bivouac on the banks of the Belbec on the 23rd, it was decided by Lord Raglan and his French counterpart, St Arnaud, not to proceed with an immediate offensive from the north, but instead to make a flank march around the city and co-ordinate the assault from the south side, which was less heavily defended than the north side. This entailed some risk, not only because it might waste an opportunity of pressing the advantage against the dispirited Russians, but because it entailed a march through the densely wooded interior of the Crimea, well away from their supply lines. At least on the open plains near the coast the army could observe any potential threat and easily maintain battle readiness. Also, by the coastal route one side was always protected by the sea and in the event of a major engagement the navy's guns could be used to good effect.

The reason for this change of plan was that Lord Raglan had been unable to persuade St Arnaud to take the northern forts of

Sebastopol by a *coup de main*. The latter felt that the army was not in good enough condition to undertake such a task and believed that an immediate assault would be too costly. His judgement was affected by his own failing health; he was in fact invalided back to Scutari a few days later and he died from stomach cancer, exacerbated by cholera, *en route*. Lord Raglan was perhaps not forceful enough in pressing his own point of view, but he was under strict instructions from London not to endanger the alliance and, without the French, an immediate *coup de main* by the English alone was impossible.

This fateful decision was immediately controversial. After the war it became known that the north side of Sebastopol was actually very lightly defended, mainly by sailors and marines, and that if the Star Fort commanding the harbour could have been neutralized by a combined attack from land and sea, the town would probably have fallen.

So, through thick brushwood and dense oak forest, the army marched south-east in dense columns. A Coldstream Guards officer described the difficulties:

> Everybody who has seen beaters pushing their way through a thick cover may form a faint idea of the difficulties which beset, and the obstacles which retarded our progress. The heat was overpowering, not a breath of air percolated the dense vegetation. You scrambled on with arms uplifted to protect the face against the swinging back-handers dealt by the boughs; now your shako was dashed off, now the briars laid tenacious hold on your haversack, or on the tails of your coatee. It was as much as you could do to see the soldiers immediately on your right and left. For the time, military order was an impossibility, brigades and regiments got intermixed. Guardsmen, Rifles and Highlanders struggled forward blindly, all in a ruck. There was much suffering, and some stout soldiers dropped involuntarily to the rear, to be heard of no more.[1]

The only contact with the enemy on the flank march was a chance encounter with a Russian column. Lord Raglan and his Quartermaster General, Airey, suddenly found themselves at the edge of a wood by the road near Mackenzie's Farm (so named after a Russian admiral of Scots origin who settled there). They stumbled within a few yards of some Russian soldiers who were quietly ambling beside an enormous baggage train. These Russian privates were understandably astonished at suddenly seeing two curiously unprotected English generals at the edge of the trees and rushed off to report the apparition to their superiors, giving Lord Raglan's aides enough time to get him out of the way. The vanguard of the British army had run into the tail of a large Russian column making its way out of Sebastopol along the road to Simferopol in the interior. There was a brief exchange of fire by both sides, but the Russians continued on their way, hastened by a volley of Minié bullets in their rears. Lord Raglan would not allow the cavalry to pursue them, continuing his policy of extreme caution with regard to that particular force, which rather unjustly resulted in Lord Lucan, who commanded the Cavalry Division, being nicknamed 'Lord Look-on'. Raglan considered the cavalry to be a valuable and scarce resource and was reluctant to risk it unnecessarily; there were only two Brigades, and both were short of horses.

Nobody could divine much intelligence from the captured rearguard of the Russian column. There was a Russian officer found in one of the carriages; he was in a very jovial mood, but so drunk that it proved impossible to get any sense whatever from him as to the reasons for the departure of this column from Sebastopol. The contents of what it transpired was the Russian commander Prince Mentschikoff's baggage, were, however, rather interesting: they included bottles of brandy, champagne, brand new hussars' jackets laced with silver, sheepskin coats, women's underwear, erotic novels and pornographic pictures – the latter perhaps all the more surprising since Mentschikoff had been castrated by a Turkish cannonball on a previous campaign.[2]

The departure of the Russian army from Sebastopol was an indication of the state of its fighting ability following the defeat at the Alma. Mentschikoff feared that the army might become trapped in the city and cut off from supplies and ammunition. So, rather than stay and defend it, he left it to the navy, under Vice Admiral Korniloff, and the talented Lieutenant Colonel of the Engineers, Franz Todleben. The latter would comment after the war that, in his opinion, Sebastopol could indeed have been taken by the allies by an immediate assault directed from the north side.

By the 25th the British reached the valley of the River Tchernaya, which flows into the eastern end of the Sebastopol roadstead; they were almost within sight of their objective, the small fishing port of Balaklava, about eight miles south of Sebastopol. This they reached and made their headquarters on the following day, the Royal Navy already having taken it after a brief skirmish. The flank march, however, had taken its toll. The Grenadiers had lost several men to cholera and Colonel Hood's strict discipline allowed no hope of rest to other sufferers until it was too late. Higginson said of Hood's attitude, 'Although to the sentimentalist it may seem heartless, it will commend itself to all those who understand the value of stern resolution exercised at a critical moment.'[3] That same evening Higginson himself was ticked off by Colonel Hood for not complying with the strict letter of an order to see that the men had had their dinners: the adjutant had provided their food and left them sitting down to eat – but he did not wait to see that they had actually had their fill before reporting back to his colonel. The Grenadiers had also lost their first officer and senior Captain, Lieutenant Colonel Augustus Cox, who had been so magnanimous to Sir James Fergusson when he decided to transfer to Henry Percy's company. Higginson later recalled that Cox was 'lifted from the ground, his limbs paralysed and features of an ashen grey, absolutely incapacitated from any further exertion A battery of artillery was passing by our flank, and our poor comrade was lifted on to a gun limber after a hasty and sad farewell to us all. He was thus carried in to Balaklava and died that night on board the *Caradoc*.'[4]

Tempers too were strained. Henry Percy, who was still struggling on with his disabled arm, recorded later:

As for HRH [the Duke of Cambridge] he has amply shown that he has neither coolness in the field or the camp. All are of the same opinion. We had a tremendous march one day, and arrived late at night at our bivouac, and he came and laid down at my fire, when I was eating biscuit and water, and going without dinner to be able to cook a poultice in my own pot, and he grumbled and complained so querulously about not getting his baggage, that I was quite disgusted. He said he was dying of hunger, and so cold. I offered him biscuit & water, which he refused and went on moaning and groaning till we were right glad to get quit of him. It was cold & we were tired & hungry, but he ought to have set an example.

27

Henry Neville wrote the day after they reached Balaklava:

> We marched in a south-easterly direction, through a thick forest, and had a most tiring march of more than fifteen miles, which was enlivened by a scrimmage with some troops under Prince Mentschikoff, who were leaving Sebastopol. We were not engaged, as the Russians bolted as soon as our artillery fired upon them . . . . It was the hardest day's work I ever had, as we were under arms from 5 am till eight in the evening, when we encamped at a small river. The men were awfully knocked up, but marched very pluckily . . . . Poor Colonel Cox died this morning . . . . Percy's wound is going on very well, and he has come on with us.

However, his company commander's arm was still disabled and he could not even write letters home, let alone carry anything or help pitch tents in the hard and stony soil where they set up camp near Balaklava. So, on the 30th, ten days after receiving his wound, he was forced to go on board the hospital ship *Hydaspes*. Though *Hydaspes* was in theory reserved for officers, the scene on board was frightful. Hospital ships had no nurses and not nearly enough surgeons; rotting flesh was infested with maggots and those who were wounded in action were placed hugger-mugger with cholera victims. The life expectancy of the patients was not good under such circumstances. William Howard Russell, *The Times* correspondent in the Crimea, had already shocked readers at home with his vivid description of the aftermath of Alma. His colleague at Scutari, Thomas Chenery, described conditions on board the hospital ships and the following article, published in *The Times* on Friday 13th October, caused a huge row in England:

> It is impossible for any one to see the melancholy sights of the last few days without feelings of surprise and indignation at the deficiencies of our medical system. The manner in which the sick and wounded have been treated is worthy only of the savages of Dahomey. The sufferings on board the *Vulcan* were bad enough. There were 300 wounded, and 700 cholera patients, and these were attended to by four surgeons. The scene is described as terrible. The wounded seized the surgeons by the skirts as they picked their way through the heaps of dying and dead; but the surgeons shook them off. It may be expected, and perhaps right, that the officers should receive the principal attention, and they probably required the

almost undivided labour of four men; but someone must be in fault when large bodies of wounded men are put on board a ship with no one to give them surgical assistance, or even to supply their necessary wants. Numbers arrived at Scutari without having been touched by a surgeon since they fell pierced by Russian bullets on the slopes of the Alma. Their wounds were stiff and their strength exhausted as they were lifted out of the boats to be carried to the hospital, where, fortunately, surgical aid may be obtained. But all horrors sink into insignificance compared with the state of the unfortunate passengers by the *Colombo*. This vessel left the Crimea on the morning of the 24th. Wounded men were being placed on board for two days before she sailed, and when she weighed anchor she carried the following numbers: – 27 wounded officers, 422 wounded soldiers, and 104 Russian prisoners – in all 553 souls. About half of the wounded had received surgical assistance before they were put on board. To supply the wants of this mass of misery were four medical men, one of whom was the surgeon of the ship, – sufficiently employed in looking after the crew, who at this place and season are seldom far from sickness. The ship was literally covered with prostrate forms, so as to be almost unmanageable. The officers could not get below to find their sextants, and the run was made at hazard. The vessel was at sea 12 hours longer through this mischance. The worst cases were placed on the upper deck, which in a day or two became a mass of putridity. The neglected gunshot wounds bred maggots, which crawled in every direction, infecting the food of the unhappy beings on board. The putrid animal matter caused such a stench that the officers and crew were nearly overcome, and the captain is now ill from defects of five days' misery. All the blankets, to the number of 1,500, have been thrown overboard as useless. Thirty men died during the voyage. The surgeons worked as hard as possible, but could do little among so many, and many an unfortunate fellow first came under a medical man's hand, on his arrival at Scutari, six days after the battle. It is an ungracious task to find fault and to speak of the shortcomings of men who do their utmost, but an unfortunate neglect has occurred since the arrival of the steamer. Forty-six men have been left on board for two days, when by some extra exertion they might have been safely placed in the hospital. The vessel is quite putrid, but a large number of men will be immediately employed to clean and fumigate her, and thus avoid the danger of typhus, which generally arises in such conditions. Two transports were towed by the *Colombo*, and their state was nearly as bad.

Among the objects of philanthropy for some time past has been the improvement of the conditions of the soldier. Progress may have been made in some respects, but how much remains to be done will be recognised by every one who has seen the condition of the sick and wounded during the last fortnight. No blame is due to the medical men or the officers in command. They work early and late, are worn and harassed, and feel as much pity as any one for the unfortunate dying creatures; but our whole medical system is shamefully bad. The worn-out [Chelsea] pensioners who were brought out as an ambulance corps are totally useless, and not only are surgeons not to be had, but there are no dressers and nurses to carry out the surgeon's directions and to attend on the sick during the interval between his visits. Here the French are greatly our superiors. Their medical arrangements are extremely good, their surgeons more numerous, and they have also the help of the 'Sisters of Charity', who have accompanied the expedition in incredible numbers. These devoted women are excellent nurses, and perform for the sick and wounded all the offices which could be rendered in the most complete hospitals. We have nothing. The men must attend on each other, or receive no relief at all. The least that could have been done would have been to send out an efficient staff of surgeons. Surely the battle has not come unexpectedly. The army has been at Varna for months, and the expedition to Sebastopol has been long prepared. Nor are medical men rare, or their services ruinously expensive. There are hundreds who would be glad to come out to Turkey on temporary employment, with the chance of some permanent situation in future. But, though cholera gave due notice of its presence – though fever at first attacked a few, and increased its violence day by day – hardly any increase of the medical staff took place. In Varna lately 400 sick were attended by four men, and now vessels are sent on a voyage with a surgeon to 120 wretches. As the worst is not over, and indeed has hardly commenced, the attention of the Government may be well directed to this pressing want.[5]

The steamer *Hydaspes* was moored at Balaklava, and unlikely to have been as bad as *Colombo*, but it was still 'beastly and crowded'. Percy was walking wounded and in control of his senses, so at least he could escape *in extremis*. In the event, he only had to endure one night of discomfort as, by a stroke of luck, a family friend, Captain James Drummond* of HMS *Retribution*, found

* Hon James Drummond (1812–1895). He later became Admiral Sir James Drummond.

him out and gave him a berth on board his small steamer. He was an old hand in the Black Sea, as under him *Retribution* had been the first British warship to reach Sinope after the destruction of the Turkish fleet in 1853. Henry was eternally grateful for Drummond's kindness which, given the numbers that died in hospital, may even have saved his life; in the warm confines of the *Retribution*, moored in Balaklava harbour, he recovered well. The surgeons told him he had been lucky not to lose his arm.

The first letter that Henry was able to write in his own hand since before 20 September is dated 8 October, and the handwriting clearly displays the tortuous effort this short note involved:

HMS *Retribution*
Balaklava
Oct 8

My dear Father,
    I am getting well, but was ordered to go on board ship for some days, as operations could not commence; they have not commenced yet. We are I fear slow, and have given the Russians good opportunities of making a stronger resistance than at first anticipated. Sir John Burgoyne* is thought to blame – he certainly. I said we should be in Sebastopol in 48 hours. Captain James Drummond of this ship has been <u>most kind</u> finding me out, to take me on board. His surgeon has done me much good. Tell Isabel her handkerchief was my first bandage and it came indispensable. I cannot write any more but hope you are quite well. Give my love to Louisa† and everybody. In 3 days I go back to camp, but my arm will not be fit for use – but the danger of ulcers and sinuses will be quite gone.
    Your most affectionate son,
        H. Percy

While he was on board *Retribution* in Balaklava harbour the allies were setting up their camps and digging in around Sebastopol. The intention was to prepare artillery batteries all along the front in

---

* Lieutenant General Sir John Burgoyne (1782–1871), a distant relative of Lieutenant Montague Burgoyne in the Grenadier Guards, was Lord Raglan's Chief Engineer and advised him against an immediate attack from the north. He incurred widespread criticism during the Crimean campaign and was recalled home in February 1855.
† Henry's eldest sister, Lady Louisa Percy (1802–1883).

preparation for an enormous barrage which would precede an armed assault. The centre of activity was the uplands of the Chersonese, the peninsula which juts out into the Black Sea between Sebastopol on the north side and Balaklava on the south side. The French took the left of the line, using the bay of Kamiesch as their harbour – a wide sandy bay, well suited to the enormous number of ships unloading supplies and ammunition. The British took the right of the line (i.e. the section furthest from the sea), and used as their supply base Balaklava, which had very limited capacity. Balaklava is only about four hundred yards across at the widest point and it is so completely enclosed by high cliffs on all sides, the entrance from the Black Sea being a dog-leg, that the small expanse of water beside the village looks from most directions like an inland lake.

Moreover, the fact that the British end of the line, facing the valley of the Tchernaya, was exposed to the interior of the Crimea made the British position more precarious than that of the French, who were protected by the sea on their left flank. The British also had to contend with a greater distance from their harbour to the front line, which involved carrying everything up the Sapoune escarpment, which is up to 700 feet high in places.

Soon the Guards were doing duty in the trenches, and in the most exposed positions the work had to be done at night; little did they know in these early days how thin would wear the novelty of this routine. Henry Neville recorded on 12 October:

I made my first appearance in the trenches in charge of a covering party the other night, and a most disagreeable duty it was, as the moon was very bright. We paraded at 6 p.m., and proceeded to the place appointed for the battery; there we found the working party, who at once proceeded to commence operations, while we were extended on the crest of a hill to the left to protect them from a sortie. We were obliged to lie down, and were not more than 2,000 yards from the town, and indeed where our advanced sentries were placed, we had a most beautiful panorama of Sebastopol by moonlight, and I have no doubt that it will soon appear at the Colosseum. About twelve o'clock, when we were all very drowsy, we were awoke by a shell which burst close to us, succeeded by seven or eight others, all equally harmless. The working party took the hint, and immediately absconded (N.B. – they were not Guardsmen), and left us to take care of their half-finished work. Whether the Russians were alarmed at the noise of their own cannon, I know not; but they fired no more, and the only disagreeable part was the lying on the damp ground, shivering with cold, not daring to run about to warm oneself for fear of being seen. This was my first night in the trenches, and truly grateful am I to have escaped, and trust that, under Providence, I may be equally fortunate next time.

Those not on duty in the trenches were employed in manufacturing fascines and gabions. Fascines were bundles of sticks woven together to form portable platforms / pathways for use in crossing the enemy's trenches and broken earthworks. Gabions were enclosed wicker baskets in the shape of a small barrel, used in place of and in addition to sandbags when strengthening earthworks, lining trenches or fortifying gun emplacements.

Henry Percy, though, missed out on all these initial preparations.

HMS *Retribution* / Oct 14

My dear Father,

I am now able to use my fingers though my arm is not very move-able or useful. I have had a very good time of it not having had any fever or inflammation of any consequence, which is I think attrib-utable to the hard condition I was in, and to the necessity in marching on for 10 or 12 days though it was very hard work in the sun all day, and sometimes sleeping *a la belle étiole*, but I shaved myself, rejoicing that I escaped fever. I did not touch meat for 18 days but lived on rum, tea and cocoa.

The parallels are being opened daily, but no batteries commenced as it is apparently the intention of the authorities to commence with a general and tremendous fire – but the Russians have had ample time to entrench themselves. They shell us all day long but have done no damage. The weather is getting cold and the sooner we finish the job the better. Sickness is abating; indeed it need never have attained the frightful height it did if the authorities had chosen to prevent the men from gorging themselves with grapes and fruit. But they are really too unpractised, and Lord Raglan cannot see to everything. They forget or disdain minor precautions . . . .

I forgot to thank you for my mail which have arrived today and are a comfort. I hope you are quite well. Give my love to everybody.

Your most affectionate son,

H. Percy

Later that day Percy was allowed up to the Guards' camp, but he was still somewhat incapacitated by severe rheumatism and in great pain. He could not yet experience the perils of trench warfare which were fast becoming apparent. On 16 October a number of Guardsmen were employed in Gordon's battery – so named after the Engineer in charge of its preparation, who, as he walked up to his station, appeared to be quite impervious to the hail of round shot coming from the Russian lines, as it struck the ground all around him. It was here that the Grenadiers lost their first officer killed in action. They were on duty in a small chalk pit just outside and in front of the battery, under Captain Rowley. During one cannonade a spent shot struck the parapet, bounced up off a large stone and fell perpendicularly onto the back of Rowley, who was lying below. The ball did not even break his skin, but his spine was broken and he died instantaneously, without uttering a word.

The following day was the one they had all been working towards; all the English and French batteries were ready for the bombardment. It was intended that the combined English and French artillery, together with the navy, should be ready at 6.30 am for one coordinated and massive barrage. Unfortunately, as dawn broke, the Russians were able to see that embrasures had been opened up all along the lines in readiness, so they opened fire first, thus depriving the allies of a certain psychological advantage. The allied guns therefore started their fire with a coordination that was slightly disappointing, where they had intended to deliver one abrupt and instantaneous fire from all the batteries together.[6] Nevertheless, the exchange continued furiously for most of the day and there were some notable successes against two key Russian bastions – the Malakoff tower and the Great Redan. The former's stone structure crumbled and one of the Redan's powder magazines was hit by a shell, killing over a hundred men on the spot, shattering gun carriages all around. Admiral Korniloff, who gallantly insisted on directing Sebastopol's defences right from the front, was killed at the Malakoff. By the middle of the afternoon the British were ready to capitalize on their successes, and make the assault. The French, however, would not go in; the Flagstaff Bastion opposite their sector was still intact and they in turn had taken a heavier toll from the returning Russian fire. One of their own ammunition dumps had been hit, causing the ground to shudder a mile away; another blew up as a result of an accident. As only a combined attack could be contemplated, it was resolved to try again the next day.

That afternoon and evening the Grenadiers, who were in reserve, had plenty of time to write home describing the events of the day. Although Sebastopol had not fallen, the day had been a success, achieved with minimal casualties in the British sector. Higginson wrote to Captain Hatton, the Regimental Adjutant at Horse Guards:

It is an exciting moment to choose to begin a letter to you, for my ears are deafened as I write by the most tremendous cannonade that perhaps has ever been heard since gunpowder became an element of war. At half-past six this morning the French and English batteries, each numbering 73 guns, opened fire on Sebastopol simultaneously, and have now been hard at it for six hours. The stillness of the day and the little wind prevented our seeing much, except at the point just opposite us; but, if I may judge by the slackened fire, our guns have already told severely on the earthworks of the Russians, and I can see with my telescope that the 'Tower' which forms the centre of their principal battery is completely silenced. The fleet are at this moment approaching the sea forts, and I expect to hear them open their broadsides very shortly . . . . I believe it is the intention of the admirals to force an entrance into the port so soon as their broadsides have silenced the stone forts at the entrance.

The firing at this instance is perfectly <u>awful</u>, just in front of me I see rising some 200 feet into the air a huge tree of white smoke caused by the explosion of the magazine in one of the Russian batteries . . . . Our casualties for the whole day in the English Army have been one officer, a surgeon of the 68th, killed and 18 men slightly wounded.

You will readily understand that our Grenadiers have had no easy time of it for the last five or six days. They have been in the trenches, either as working or covering parties, almost incessantly; such luxury as six hours' continuous rest being positively unknown. Yet the urgency of the moment, and the real British pluck, choked off any grumbling that might naturally arise to the lips of some fine fellow, who after returning off twenty-four hours of outpost, found himself named for twenty-four hours of covering party in No. 1 battery.[7]

35

Colonel Hood chose to write to his wife, whom he cautioned again not to believe all the rumours she heard in England, the electric telegraph being the provider of only very scanty details: 'This morning I have been told that I was <u>dead</u> for 4 hours in London – a soldier had written to his wife "Poor Colonel Hood is dead" . . . pray do not give credit to such stories until official information reaches you. I have told you this before. I repeat it again.'[8] It was a prescient warning.

Henry Percy, though his handwriting was now almost back to normal, was in no mood to write much at all:

<u>Lines before Sebastopol</u>
<u>Oct 17</u>

My dear Father,

Siege began today before 7 am. I came up with my wound nearly healed the other day and was directly seized with a most violent rheumatism obliging me to be carried about by my servant in his arms even to perform the basest avocations. I suffer dreadfully from pain and sleepnessness and am on the ground in a tent with 4 other officers, but my mental annoyance beats all.

Oct 18: I am a little better. The place is not taken yet. I cannot write more.

Your most affectionate son,

H. Percy

As dawn broke the following morning allied troops were astonished and disappointed to see that the havoc caused in the Russian defences the previous day had largely been repaired during the night. The English bombardment continued, but the French were still in disarray as a result of the previous day's disasters, so the assault again had to be postponed. On this day, the second of the bombardment, the Regiment suffered a tragedy. Colonel Hood was superintending a large covering and working party, which included a detachment of the Grenadiers, in the trenches. Higginson had gone up with him as far as the first parallel, before being sent back to camp on an errand. At one point during this morning in the trenches Hood rose from his seat, intending to look through his glass over the half-complete parapet at the Russian battery opposite. As he peered over, he was killed instantly by a round shot in the chest.

Rowley had been killed at almost the same hour just two days before. On that occasion Hood had forbidden a detachment to go up to the trenches to retrieve the body until after dark, in order not to expose men to needless danger. Higginson, as he later explained in a letter to Mrs Hood, now had the unhappy necessity of following the same procedure for his commanding officer and it was not until after midnight that an ambulance wagon brought him down.[9] In his memoirs, written more than sixty years later, Higginson recalled:

A litter was laid at my tent door, by four Grenadiers, which contained the body of my honoured colonel . . . . As I lifted his remains in my arms and carried them into his tent all other feelings seemed to be merged in the consciousness that we had lost the man whose firmness and calm leadership were so conspicuous at the battle of the Alma. Though of a reserved nature, he yielded freely at times to a love of friendly intercourse. I had lived on terms of the greatest intimacy with him, and although he treated me in all matters of duty with a sternness approaching severity, his kindly bearing and language while we were enjoying our simple meals together confirmed my early belief that in him I had found a true friend. Had he lived, he would, I am confident, have succeeded to very high, if not the highest, command.[10]

Following so close upon Rowley's death, the loss of the Grenadiers' commanding officer cast a gloom over all the Guards; the entire Brigade attended Colonel Hood's funeral on the 19th, a day on which three more Grenadier officers were put out of action. Prince Edward of Saxe-Weimar and Lieutenant Davies were hit by splinters from an exploding shell while serving in the trenches; while the Prince recovered from the contusion brought about by this in a few days, Davies received a compound fracture of the leg below the knee and subsequently died on the voyage home.[11] Another casualty was William Cameron. He was leading a party of twenty-three volunteer sharpshooters on the second day of the bombardment. They were detailed to go out into no-man's-land as far forward as they could, using the wooded ravines as cover, in order to pick off artillerymen in the Russian batteries. During the course of these duties they were surprised by a party of Russians and in a brief exchange of fire Cameron was shot below the elbow.

37

Fortunately, like Percy, the bone was not broken, but he was invalided home.*

On the very day that Colonel Hood was killed, Henry Percy's aunt and uncle, Charles and Caroline Greatheed-Bertie-Percy, who were friends of the Hood family, posted letters to their nephew:

Guy's Cliffe. Oct 16 '54

My dear Henry,

Beverley wrote me a word that he had an opportunity of sending letters on the 18th. So the bag shall not go without a word of congratulation from me on your escape from worse peril in the glorious victory of the Alma; though, poor fellow, I dare say you have suffered quite sufficiently from your wound, and the skilful and successful, but very painful march on Balaklava. We hope to hear from B. that all these have not exasperated your wound, and that the spirit that led you to press forward even though a grand imprudence has had no unfavourable results. We are all very proud of you, our gallant and spirited relative, as Grosvenor Hood called you. Forty years of Peace has not impaired the courage or discipline of the British Army, and no one speaks of what has been achieved, and of the individual tales of gallantry, and courage, which have been exhibited without tears in their eyes. Our hope is that the panic caused by such exploits as the Alma and the march on Balaklava may have intimidated the Russians either to surrender to invincible assailants, nor to oppose them with the energies of despair! You cannot exaggerate the intense anxiety with which further intelligence is awaited at home; or the sorrow that is felt for the glorious dead.

I was delighted to hear that my old friend, Bobby Lindsay, has had the opportunity of showing his young courage! If he is a friend of yours, tell him so with every expression of good wish from me. I am very sorry to hear that Augustus Cox has fallen victim to fatigue, having escaped in battle, and how sad are the deaths from cholera immediately succeeding the perils of 20th Sept. May God offer mercy, avert their and all other dangers from those who are fulfilling their arduous duties with such unflinching magnanimity, and bring this campaign to an end without further bloodshed and loss . . . .

I have nothing to tell. We think of nothing but the Crimea and our gallant friends there. Our neighbour Mrs Gregory [Colonel Hood's

---

* Cameron survived, eventually became a general and lived on until 1913.

38

sister] is in despair as her young son in the Coldstreams* is ordered off to the East and is to sail immediately – he is a snotty youth, <u>rather green,</u> and I believe a very amiable son to his widowed mother, the widow of a soldier. He is a nephew of Grosvenor Hood's – if you have any opportunity of showing him a kindness, I shall be much obliged to you if you will do so, as both father and mother have been long friends in this house. Caroline had a very nice letter from Miss Charlotte Somerset† the other day expressing herself in her own and family's name very kindly about you and your honourable wounds. I shall leave the other side of the sheet for a word from Caroline herself. God bless and preserve you, my dear Henry.

Yours affectionately,
Charles B.P.

My dear, gallant nephew,

Charles has left me a page to express all my congratulations to you, although he has forestalled everything I had to say, even to the mention of the simple youth Gregory – and my letter from Charlotte Somerset. There is nothing left me but to talk of <u>rags!</u> As there are so many appeals for them in <u>*The Times*</u>, I have collected a large bundle to send. But as I would rather they reached <u>you</u>, and were useful to any of <u>your</u> poor sufferings, I have written to ask Lord Beverley if he has any suggestions to give me as to how this can be best effected. If not, I shall send them as the paper directs, and you will know that at least somebody will be the better for my <u>old shifts</u>. I wish we were in London just now, to hear all that can be heard from the Crimea. Poor Louisa's eyes prevent her from sending us as much of the <u>*on dits*</u> as she otherwise would.

God bless you, my dear Henry, and preserve you from further misery, and may you win many more laurels.

Ever yours affectionately,
Caroline B. P.

Clearly by mid-October full details of the battle of the Alma had reached England. The electric telegraph referred to by Hood in his last letter to his wife did not have the capacity to wire more than the basic necessities back to the Government at home and, in any case, at this stage in the campaign the closest telegraph station was at Kronstadt on the Austrian border with the Ottoman Empire

* Arthur Gregory was actually in the Scots Fusilier Guards.
† Miss Charlotte Somerset was a daughter of Lord Raglan, who was affectionately known as 'Rag', hence the pun in Caroline's letter.

(now Brasov, Romania). There would be no direct link from the Crimea to London until April 1855, so until then the quickest official communication still took six to ten days[12] and the conventional mail typically took between two and three weeks to reach home. In late October, therefore, the battle of the Alma and the flank march were the major topics of discussion between Henry and his family. He had plenty of time to think about *post mortems* of the battle, as he was still forbidden to do duty on 22 October: 'My last told you how ill I was; I suffered fearfully but I am better – but they will not let me on duty as they say I can't. I say I can.'

Lines before Sebastopol
Oct 27

My dear Father,

I am very much obliged to you for your munificence, your kindness & that of everybody. But I must put you right upon one subject which is that I did <u>not</u> conceal my wound, but I did not go to get dressed [until] after the action was over for fear of being huddled away and then I told the doctors point blank that I would not upon any consideration leave the Battalion till the fighting was positively over as I expected that at Katcha & Belbec we should have another battle. The Duke of Cambridge wanted me to go, but I declined and there is the entire history upon which I need not dilate any more. I now want to tell you a fact which I see the papers leave in uncertainty and which I beg you will spread. *Viz.* that the 33rd took the gun and were forced to relinquish it, but the <u>Grenadiers, not the Fusiliers</u> took the Battery. The right of my company was on the gun's right and the left of 7th company on its left, and that I halted my company till I got over the parapet to see whether there was a mine – and I could have touched the gun but my right arm was disabled. Pakenham, who commanded the other company, actually scratched 'No 7 Grenadier Guards' on the gun. I was thinking too much of going on to do so. Pray state this to every one, with the exception of my own particular performance, as it is feared the Regiment is to be deprived of the honour of capturing the gun. This I am ready to swear before any court. My Battalion was the only Battalion that did not *romper en arrière*. The Fusiliers retreated by order and to that circumstance they owe their greater loss. My company dressed back and took the Russians who were pursuing the Fusiliers in their flank, and they went down like corn before the wind. I had about 30 men including myself *hors de combat*, and others were hit but not too significantly. One of my officers had his cap shot through, the other had his epaulette partly carried away. I ought to have been returned 'shot through the arm' and Burgoyne, who carried the colours, had his leg broken – and forsooth was released by this muff of a surgeon as 'slightly wounded' – at which we are all savage.

Please thank everybody for their kind wishes. The Naval Surgeon told me that if I had not been in good condition and [had] good flesh, I should have had inflammation of the joint for a matter of months. My wound was right through the sword arm – a large double orifice – just shaving the joint. Had it broken it, I must have lost my arm. I was wounded early the 20th but being pretty close the shot came so sharp that it carried coat, silk waistcoat and shirt bang out with it, which was very lucky. I was hit by a spent ball in the shoulder strap. And again in the water bottle, glancing off the buckle of my belt, which made me jerk down a bit. With the few officers wounded in my Battalion, I hasten to say almost every officer was shot in his garments, and one twice, one of which was his breastplate.

My rheumatism has gone and I am doing duty. Poor Hood and Rowley were killed in the trenches and two others wounded severely, one slightly – pretty well out of 18 [of us]. The weather continues beautiful. Constant alarms, which all turn out bosh and are in a great measure owing to the Duke's fidgeting. I have no conveniences for writing, so you must make my excuses to Louisa and Margaret* for not writing at present. I wish we had five Lord Raglans, we should be better off. He is wonderful but seems to have an English shyness in showing himself, <u>except when in action</u>. My principle suffering [is] from want of sleep for I have never slept well since the Alma, why I don't know. I don't mind bivouacking but I don't like being five or six in a tent at all. I hope Lovaine's child is better. Give my love to Louisa. I hope you will continue well and believe me your most affectionate son,
    H. Percy

Henry's father, Lord Beverley, wrote to him fairly regularly, but his handwriting is that of an elderly man and not easy to read. Also, like his son, he was often more interested in the tactical arrangements than the human elements. However, Henry's fifty-two-year-old unmarried sister had more down-to-earth concerns:

---

* Louisa's younger sister (1813–1897), who was married to Lord Hatherton.

23rd October
Portman Square

My dear Henry,

My eyes are much worse, so I will only write a line, as Arthur Gregory consents to take it – indeed I have nothing to say. Not being of a sentimental turn, you will not care to hear how my father sits, all day, thinking of Sebastopol, and watching for news. Your letter of the 8th arrived today, and was a great comfort – for we both dreaded fever coming on from your neglect of your wound, and it is a consolation to know that you are well cared for and quiet on board ship. We are so pleased and proud at hearing so much of your gallantry. Charles Bagot* sent me word that at the Guards Club you were talked of as one of the most distinguished, where all were so distinguished for bravery. I think I mentioned Colonel Hood's kind and flattering note to Algernon. *The Times* published 10 days ago[†] a frightful statement of the neglected condition of the wounded. The Director General of the Medical Board put forth a counter-statement, which the villainous *Times* refused to insert till shamed into doing so by its appearance in all the other papers! I should like to know whether there was any truth in *The Times'* account, for I believe not one word said by officials.

I went the other day to the Miss Somersets; they told me that their father[‡] had mentioned your wound in his first letter to them, and that he had been much pleased with you during your visit to him at Varna. They were extremely kind and promised to send me news whenever they heard anything. We are staying in London till after the fall of Sebastopol. I hardly ever see anybody, and when we do, nobody speaks of or thinks of any events except those in the Crimea.

My eyes forbid my saying more now. My father has sent you another air cushion, and I have added a small parcel of fine hand-kerchiefs which may be a comfort to your poor arm. So many people have written to enquire that I do nothing but answer notes, to the great detriment of my eyes.

Your most affectionate
L.P.

---

* Charles Bagot (1808–1881), was married to Henry's cousin Sophia (Vice Admiral Josceline Percy's daughter).
[†] See extract above, pp28–30.
[‡] i.e. Lord Raglan.

The small parcel is sent to Captain Hatton, who promises to do his best for it. I would have sent you many more handkerchiefs, but the parcel was to be <u>very</u> small. Arthur Gregory is a neighbour and good friend of the B. P.'s. I fear, though you do not say so, you have suffered much. God bless.

But just as those at home were thinking about Alma, which had happened five weeks previously, on the front line things were moving apace once more. What became known as the First Bombardment continued for a week, but every night the Russians repaired their defences enough to preclude an assault, despite the fact that the south side of the town was rapidly becoming a pile of rubble. The Russians undoubtedly took the heaviest casualties, but, just as the defenders of the town could not take indefinite punishment, the besiegers did not have sufficient ammunition to maintain the intensity of their fire indefinitely; nor could their troops continue to rise day after day at two in the morning (having had only a few hours sleep on the stony ground inside their tents) so that they should be in position in the trenches by dawn, without getting some longer period of rest. Lord Raglan was content to see the cannonade wound down on the 24th as he had received intelligence of a fresh Russian force under General Liprandi, which had just arrived in the Crimea from Bessarabia. He simply did not have the manpower to continue intensive siege operations at the same time as protecting the right flank from this new threat. The next day Liprandi did indeed launch an attack on Balaklava from the direction of the valley of the Tchernaya. As the allies had always known, their weakest point was on the plain below the Sapoune ridge, where they were vulnerable to an attack from the interior of the Crimea. Any such attack had the ability to cut the British end of the siege lines off from the port of Balaklava, which, if it was recaptured by the Russians, would have been disastrous. The entrance to Balaklava was protected by a line of six redoubts, temporary gun emplacements, about two miles out from the harbour itself, along the Woronzoff road. These redoubts were manned by Turkish troops, but they only had nine field guns between them. A body of British infantry, the 93rd Highlanders, protected the immediate approach to the town.

More must have been written about the battle of Balaklava than any other, so, given that the Guards were not involved, there is little relevance for this narrative in giving more than a skeleton account. The Russians attacked at about 6 am; by 7.30, they had captured Redoubt No. 1, at which point the Turks in Redoubts 2, 3 and 4 fled. This first line of defence being overcome, the way was open for Russian cavalry to move in on Balaklava proper. The Russian horsemen were repelled by volleys of rifle fire from the Highlanders (the episode which immortalized the expression, 'Thin Red Line') and then charged by the cavalry's Heavy Brigade; British casualties were astonishingly light, with just a handful killed – but Grey Neville was one of the unfortunate few in the Heavies to be severely wounded.

Lord Raglan then ordered the cavalry to press the advantage, re-take the redoubts and prevent the Russians from carrying away the guns they had captured there earlier in the day. Owing to a combination of misunderstood orders, the impetuosity of Captain Nolan and the confused geography of the area (which meant that Lords Lucan and Cardigan had very different and incomplete views of the battlefield when compared with Lord Raglan's own viewpoint high on the Sapoune ridge) the Light Brigade of the cavalry charged on the most insane objective – a line of Russian guns on the *enemy's* side of the redoubts, overlooked by Russian artillery on both flanks.*

The result of this catastrophe was the loss of one of Lord Raglan's two precious cavalry brigades as an effective fighting force and, while the main Russian attack had been beaten off, the enemy retained control of the three easternmost redoubts and consequently commanded the Woronzoff road. This would have serious repercussions during the winter.

Aside from the engagement of the thin red line of the 93rd Highlanders, the battle of Balaklava was almost exclusively a cavalry engagement. The 1st Division of Infantry under the Duke of Cambridge, including the Brigade of Guards, made quick time from their camp four or five miles away on the heights above

---

* Henry Percy's verdict on this episode was that Lord Lucan should have been more strong-minded in resisting Captain Nolan's representations to charge. He said that if he had been in Lucan's position, he would have retorted: 'I will not have my young <u>men</u> killed'.

Sebastopol to arrive on the scene mid-morning in time for a grandstand view of the charge of the Heavies. But, although they were on the battlefield and subsequently qualified for Balaklava clasps on their campaign medals, they remained in reserve just outside Balaklava. The 4th Division, under General Sir George Cathcart, who Lord Raglan urged to come as quickly as possible so that the Light Brigade should have infantry support in retaking the guns, did not arrive on the scene until it was too late. Cathcart was having breakfast at the time he received the instruction, and failed to react with the urgency that was undoubtedly required.

Nevertheless, the Russians had plenty in store for the infantry at the Battle of Inkerman, who caught a taster of this at dawn the day after the Battle of Balaklava, when the Russians chanced a sortie out from Sebastopol against the right-hand end of the British lines, known as the Inkerman Heights. It was a half-hearted attack, perhaps just probing the strength of the British in that sector of the line and testing the possibility of bringing artillery within range of the enemy without being heard. In that it gave them information that would come in useful at a later stage, 'Little Inkerman', as it came to be known, was a success for the Russians. But the cost to the Russian attackers was dear: they took five or six hundred casualties, against less than a hundred allied killed and wounded.

October 28 '54. Lines before Sebastopol

My dear Father,
   I sent a very hurried letter by today's post to you. So I begin more at leisure today. The action that took place at Balaklava on [the] 25th began by the Turks being attacked in some earthworks about 1 mile in advance of Balaklava which they gave up without apparently a struggle. These earthworks were faultily made, the gorge* on the right flank, and would you imagine it, no gate – not even a tree cut down and thrown across. One would have thought that after the numerous instances of earthworks being taken by cavalry from the absence of means of closing the gorge, Smolensk† to wit, our engineers might have seen that they might have also

---

* Gorge: an entrance to a redoubt.
† The Battle of Smolensk, 1812, when French Cavalry successfully stormed the Russian city.

connected the redoubts with a deep ditch – which would have stopped cavalry effectively.

The Russian cavalry advanced after the capture of the redoubts and were received by the 93rd, who sent them to the right about. The Heavy Brigade of our Cavalry charged with success, and afterwards the Light Brigade, who charged foolishly but most gallantly captured 12 guns, and in their turn were shattered to pieces by some Russian artillery in reserve. We advanced along the Heights seeing the whole of the action and descended to Balaklava where we formed in line and the Russians never advanced a bit. We marched back half-starved and I myself was dead beat in the legs.

People are very angry with the Turks, but considering their being new troops, we are to blame for placing them so far in advance, in works of so paltry a profile. An English hunter could have cleared the ditch* and, considering the French are wonderful diggers, they might have made them very strong had care been taken to point out the way to them. The more I see, the less I think of Lord Raglan's immediate subordinates (except Cathcart, Campbell and one or two more), and the more I think of my lord himself.

On the 26th Gortschakoff, who commanded in the city, assembled the troops saying he desired the destruction of English Cavalry and the troops demanded to be led forth. They were given drink, came forth – and got a most rare thrashing, of which I saw little as we were sent to guard a weak point, where they never could reach, our artillery was so well served. Shot and bullets, however, came near enough to be unpleasant. The deserters and prisoners confessed that they would never have thought of attacking the redoubts on the 25th if the allied army had held them, but seeing Turks only, they thought they would chance it. The Russians menace Balaklava but have as much chance of getting in as of flying, as we have a Highland Brigade, several marines and sailors, and Batteries on all the bare points. I am afraid the inconvenient position I write in must make this nearly illegible.

29th Oct. Today we have a severe cold North wind which has made us all very uncomfortable, more especially as the soil is so thin that our tent pegs will hardly hold; the total absence of fuel is much felt. The night before last a strong patrol fell in with the Russian Cavalry with their horses picketed, fired into them, frightened their horses till they broke loose and captured about 180 horses, besides

---

* Henry did in fact borrow a horse and have a close look at the redoubts after the battle, and had no difficulty jumping the ditches.

those that ran away. The loss of the Light Cavalry (ours) is esti-
mated under 300.* They said 600 at first . . . . In the sortie [of Little
Inkerman], the Russians lost over 600 men killed – we very few.

Believe me, my dear Father, your most affectionate son,

H. Percy

The actions of Balaklava and 'Little Inkerman', while not decisive
for either side, had not unduly damaged the morale of the British.
One Coldstream Guards officer wrote: 'Far from drooping in
spirits, most of [our wounded] were in buoyant spirits. Sometimes
a fine youth with a badly fractured arm, hurra-ed lustily as he
passed; another whose thigh a round shot had smashed, would –
faint as he was – raise himself up a little on his litter, and brandish
his rifle triumphantly. I observed that nearly every man, whether
slightly or sorely hurt, still clutched his musket.'[13]

---

* The actual numbers are as follows: of 664 who charged, 298 were lost – 110
killed, 130 wounded and 58 taken prisoner. Thus forty-five per cent casualties,
all in a few minutes – for nothing. Additionally, fifty-four per cent of horses,
already an incredibly scarce resource, were lost. (Adkin)

Chapter 3

Inkerman

The day after the Battle of Balaklava was Henry Neville's thirtieth birthday. As soon as he could that morning, he went down to the village to find his brother Grey, who was by this time on board a hospital ship awaiting transport back to Scutari. He found him propped up in bed because his wounds, including a deep penetration from a lance in his side and three other smaller ones in his back, prevented him from lying flat. However, although he was having some difficulty in breathing, he did not believe that his chest was penetrated and the stimulants he was being given brought him great relief. All in all, and considering the severity of his wounds, he was in relatively good spirits. It transpired that Grey had had a very lucky escape and had only made it back to the British camp owing to the humanity and courage of a private soldier in his regiment, Abbott.

Grey explained that he had led his troop to the charge, passing through the first line of Russians, whereupon, after a second or two of continuing on to the second line, he ceased to hear the tramp of his troop behind him. On looking round, he saw that the others had turned around and charged back through the first line whence they came. He thus found himself cut off, with several of the Russian cavalry now riding towards him. Thinking that the best thing to do was attempt to ride through them, he went with all his horse's might bang into the middle of them. The impact knocked both him and the man he directly clashed with off their horses; on falling, he had thought he was a dead man. Wounded, he lay still, with his face to the ground. The Russians clearly thought he was done for and Grey soon heard them moving away. Believing they were gone, he raised his head to have a look. Unluckily, a Russian dragoon saw him move, dismounted and cut him over the head with his sword. The Russian cavalry in the Crimea had notoriously blunt swords, to the extent that they would frequently glance off a thick coat, so Grey's helmet saved his scalp, but his right ear was cut into.

Shortly afterwards, his own cavalry came back over the place where he had fallen, causing his assassin to sheer off. Grey, unable to get up, was hit a number of times by horses' hooves. As his own troop came near, he shouted out for them to pick him up, but they couldn't hear him. One man, Abbott, however, did find him, dismounted from his horse and lifted him from the ground. Abbott made his officer stand for a moment, but Grey was so weak that he could not walk and fell back down again. The soldier would not leave him, but continued to urge him by every persuasion to try and move; eventually he was forced to drag Grey by bodily strength to a place of assistance and safety.

Once on board ship the two brothers had but a few minutes with each other, as the vessel was already under weigh and Henry was under orders for a twenty-four-hour spell in the trenches. Whilst Henry was under no illusions as to the severity of his brother's wounds, he felt able reassure his father that Grey 'has spat no blood and I trust that none of the internals are injured. I was glad to see him looking pretty well and cheerful, and able to talk and breathe without pain . . . . I hope the family will not allow themselves to be uneasy about the young "Heavy", as I sincerely trust there is nothing serious.' He packed him off to Scutari in the knowledge that he was unlikely ever to return to the Crimea, but should soon be invalided home.

In the meantime the Army of the East continued in much the same way as it had before the battle of Balaklava and Henry Neville recorded spending the rest of his 'miserable' birthday crouched under an earthwork with shot and shell flying all about. The fact was that neither the general engagement at Balaklava nor the Russian sortie of 'Little Inkerman' had really changed anything. The siege lines and the base at Balaklava were still intact, but the British cavalry were now a spent force. They had always been regarded as primarily an offensive weapon and such was the stalemate in the trenches that any further opportunity for using cavalry looked like a distant prospect, even if it had still been available. The continuation of the siege of Sebastopol depended upon infantry manpower.

Both the Brigade of Guards and the regiments of the Line carried on with their increasingly monotonous routine of regular outpost duty – day and night – interrupted by regular false alarms and urgent cries of 'Stand to!' The troops still had not seen any meaningful extra supplies, but a few small comforts that they had left behind on ship when they first landed at Calamita Bay had gradually filtered through to the camps, such as an extra shirt or two and the odd blanket. The men had recovered their knapsacks, though many had somehow lost their contents. The officers, who often conducted parades in the early hours of the morning, were becoming used to walking down the ranks by lantern light, where they could dimly discern the men's feet protruding out of their worn-out or mud-rotted boots, their ragged trousers tied around the ankle with string. But, with a tot of rum given to each man, they would all happily set off with pork and biscuit in their haversacks, often not to return for twenty-four hours.[1] Lord Balgonie described the British officer's routine in October 1854:

The last few days have been very cold, with a biting north wind that penetrates tents, great coats and blankets – so you may fancy the hour I spent between 2 and 3 this morning was not one of unalloyed pleasure; [nor is the fact] that a piece of salt pork about the size of a Latin Grammar is given to the British officer during very hard work, as his sustenance for 3 days. Biscuit is added, and just rum enough to make him wish for more. The first thing the 'British Officer' does on receiving his pork is to see if there is any lean. Finding of course that there is none (there never is in Continental Pork) he soliloquies 'all fat' and makes notches dividing it into 3 equal parts, one for Monday, and etc. according to the number of days his 'dollop' of fat is to last. Having been 2 nights out of bed, he flatters himself he is in for a good snooze and turns in at 8 o'clock. At 9 he is waked up with the pleasing intelligence that 'an officer has been hit in the trenches, and he must fill his place,' or that, 'the enemy is threatening our rear, and an extra Picquet is wanted.' Knowing that expostulation is vain, he shoulders his great coat and blanket, secures a large supply of tobacco and a short pipe, hesitates about taking a pistol, but eventually takes it 'in case the beggars should come near enough', and sallies forth feeling very like a martyr. In spite of the want of Romance attending the stern realities of war, there is a sort of pleasing excitement to a man who can laugh at salt pork and scorn the want of sleep.[2]

The shelling continued intermittently on both sides. But despite the allies' determination to set fire to the city by firing incendiary rockets into the dockyards, they never had much success. The citizens of Sebastopol had removed wooden doors and window frames, and flammable roof material was replaced with metal sheeting.[3] Although cracks in the city's defences would appear by nightfall, they were almost miraculously made good by morning. Again, Lord Raglan and his French counterpart, Canrobert, discussed the possibility of an assault, provisionally fixing a date of 7 November. They would meet for detailed planning on the evening of the 5th.

The night of 4–5 November was wet but still. It was so quiet that even right away up on the British lines, the bells of Sebastopol were heard tolling long before dawn, summoning the enemy's garrison down below to mass. During the course of the previous few days there had been increased activity from the Russian army building up the other side of the Tchernaya Valley over to the east; the high command suspected that something was afoot, but there was no indication of an imminent attack. Early on the morning of the 5th the night picquets returned from their outposts without incident. Some thought that they had heard rumbling noises in the valley below, but the sounds were too indistinct beneath the pattering of rain to be worth reporting.

As dawn broke, at about 6 am, the fresh picquet companies – a few men each from the Coldstream Guards, the 23rd (Royal Welch Fusiliers) and the 41st – who had only just relieved the previous lot at their posts a mile or so in front of the British camps, suddenly saw through the mist an enormous Russian column heading straight for them up the main Careenage Ravine. This was no 'sortie', for they were bringing with them heavy field guns, whose wheels had been muffled so that they could be brought close quietly overnight. Furthest out in front, and well down Careenage Ravine, was Captain Gerald Goodlake of the Coldstream Guards. He knew the value of this position well, as he had prevented a

51

major incursion from a column coming up this way on 26 October, for which he was subsequently awarded the Victoria Cross.

Goodlake and his sharpshooters now fired the opening shots of the Battle of Inkerman. Up the hill to the right of Goodlake was Captain Hugh Rowlands* of the 41st:

> On the morning of the 5th, I and the company were for outlying piquet . . . . I halted my company and went out to plant sentries about 150 yards over the hill. Having done so, I returned to the company which had just piled arms and ordered the men to take off packs, when the sentries commenced firing in a most determined way.
>
> I ran up to enquire the cause when one shouted that there were columns of Russians close to them. I stood to my arms and advanced in extended order, thinking it was a sortie something like that of the 26th. On getting to the top of the hill I found myself close upon, very truly, thousands of Russians. I immediately gave an order to retire, which was done for about 200 yards, when I halted on the next high bit of ground and lay down quietly waiting for them . . . .
>
> When we retired the Russians came on with the most fiendish yells you can imagine. We commenced firing. To my dismay, I found that half the firelocks missed fire, which dispirited the men. At this period the Russian columns opened fire with their field pieces, pouring in grape and shell. We then got some reinforcements from the 55th and the 30th, but were gradually obliged to retire . . . . After a little hand-to-hand work we turned them and drove them back about 500 yards, when we were met by a fresh column and compelled to retire.[4]

The outposts had more than done their duty. A picquet was no more than a company of men (at this time under-strength and probably numbering no more than sixty or seventy) whose role it was to observe the enemy and, in the event of an attack, warn the camp as quickly as possible. In the meantime they were to buy as much time as they could by harassing the enemy with rifle fire. In the Peninsular War picquets perfected the art of retiring intact while under fire; at Inkerman they were rusty on these tactics and instead fought as if every inch of ground was precious.[5]

Before continuing with this account, it is necessary to step back and describe the deposition of the opposing armies and the lie of

---

* Captain Rowlands was subsequently awarded the Victoria Cross for rescuing a wounded man later in the action.

the land. The Battle of Inkerman was probably the hardest-fought clash of arms on European soil in the hundred years between Waterloo and the First World War. However, it never captured the public imagination as, for example, Balaklava did, which may in part be because it is so difficult to depict or describe. Unlike Waterloo, Alma or Balaklava, Inkerman was no set-piece battle managed by the General Staff from a vantage point. It came to be known as the 'Soldiers' Battle' as it was entirely owing to the initiative of regimental officers (chiefly company commanders and their subalterns) and the sheer guts and determination of their men that the day was saved in the face of overwhelming odds.

Total allied forces at this time numbered about 40,000 French, 25,000 British (including the Naval Brigade) and 11,000 Turks.[6] The Turks, however, were excluded from active duties by Raglan and Canrobert after they had fled the redoubts at Balaklava, despite their proven capabilities as warriors, as had been seen at Silistria in the Balkans. So, in practice the allies only had 47,000 of infantry[7] with which to meet the impending crisis. In contrast, throughout October, Russian troops had been pouring into Sebastopol, and Prince Mentschikoff's total force now numbered some 120,000 men.[8]

Quite apart from being outnumbered, the chief difficulty for the allies was that their troops were thinly dispersed all around the south side of Sebastopol from just north of Kamiesch Bay, right round to the heights of Inkerman overlooking the Tchernaya valley, and then back again to the Sapoune ridge and down towards Balaklava – a front stretching twenty miles. The British, and more particularly the Guards, were at the apex of the most vulnerable point at the eastern end of this line, potentially exposed to the enemy on three sides.

Mentschikoff's plan was to concentrate his attack here, with his force split in two; Dannenberg would attack the British from the north, using the Post Road through Quarry Ravine and a track up the Careenage Ravine to get his troops, and more importantly his artillery, up onto Shell Hill (so named because of the peculiar preponderance of small white snail shells found there). Prince Gortschakoff would move up the Tchernaya Valley, covering the main attack with artillery, and then move on to the plains of Balaklava, driving a wedge between the main allied force and its back-up at Balaklava. Gortschakoff would also endeavour to seize a position on the Sapoune ridge behind the British camps. In short, a classic pincer movement. The Russians were very confident that their overwhelming odds would win the day. Two Grand Dukes, sons of the Tsar, had just arrived in the Crimea to encourage the troops – hence the unusual degree of activity seen the previous day over the other side of the valley.

The only way to grasp fully the complexity of the ground at Inkerman is to study closely a map, of which there are no fewer than eleven in Kinglake's 500-page volume on Inkerman, and then visit the site. A detailed description of all the slopes, escarpments and meandering, interlacing ravines serves little purpose. Suffice to say, however, that the area where the fighting took place covers the easternmost square mile of the hills overlooking Sebastopol; this ground also looks down to the right onto the Tchernaya River some seven hundred feet below. The whole range, besides being punctuated throughout by watercourses and gullies, is covered over much of its area by dense brushwood.

There were no real fortifications (perhaps there should have been after the events of the 26th: surely the Engineers, of whom there were plenty, Henry observed, could have used the Turks to build earthworks etc?) – merely a barrier of stones across the Post Road at a strategic place in front of 'Home Ridge', and a Sandbag Battery a few hundred yards to the east, on a slightly flatter piece of ground on the Kitspur, which commanded the valley below. This Sandbag Battery had been designed by the Engineers to take two guns, the idea being to counter a Russian battery across the valley, near the ruins of Inkerman. However, as Henry's eighteen-year-old cousin Archer Amherst,* who was a lieutenant in the Coldstream Guards, observed, it was 'a very good Battery no doubt, but one from which our guns could no more reach the Russians than if they had been at Woolwich'.[9] Therefore, since it covered neither Sebastopol nor its approaches, the two eighteen-pounders were removed to be employed more usefully elsewhere. The work itself, about twenty yards wide and made of earth and sandbags built up to a height of up to ten feet,[10] remained a feature on the skyline. Despite being completely redundant the Sandbag

* Hon William Archer Amherst (1836–1910), later 3rd Earl Amherst. His mother, Lady Holmesdale, was Henry Percy's first cousin.

Battery was perceived by the Russians at Inkerman to be a primary objective, and it was there, as well as at the Barrier and the Gap between them, that the fiercest hand-to-hand fighting took place.

The Second Division was encamped behind Home Ridge, astride the Post Road. The Guards' Camp was about a mile behind, near a ruined windmill. As dawn broke, therefore, there were only about 4,500 men in this sector: for the moment it would be up to these men alone to hold the line against up to 40,000 enemy who were about to be pitted directly against them. Having heard the repeated firing coming from the outposts in front and soon realizing that this was a full-scale Russian offensive, General Pennefather of the Second Division immediately mobilized.

The three Guards battalions, which now amounted to only about 1,400 men (about half their full strength), were also under way in no time; not a man had time for breakfast. Of the Grenadiers, three of the eight companies were out of the camp on outpost duty. One of these was led by Prince Edward of Saxe-Weimar, who had arrived at his post on a spur commanding one of the southernmost fingers of Careenage Ravine, known as the Wellway, at about 5:30 am. His company had been placed there, well outside the general system of English outposts, by Bentinck, the Brigade commander, as a fail-safe purely to protect their camp. He never imagined that his isolated watch would prove to be the front of the battle, but suddenly there appeared through the gloom a column of 2,000 Russians, snaking its way up the bed of the Wellway, imminently threatening the rear of the main British defences.

On the other side of the ravine a young Rifle Brigade officer, Lieutenant Henry Clifford,* also saw the danger and immediately launched a bayonet charge; as an ADC, he only had twelve men with him.

'Come on,' I said, 'my lads!' and the brave fellows dashed in amongst the astonished Russians, bayoneting them in every direction. One of the bullets in my revolver had partly come out and prevented it revolving and I could not get it off. The Russians fired

* The Hon Henry Clifford (1826–1883) was later awarded the Victoria Cross for his part in the Battle of Inkerman.

their pieces off within a few yards of my head, but none touched me. I drew my sword and cut off one man's arm who was in the act of bayoneting me and a second seeing it, turned round and was in the act of running out of my way, when I hit him over the back of the neck and laid him dead at my feet. About 15 of them threw down their arms and gave themselves up, and the remainder ran back . . . . Out of the small party with me (12), 6 men were killed and 3 wounded, so my escape was wonderful.[11]

Simultaneously, Prince Edward placed his men in skirmishing order and made them lie down partly concealed by the brushwood, and fire volley after volley into these Russians' flank, so making them think that his eighty or ninety men were the advance guard of a much larger force. He kept this up for three-quarters of an hour, gradually pushing them back down the Wellway.

Meanwhile, the bulk of the Grenadiers were resting in camp that Sunday morning. They awoke at daybreak to the sound of intermittent gunfire and, as they all slept in their clothes, it took just a minute to don swords and revolvers; by the time they mustered in the drizzle more general gunfire, including artillery, could be heard.[12] With Lieutenants Sturt and Verschoyle carrying the colours, up they went through the Second Division camp, already receiving fire from Russian artillery on Shell Hill, towards their comrades now engaged on Home Ridge. The Barrier on the road was another point on which the enemy concentrated its fire and big gaps in the line were already appearing. The Guards moved to support the right flank of the Second Division, advancing in lines through the thick brushwood towards the Sandbag Battery. Captain Harvey Tower of the Coldstreams, who arrived on the scene after the Grenadiers and the Scots Fusiliers, recorded in his diary:

Several times I saw the heads of Russian columns coming swarming through the bushes, the Officers in front waving their swords and shouting to the men; but directly they saw us there was a hesitation, a huddling together, and indecision, and a decided tendency *not* to come on. They fired quickly and nervously, and generally over our heads; they were so close to us before they saw us, and they were on lower ground than we were; if they had advanced in anything like a decided manner, we *must* have been entirely swamped and annihilated. But our fellows stood their ground manfully, and the more the Ruskis came up, the quicker our fellows rammed down their cartridges and blazed into them . . . .

The numbers in front of us increased every second, and we were really hand to hand with them; the bushes were full of English and Russians mixed up together. The groans of the wounded, Officers yelling and screaming at their men, the soldiers shouting at one another, and (I have no doubt) using their favourite expressions, and the firing almost deafened one.

The Brigade was getting very much mixed up now . . . . Several other regiments and men of the Second Division picquets furnished us with stragglers who were of the right sort. Our Brigade line, or remnant of our line, was the rallying point of everybody who was animated with a right spirit. Oh, for breech-loaders* at the moment, how we could have swept them off as they came up the hill! . . . I kept taking ammunition out of dead men's pouches to feed the pouches of the living, screaming if I saw any fanatic Ruski that required shooting.

When the Grenadiers reached the Sandbag Battery, bitter hand-to-hand fighting was testament to the desperation of those who know there is no support if they fail, alternately slashing and stabbing with their bayonets, and smashing with the butt-ends of their rifles. In Christopher Hibbert's words, 'The whine of bullets, the damp whistle of shells, the screams of agony and rage, even the constant raucous shouting which those who fought at Inkerman afterwards remembered more clearly than anything, were muffled by the thick and suffocating air . . . . Dark shapes heaved out of the whiteness with the suddenness of apparitions or melted away into it silently . . . . Men looked like bushes, bushes like men. On both sides they were wearing overcoats, and it was almost impossible to tell who were friends and who were enemies. It was like fighting in a nightmare.'[13]

Soon after arriving on the scene Percy found himself isolated in single combat with a Russian, whom he ran through with his sword when he would not submit to be taken prisoner. As the battle waxed and waned throughout the morning, the Battery

* Breech loaders were beginning to come into use at this time, but the army's Minié rifle, despite being a modern invention, was muzzle-loading and slower to reload than the old-fashioned Russian muskets.

changed hands countless times. The mounted officers had their horses shot from under them almost immediately, so the entire struggle was directed from on foot, although in this conflict, the actions and initiative of individuals counted far more than orders from above. The officers who were ordinarily on horses but now joined in with the rank and file included Colonel Reynardson, who had taken over from Hood in command of the Grenadiers in the Crimea, and Captain Higginson.

When a fresh onslaught of Russians emerged out of the brushwood below, Neville was shot through the body, the ball striking his spine, paralysing him. As they fell back, his friends saw one Russian soldier move to bayonet him on the ground, but he was dissuaded from doing so by his own comrades. When the Guards, however, gained the upper hand again, Henry Neville's assailant stabbed him three times before retiring.[14] Not long after, Lieutenant Napier Sturt, carrying the colour, was severely wounded by a musket ball, but before falling he handed the flag to another. Sturt was in such a position that he could immediately be carried away on stretcher, but Neville would have to wait, still alive but completely helpless.

The Coldstreams soon made their appearance and were received by cheers from the two other regiments. Some Grenadiers then passed poor Neville as he lay prostrate and unable to move, as they charged once again into the Battery. And so the conflict ebbed and flowed, with occasional lulls, for nigh on three hours.

When the Guards had been in action for scarcely an hour, albeit after a hasty march up onto the heights and without breakfast, they were already showing signs of fatigue and battle-weariness. Reynardson and the other officers could see the Brigade's resolve failing. Lieutenant Colonel Henry Percy therefore took it upon himself to rally the faltering troops and, waving his sword, he called upon his 'boys' to do their duty now in this hour of need, or they should all, himself included, regret it as long as they lived. With this entreaty, he charged forwards in front of them all. Higginson, in a private letter to Captain Hatton at Horse Guards, described Percy as being 'a full 10 yards ahead of anyone'.[15] Another eyewitness, in an anonymous letter to *The Morning Herald*, said: 'He went bang into the Russian masses and disappeared; his men followed and disappeared also.' Among the

Grenadiers who charged on this occasion were George Cadogan,*
Sir Charles Russell and Charles Lindsay.†

On reaching the battery Percy jumped onto the parapet and tried
to crane over it to shoot the first Russian with his revolver, and
with his sword 'exchange thrusts' (as he put it) with those under-
neath. With the parapet being so high, both sides found it difficult
to fire their rifles effectively at the other, except where the two
embrasures had been made. Percy, having fallen back from the
parapet, crouched under it with two others, their heads only inches
beneath the muzzles of Russian muskets. Here they found that the
enemy were unable to depress their barrels sufficiently to shoot
them, but the three of them, on the other hand, could fend off with
their revolvers and swords any of their adversaries who leant over
in an attempt to kill them.[16] This tactic, however, was not in-
fallible; as the enemy were unable to neutralize Percy and his
indomitable vanguard with either hot lead or cold iron, they
resorted to other missiles. When he turned round briefly to give an
order, Percy was hit on the back of the head by a large stone that
had been hurled over the parapet by one of the Russians, who were
resisting the attack with anything they could lay their hands on.
Meanwhile, a few yards away more enemy infantry were blazing
away through the embrasures at the Grenadiers, while others had
climbed up onto the parapet to fire down into the mass of
Guardsmen at their feet. In the words of W. W. Knollys, author of
The Victoria Cross in the Crimea, 'Col. Percy, being of a fiery
disposition, could not submit to this, as it seemed to him imperti-
nence, and himself climbed up [again] to the top of the parapet.'
He immediately received a blow from another stone about the size
of a man's fist, which bloodied his nose and smashed his eyeglass
into his face. He collapsed onto the floor of the work and lay in a
state of semi-consciousness for a length of time which he said
afterwards must have been about a quarter of an hour, his only

* Cadogan had already had a busy morning. He had been on picquet duty in
Canrobert's Redoubt, which had a panoramic view of the open plain behind the
Guards Camp. On discovering that a major attack was under way, he had ridden
over to the French General Bosquet, and appraised him of the situation. He had
then made his way up to the battlefield, having been obliged to leave his horse
behind, owing to the rough ground.
† Hon Charles Lindsay (1816–1889), a cousin of Robert Lindsay.

recollection of which was a subaltern taking time in the mêlée to administer him some brandy.

While Percy was lying dazed on the floor of the Battery, the hand-to-hand fighting reached a crescendo. Captain Sir Charles Russell, near the left embrasure, was particularly hard-pressed:

> The air was thick with huge stones flying in all directions, but we were too much for them and once more a mêlée of Grenadiers, Coldstream and Fusiliers held the Battery their own, and from it on the solid masses of Russians still poured as good fire as our ammunition would permit. There were repeated cries of charge, and some men near me said, 'If any officer will lead, we will charge', and as I was the only one just there, I could not refuse such an appeal, so I jumped into the embrasure, and waving my revolver, I said, 'Come on my lads. Who will follow me?' I then rushed on, fired my revolver at a fellow close to me, but it missed fire; I pulled again, and I think I killed him. Just then a man touched me on the shoulder and said, 'You was near done for.' I said, 'Oh no, he was some way from me,' and he said, 'His bayonet was all but into you when I clouted him over the head,' and sure enough the fellow had got behind me, and nearly settled me. I then for the first time discovered that only this man by some mistake was with me, but I saw on my right some Bearskins, and joined Colonel Lindsay, who was most gallantly leading a charge. The Russians were by now in full retreat and we kept picking up ammunition from the dead and dying, and firing it into masses, without exaggeration, 20 times our number; we were joined by men of all sorts of regiments, and pushed on at them, slaughtering them most fearfully.[17]

Somehow Sir Charles, who was not a large man, managed also to tear a rifle from the hands of a Russian soldier, which he kept to the end of the day.[18] The Private who had helped him, Anthony Palmer, was publicly promoted to Corporal the next morning. Russell and Palmer were both later awarded the Victoria Cross.

At the same time as Sir Charles Russell sallied forth, Captain Edwyn Burnaby, commanding the right flank company of the Grenadiers, performed a similar act of gallantry. Concluding that such a strong, determined body of Russian infantry were not going to be beaten off by the trivial fire of a few men with nearly empty ammunition pouches, he also resolved to make a bayonet charge.

So, jumping to the top of the parapet, he called upon his men to follow and ran forward a few paces, but, finding himself alone, quickly retired. Back at the sandbags, another knot of Russian soldiery was striking at them from the right and one of them reached the parapet. Captain Burnaby laid him dead with his sword and again appealed to his men, 'We must charge!' He clambered up the parapet once more and this time a few men followed. One of them, Private James Bancroft, later told his story:

> I bayoneted the first Russian in the chest; he fell dead. I was then stabbed in the mouth with great force, which caused me to stagger back, where I shot this second Russian and thereupon run a third one through, and brought him to the ground. A fourth and fifth Russian then came at me and ran me through the right side. I fell, but managed to rise and run one of them through, and brought him down. I killed him, or either stunned him by kicking him, whilst I was engaging my bayonet with another. Sergeant-Major Algar called out to me not to kick the man that was down, but not being dead he was very troublesome to my legs; in fact, I was fighting the other over his body. I returned to the battery and spat out my teeth in my hand. I found only two.[19]

Outside the Battery Burnaby and his original party of about seven were joined by a number of others, including Robert Lindsay, Scots Fusilier Guards (of Alma fame). Together with Russell and his bevy, they now held the ledgeway in front of the sandbags.

The time was shortly after 8.00 am. No one knows who gave the order; more likely it was a simultaneous cry from a number of officers, as there was no regular formation to command. But when Percy heard the shout, 'Charge!' he staggered to his feet and, together with about 90 officers and men, pursued the Russians down the hill, tumbling over the stones and brushes towards the steep incline of St Clement's ravine. Also involved in this pursuit, but in disparate bands, were Russell, Cadogan, Burnaby and Charles Lindsay, and there were others from the 2nd Division with them. Robert Lindsay was not far away and recalled coming across one distinguished-looking Russian officer on the point of being impaled by several guardsmen's bayonets. He appeared to be carrying a bag of money over his shoulder and Lindsay, instead of allowing things to take their natural course in the field of battle, intervened on the basis that a man being killed for his money was 'outside the scope of warfare'. So, sword in hand, he threw up the barrels of the guardsmen's guns and, in a moment, the man was 'striding away towards Sebastopol, making signs of gratitude as he fled'. One officer of the 95th, Lieutenant Colonel Carmichael, described overtaking several Russians who threw down their arms, kneeling for mercy, pleading 'Christos!' As far as possible, he said, these were taken prisoner, but the pursuit carried on down the hill:

> I thought the battle was won, and the men were also exultant. A fine young soldier of the 95th, Lance Corporal Purcell came up to me saying, 'We are driving them again, Sir,' alluding to the repulse of the sortie on the 26th October, and at the same time was about to run his bayonet into a Russian's back who we were overtaking. I cried out, 'Don't kill him,' and he instead seized him by the belt behind, and flung him to the ground and took his weapon off him. I don't know what became of Purcell subsequently, but he never came out of the fight, and his body was found months afterwards on the other side of the hill, facing the ruins.[20]

Henry Percy also remembered passing over ground strewn with the bodies of the enemy, many of whom were only wounded. He and those who charged with him continued on down the incline of the Kitspur to where they found another posse of British soldiers from a variety of different regiments who had also become separated from their units. Evidently, as they had rushed headlong out of the Sandbag Battery none had heard behind them the officers' urgent shouts for restraint. The men whom Percy came across were preparing now to charge down the steep incline of St Clement's Ravine at a large body of Russians, which completely clothed the other side in a mass of bayonets. Whether he himself had heard the order not to charge too far or whether he simply worked it out for himself is not clear. By the time he had reached the edge of the ravine he could sense that they were all in danger of being cut off – even though he could not see very clearly, given his black eye, broken eyeglass and bloodied face. He was the senior officer in the vicinity, so by repeated efforts he stopped the 'mad gallantry' of these men; many who had got this far forward had already been surrounded and slain. Percy's account of the action, which was never printed, is written in the third person, but in his own handwriting:

The writer arranged them in a line on the edge of the pitch and ordered them to keep up a steady fire on the descending Russians in their front. The position was as follows: the opposite side of the whole ravine was completely clothed with a mass of bayonets, partially shrouded by mist and smoke, advancing with the usual Russian sloth; on the left, nothing visible but mist and smoke; the Valley of the Tchernaya on the right. As the Russians came near the bottom of the ravine, whether they heard that our position was strong, I know not, but they turned to the right. Every shot of our men must have hit, the distance nothing above 100 yards at most, and no possibility of missing. The writer found a great many Russian muskets to help the men. The writer, being half blinded, ordered a Sergeant to keep down and do nothing but attentively watch the enemy positions and this NCO suddenly, as a puff of wind cleared the mist on our left said, 'Sir, the Russians are surrounding us'. The writer saw that the Russians had quite got round the left flank and were making for the Sandbag Battery. He formed up his men to face the Russians and ordered the fire to continue. [He was] intending to have advanced and charged through them to rejoin the remainder of the Brigade, of whose position he was uncertain through the mist and smoke, when the men said they had no more ammunition. Another painful moment – but an instant's reflection made the writer think that if he could head the men under the bank by the precipitous right flank of the Spur, he would by hugging the steep descent escape either the notice or the fire of the enemy, and clamber [back] up to the right where ammunition was, and recommence the combat. He has every reason to thank Heaven for sending him this order, for a few moments more, the men would have been either prisoners or killed, as the odds were fearful.[21]

He recalled a sheep track which led round the extreme right flank of the Kitspur, passing beneath the knoll on which stood the Sandbag Battery. Here, at a distance of forty yards or so, he and the men he was leading, of whom there were about fifty by this time (others of the original party who had charged out of the Battery having dispersed elsewhere through the thicket), were received by a brisk fire from the Battery, apparently coming from their own Grenadiers. So he clambered up the steep ascent and shouted at them to stop firing, only to be answered by a redoubled volley of fire: the Russians had occupied their perceived trophy once again. The brushwood at least provided some cover; he briefly wondered whether it would be possible to make a desperate bayonet charge, but the ground was impossibly steep and round shot and shell were coming in all around. They therefore continued in single file, following the path. By good fortune, it more or less took them directly back to the camp, and more ammunition.

On the way, they met a mounted staff officer. The man, 'seeing me a black and bloody cyclops, treated me with general hauteur, and . . . looked at me quite as if I was a dirty fellow.' Percy asked him where they could find some more ammunition. All the staff officer could say was ''pon honour, I don't know,' instead of, 'I'll ride over and see.' Henry could not help being reminded of Shakespeare's reference to his Percy ancestor Hotspur's 'perfumed noblemen' in *Henry IV, Pt. 1*, and for the rest of his life he (perhaps unfairly, but not unusually for regimental officers) felt that this incident epitomized the attitude of the Staff in the Crimea.

On reaching the camp they met the Duke of Cambridge in a state of high anxiety, who, when he had last seen the rest of the Guards near the Sandbag Battery, was afraid they were going to be surrounded. His depression had hardly been assuaged by a young officer cheerfully reassuring him that, 'The Guards, Sir, will be sure to turn up.'[22] The Duke could well believe it when another officer told him that the small parties of men attached to Percy and Cadogan (who had arrived back shortly afterwards with Russell via a slightly different route) were all that remained of the entire Brigade. In any event, HRH congratulated Percy on his performance and, at the request of Canrobert, ordered him to return with his men to support the French artillery which had now arrived back on the heights. The situation there was serious, with Russian artillery raking the British and French positions mercilessly. The Duke personally led this depleted band of men up to where the French guns were, to the left of the Barrier. Because of the rate of incoming fire, it was all they could do to lie down and keep out of the way of the flying cannon balls and shells.

While Henry Percy, like so many other regimental officers that day, had been engaged in his own private skirmish on the edge of St Clement's Ravine, the Grenadiers' Headquarters, together with a small number of others, found themselves in as desperate a plight. There had been a brief interlude in which a few of them had got a modicum of sustenance: Quartermaster Sergeant Hill, knowing that most of the men had gone into action without food since the previous night, made his appearance in the Battery, regardless of the firing all around him, and his thoughtfulness was thoroughly appreciated.[23] However, they were quickly low on ammunition and, because of the dense brushwood, the mist and the lie of the land, they could not see to what degree they were being surrounded by ever-growing numbers of Russian troops. Moreover, the fact that the Grenadiers were holding their Colours high only encouraged further efforts on the part of the enemy. The Duke of Cambridge, when he had been near the Sandbag Battery and seen Percy's and Cadogan's detachment pursue the Russians down the hill, had wanted the remainder of the Guards to be recalled. But there were no mounted officers to co-ordinate such a manoeuvre, and in any case the few men who remained with the Colours were too hard-pressed to do anything except try to hold out against a new Russian column which had appeared between them and Percy's contingent out on the Kitspur.

The Grenadiers who remained in the Battery, what with their losses, amounted to little more than 100 men, including their commanding officer and his adjutant. They were attacked from behind as well as in front, for a large body of Russians had come round the head of St Clement's Ravine towards Home Ridge. These were the Okhotsk Regiment, who had just outflanked Percy. Some of the Okhotsk, on seeing the remainder of the Grenadiers still in the Battery, wheeled left with the intention of taking them prisoner.[24] Higginson's letter to Hatton of 7 November related:

> It now became to be serious – our ammunition failed and there was no reserve to hand and the havoc made to our Bearskins by the Russians, reduced us as a battalion to not more than 100 men, not including the men who had gone in pursuit and whom we thought annihilated.[25]

They had good reason to believe that Percy and his men were finished. At the same time as Percy, Cadogan and Russell were charging along the slopes of the Kitspur towards St Clement's Ravine, General Cathcart, who had just arrived with reinforcements, was ordered by Lord Raglan to plug the Gap between the

Barrier and the Sandbag Battery. Unfortunately, he took it upon himself instead to lead two regiments in pursuit down the Kitspur below the Sandbag Battery and beyond, towards the bottom of St Clement's Ravine – i.e. in a similar direction to Percy *et al*, but further east and lower down the hill, almost into the valley below. The result of this disastrous manoeuvre was that three Russian battalions got through the Gap, thereby cutting off the three entire but disparate units: the Headquarters of the Grenadiers in the Sandbag Battery, Percy and his men out on the Kitspur and General Cathcart's two regiments down below. This last party were also under fire from Russian artillery the other side of the Tchernaya and as a result were virtually annihilated. Cathcart's last words said it all: 'We are in a scrape.'[26]

Higginson's letter to Hatton continued:

> Again therefore we left the Battery, keeping a good line towards the left flank and filing up the hill until we found that the Russians had driven back the regiments of the 2nd Division on the left of ourselves and were actually <u>above</u> us between us and a large redoubt [the Barrier] which covers the height just in front of [General de Lacy] Evans' camp [i.e. Home Ridge].
>
> I looked at the colours, I thought for the last time, and I believed everyone down to the private soldiers thought that the poor old 3rd Battalion was doomed. Not a round of ammunition* was left and we were being peppered on three sides. Then followed perhaps the brightest achievement Englishmen are capable of, sticking close to the colours which Turner and Verschoyle carried like heroes, the men went up the hill at the charge and literally charged home a distance of not less than a quarter of a mile to the upper redoubt. God alone knows how thankful we were when we sprang through the embrasures and fell <u>utterly</u> exhausted in this secure rallying place; for in the meanwhile the French had arrived in very large force and tackled the Russians most nobly.[27]

Much of the credit for the saving of the Grenadier Headquarters and the Colours should be given to Captain Burnaby. He had briefly engaged in the 'false victory' along the Kitspur with Percy,

---

* F. W. Hamilton, who was also in this party of men, recorded that some of the men did have ammunition, and these few kept at bay those Russians trying to pursue them up the hill.

Cadogan and Russell, but had not gone as far as the others and, unlike them, got back up the hill before being cut off. As he raced up the slope to join the main body near the Sandbag Battery, Burnaby saw to his horror that the colours were about to be surrounded and, with no rearguard to protect them, their chances appeared to be 'almost null'. He had only eighteen to twenty men with him – some of them Grenadiers (including the now toothless Bancroft), the odd Coldstream and Scots Fusilier, together with a few men from the Line. He told them that they must somehow, by retarding their own retreat, win enough time holding off two Russian battalions to enable the colour party to rejoin the rest of the army. Burnaby remembered how, only half an hour or so before, when he had charged out of the Sandbag Battery onto the ledgeway in front, an apparently overwhelming opposing force had, after exchanging surprisingly few blows, quickly melted away into the bush. Attack therefore having been proved to be the best form of defence, he resolved to try the same tactic again. Bancroft 'thought it perfectly useless so few of us trying to resist such a tremendous lot; but, for all that, I did so.' They blasted their way through the advance party of skirmishers and on to the main body of the Okhotsk. As they fought, they inevitably fell, and very quickly there were only seven left alive – most of them wounded and lying prostrate on the ground. Burnaby himself received a bayonet thrust in the folds of his cloak, but fell only because he slipped on the wet barrel of a musket lying on the ground.

Having been overrun, and lying down in the wake of the Russian advance, the seven survivors dreaded their impending fate. They knew what to expect, as they had already seen several of their comrades bayoneted on the ground. Burnaby found himself lying alongside a wounded Russian, who tried to alert his comrades that there was an Englishman who needed to be finished off. Burnaby, however, could speak some Russian and, pointing a loaded revolver at his would-be whistleblower's head, told him in no uncertain terms to hold his tongue.

Soon afterwards the Russian column which had overrun Burnaby's little rearguard was beaten back by the arrival of a French infantry battalion. Choosing their moment in the confusion carefully, the seven of them escaped unmolested by the retreating

Russians and joined the rest of the Grenadiers, whom they had done so much to help. Higginson's account continues:

Ten minutes rest set us to right and we filled our pouches with cartridges and longed for news of our missing comrades. After we had been lying in comparative safety for an hour – I say comparative, for the Russian shot and shell only shaved our heads instead of taking them off, up rode the Duke, who almost cried with delight at seeing us and the Colours; he had given us up for lost, and was *mourning* over the annihilation of the Regiment . . . .

We got the order to move off to the left in rear of some French guns which required support, and you may fancy our delight at finding Cadogan and Percy with the main body of our missing men, who the latter had led round the foot of the hill up a bye road to our rear. The way these fellows cheered at seeing the Colours again would have done your heart good.

By this time the Zouaves and our *finest aspects* of the Light Division, assisted by some heavy guns which had been wheeled up by hand, had driven back the enemy and made the victory, so nobly begun by our 2nd Division and our very weak Brigade, complete.

We had another two hours to wait under a most galling fire of artillery until the Russians were finally routed, and when we were returned to camp it was 4pm – so that we had been fighting nine hours and a half! The Russians had at least 42,000 men opposed to us, against which the 2nd Division and our Brigade were pitted for *three* hours without support.[28]

Mid-morning, however, support was at hand in the form of the French and, most particularly for the Guards, the Zouaves. Over the course of the next few hours this extra manpower settled the day, driving the Russians from the heights of Inkerman. Lord Raglan considered the possibility of completing the victory by pursuit of the enemy down into the valley, but Canrobert (true to his nickname, 'Robert Can't') would not consent, mindful of the fire from Russian ships moored in the roadstead. He was probably right to be cautious, for it was not until much later in the day that the threat from Gortschakoff's army, which it will be remembered was to make up the other half of the pincer movement upon the allied right flank, dissipated.

The battlefield, from the ravine on the left to the redundant two-gun battery on the right, was only about three-quarters of a mile wide, but rarely had such a barrage of artillery fire been concentrated in such a confined space, and for so long. Rarely too has such dogged hand-to-hand combat, interspersed with bayonet charge after bayonet charge, been sustained for so great a length of time. Nine hours of close fighting left the victors in no mood for celebration and when the enemy finally retired there was no public rejoicing in the allied lines, as there had been at Alma.[29]

Chapter 4

Aftermath

The narrative of the previous chapter inevitably concentrates on just a few hours in one part of the battlefield, but in terms of the number of casualties sustained it represents a major portion. By the end of the afternoon the numbers of French who were on the scene roughly equalled the numbers of British troops; of the former, though, only about half were actually engaged.[1] The French therefore had only 175 killed in action, the English 635.[2] Including wounded, many of whom died in hospital in the ensuing weeks, British casualties totalled around 2,600 – about one-third of those engaged. The Russians, in far greater number, also lost about a third of their attacking force, and well over 3,000 of these were killed.[3] Of the allies, it was the Guards who had taken the brunt, with over forty per cent of the entire Brigade killed or wounded. Within this, of the 3rd Battalion Grenadier Guards who came under fire that day (i.e. excluding those who were on outlying picquet duty), an even higher proportion were killed or wounded. Russell and Percy, both writing a few days after the event, placed the Grenadiers' casualties as a proportion of the 430 men who went into action at fifty-two and fifty-five per cent respectively. Higginson, writing sixty years later, quotes a similar figure. The official returns were below this, but they listed several men as 'missing', when in fact their bodies were found later on the battlefield. Even the most conservative estimates put the Grenadiers' losses on the same scale as those sustained in the Charge of the Light Brigade.* The truth is

* Having assimilated a number of sources, it seems that the best estimate is as

that the infantry soldiers' fight for survival at the Sandbag Battery was a bloodier affair than the cavalry engagement at Balaklava, though it is the latter that has been immortalized in the British psyche and the former all but forgotten. Another testament to the ferocity of Inkerman is the amount of ammunition expended by the Grenadiers that November day – 19,000 rounds – as against 9,000 fired at Alma, when the Battalion had almost twice the number of men in the field. This is even more remarkable when one considers the effect of the drizzle on the cartridges, the number of men put out of action by the enemy, and the frequency with which those left to fight ran out of ammunition.

So just how were the British infantry, outnumbered and surprised early on that Sunday morning, able to withstand such a massive offensive? Obviously the French, with another 8,000 men, came on the scene to assist; but even so, the British on their own, in the face of repeated attacks by many times their number, had still been able to hold the line for four hours. In any case, even when the British and French forces did come together that day, they were still heavily outweighed by the number of Russians.

For one thing, the infantry knew they were 'up against it'. The allies may have thought they were besieging Sebastopol, but in reality it was they that were surrounded – the only possible escape from the enemy being into the sea. Sebastopol, it must be remembered, was open to the interior of the Crimea on the north side of the harbour and at the eastern end of the roadstead; until the whole of the Crimea was blockaded Russian reinforcements would always be able to get to the front. If the Russians had got through at the Battle of Inkerman they would immediately have destroyed the 1st and 2nd Division camps and there would have been no telling how far westwards they could have rolled up the allied lines. The entire British expeditionary force would surely have been out of the war and it is unlikely the French could have continued alone, even if they had somehow been

---

follows: of the 615 Grenadiers who qualified for the Inkerman clasp to their campaign medals, 185 did not directly take part in the action (chiefly because they were on picquet duty), leaving just 430 Grenadiers actually fighting around the Sandbag Battery. Of these, 104 were killed or died of wounds, and 130 wounded. This compares with 110 killed and 130 wounded out of the 664 who charged with the Light Brigade.

able to preserve a foothold on the Chersonese peninsula.

Patrick Mercer, in his study of the battle of Inkerman, *Give Them a Volley and Charge!,* attributes the factors governing the success of the allies on this occasion to two categories: physical and moral. On the physical side, the British had the Minié rifle, whose accuracy and range meant that Russian artillerymen on Shell Hill, several hundreds yards off, were constantly plagued by bullets and therefore did not fire as accurately as they might have done: they could otherwise have dismounted the two British eighteen-pounders which were brought up on to Home Ridge, and which proved so effective in the latter part of the fight. Also, the standard Russian infantry formation was a dense column and, given the right opportunity, concentrated Minié fire from a thin line of redcoats could mow them down wholesale, each bullet passing through several men. The experience of Percy's men on St Clement's Ravine was a perfect example of when the rifle came into its own, the pity on that occasion being that they were so short on ammunition. If it hadn't been for the mist and the density of the brushwood the Miniés could probably have wreaked greater havoc still.

The ground also favoured the British. The Russians had to climb a steep escarpment before engaging and, perversely, they knew the lie of the land less well than the defenders, for the majority of Russians who went up onto the heights of Inkerman had only just arrived in the Crimea. The preponderance of bushes favoured the defenders, trained as they were in the art of skirmishing; but the terrain did not suit the rigidity of the Russian column. The mist, too, helped the British conceal their lack of manpower.

On the moral side, it seems the Russians were already battle-weary, many of them having recently tasted defeat, either at Alma, or at the hands of the Turks in the Balkans. They were also ill-led by their generals (not that generalship counted for much anywhere at Inkerman that day), some of whom issued contradictory orders and others of whom disobeyed commands from above. Soimonoff, for example, embarked on the original assault on the British right before Pauloff had arrived to support him.[4] Finally, without wishing to denigrate the bravery of the Russian rank and file, or the leadership skills of their regimental officers (most of whom it has to be said led gallantly from the front), there is no doubt that they lacked initiative when compared with their counterparts on the other side. Sir James Fergusson summed up the culture then prevailing in the Guards when he wrote after the Battle of the Alma: 'I found I was freely giving orders to the company, though the junior subaltern, and did a good deal that would not have been permitted at a field day, but I never was found fault with, and indeed I believe I got credit for it.'[5]

There was a remarkable mutual respect and trust between the British regimental officers and their men, which enabled them all to fight incredibly effectively. As a captain in the Royal Artillery wrote of that day: 'Colonels of regiments led on small parties, and fought like subalterns, captains like privates. Once engaged, every man was his own general.'[6] Private soldiers and NCOs of the British army at this time were real 'salt of the earth' – sometimes ne'er-do-wells evading some hardship at home. Private Bancroft, for example, was repeatedly convicted for absence without leave, desertion and habitual drunkenness; but though these men came from the opposite end of the social spectrum from their officers, their company commanders were greatly fond of them. Witness the Grenadiers' new commanding officer, Colonel Reynardson, writing to Colonel Wood at Horse Guards on 7 November thus: 'Sergeant Algar amongst the first shot through the head! He died next day – a sad loss to us . . . . I hope poor Algar's wife will be recollected, as her husband has just missed what you applied for him. He was as hard working and as good a man as possibly could be, and is a severe loss to us.'[7] In a similar vein, Henry Percy's concluding words in his *Rough Notes on Inkerman*, which years later he sent to Kinglake while the latter was researching his volume on Inkerman, paid tribute to the rank and file. Recalling a night some six weeks after the action, when the condition of the army was at its nadir, he wrote that 'there was little grumbling in the army, for soldiers generally grumble . . . . On the eve of St Nicholas* we were cautioned that an attack might take place the

* St. Nicholas is patron saint of Russia and his feast day falls on 6 December. In the nineteenth century the Russians were still using the Julian calendar, twelve days behind the Gregorian calendar – so the day Percy was referring to is in fact 18 December. Colonel Ridley, who had just arrived to command the Brigade, privately lamented that, if he had been called upon that day, 'I would only bring about 40 men into the field – the rest were all on [picquet] duty: a pretty state for a Brigade supposed to be 3,000 strong.'

next morning. The men sat up singing till quite late, the only sounds of merriment I had heard for a long time.'

Late on the afternoon of the battle what was left of the Brigade assembled at Guards' Camp. After the calling of the roll, it was ascertained that the effective strength of the three battalions of guards regiments combined amounted to just 812 men. The Grenadier Guards in the aftermath of Inkerman are the inspiration behind Elizabeth Thompson's famous painting, known as 'The Roll Call'. It depicts a few bedraggled men standing in the snow, leaning on their rifles for support, the walking wounded kept upright on the shoulders of their comrades, patiently waiting to answer their names, as their weary adjutant looks on from his horse, head bowed, almost as if in submission to his charges. Higginson is the only officer portrayed in this picture, but his posture symbolizes the attitude of every company commander. For his part, Percy meticulously recorded the names of every one of the forty-four in his company who were killed or wounded on the last page of his Letts pocket diary for November, a list that would be used later in providing assistance to their families at home. It was evidently compiled shortly after his own company's roll was read out:

> My most painful moment was calling the roll of the company – killed and wounded – I had known most of the men and drilled them as adjutant for long, and their conduct on service, and particularly at Alma, was admirable for [its] cool bravery. One officer of my company was killed, two wounded, there being only 3 doing duty with it at the time.[8]

The greatest cause of anguish was the plight of the wounded. Captain Sir Robert Newman, for example, wounded near the Sandbag Battery, was held up in the air, transfixed by Russian bayonets, while still living.[9] He was brought in by stretcher that night in the most excruciating pain and died in a few hours. For ever after, Percy would be haunted by the extraordinary barbarism to which they had been subjected that day:

> The conduct of the Russians to the wounded was cruel. Captain Sir Robert Newman was brought in on a mule so hacked to pieces as

hardly to hang together. Lt. Greville (Coldstream Guards) had his face literally hacked to pieces so as not to be recognisable. Lt. Col. Pakenham was bayoneted after being wounded. Out of 35 officers of the Brigade of Guards, I think 26 to 28 had received wounds or been killed – none prisoners. A wounded major of the Russian army went about hacking the wounded English: the resistance they met with filled them with fury.

Pakenham, who commanded the neighbouring company to Percy, No. 7, and who had been, with him, among the first to reach the Russian gun at Alma, was brought in with numerous lacerations. He was alive, but insensible, and no one could catch the drift of his last words, which seemed inexplicably to be in German, obscured as they were anyway by his lisp.* Neville was sensible to the last, but suffering the most frightful agonies, from which those close to him were not sorry to see him released that night, for it was only too apparent that the gunshot wound to his spine was a mortal one. He was in a hospital tent with two other wounded officers and, in his last hours, he asked to see his oldest friends. One, Sir Charles Russell, wrote to Neville's elder brother an account of his last hours:

> On the evening of the 5th, your brother Henry (my kind and dear friend) wished to see me. I went down to the hospital tent, and found him with Captain Tipping and Sturt. I had just met Mr. Halpin, the chaplain, who said, 'I have been with Neville, and he is in a most comfortable frame of mind'. I then saw your brother. He began by saying 'He felt he was dying', but, as the doctors assured me there was no immediate danger, I hoped and believed not, and told him so. He then asked particularly about the officers, and expressed the greatest pleasure that so-and-so had escaped, or been but slightly wounded. And now I must tell you what I know will please you, – in his whole conversation there was not one word of repining; and when I was arranging his pillow for him, he tried to laugh in his old happy manner, and kept saying 'how much trouble he gave'. Even when speaking of the Russians he did not

---

* Edward Pakenham (1819–1854), one of four sons of General Sir Hercules Pakenham. His three brothers also died on active service: Robert was killed at the Siege of Lucknow in 1857, Edmund died at Fort Gwalior in 1861 and Charles died 'of decline' on *Hydaspes* in 1877.

75

use a single expression of anger or revenge; and, indeed, his mind was in a pure and settled state. He told me, 'Some drummers were carrying me on a stretcher to the rear, and the enemy so pressed them that they set me down. The first Russian who came up stabbed me in the body, a second in the arm, and a third aimed a thrust at my head, but my bearskin being on, it only grazed it,' adding, 'I cannot blame the drummers, they were so hard prest.' As I left him, he said, 'He thought he should sleep which would do him good.' It is not for me to compare my loss to your heavy sorrow, but I cannot let the memory of my dear friend pass without a tribute. He was the kindest, cheeriest, and most uncomplaining of us all; and living in the same tent with him since I was in the Crimea, you will know how much I must have understood and appreciated his character. His memory lives, and ever will, amongst the Third Battalion; and as a slight mark of esteem and affection, they have placed a little monument over his grave. It is very simple, and surmounted by a cross, – an emblem which, we hear, even the Russians will respect.[10]

Owing to Neville's precarious state at the time, not all those officers who wished to see him were admitted by the surgeons.[11] His cousin, Captain Edward Neville, was one of those who did get to speak to him:

Alas! I dread to tell you the sad news, that poor dear Henry is no more. He fell, mortally wounded, in the action with the enemy on the 5th inst., having received a bullet wound in the back which had injured the spine, as likewise a bayonet wound through the body. I saw him, poor fellow, in the hospital tent, where, with two of his brother officers, Tipping and Sturt, he was receiving every attention; and although he was perfectly conscious, and spoke to me, he seemed to be in so much pain that I did not encourage him to talk much: he said 'I am so glad to see any of the family.' I was not able to be with him in his last moments, for duty called me to our division, two or three miles distant; but on returning, soon after daylight on the 6th, I heard that he had passed away at half-past eleven the night before, so quietly that Sturt, who was close by him at the time, was not aware of his approaching end. His features in death were perfectly calm, and I trust he is now enjoying that peace in the kingdom of heaven which the Lord granteth his servants. I was present at the funeral yesterday; poor Henry and Pakenham were buried at the same time, and I was much struck with the solemnity of a soldier's burial on the field of battle. All the officers of the regiment attended, and the bodies of the gallant departed lay on and were covered with boughs (emblematic of the laurels they had won) previous to the earth closing on their mortal remains. Nothing can exceed the kindness and sympathy shown by all poor Henry's brother-officers on this sad occasion. If it please God to spare me, I long to hear that my dear uncle and aunt have not suffered in health from the severe affliction, which it is now my painful duty to make known to you.[12]

Percy, by comparison with the other five Grenadier officers who were returned officially as wounded, only had a black eye, gashes to his face and a severe contusion on the back of his head; after a day or so he was back on duty. Fergusson, being wounded in the right arm, was unable to do duty for a week, but remained with the Regiment. Oddly enough, quite a few of those in the Regiment who had also displayed conspicuous gallantry escaped apparently without a scratch, including Sir Charles Russell, George Higginson and Captain Burnaby. That the latter suffered only lacerations to his attire is truly remarkable, as, of all people, he was right in the thick of it that day.

What the returns do not, of course depict, is the psychological damage with which those who fought at Inkerman were afflicted. In 1854 the phrase 'shell shock' was as yet unuttered. Most, in the absence of any alternative course of action, muddled through. One who did succumb, however, was HRH Prince George, the Duke of Cambridge. He had already admitted to his wife after the Alma that 'when all was over I could not help crying like a child'; now, he wrote, 'the Alma was a joke' compared to what they had just been through.[13] Two days after Inkerman he was sent on board ship by the doctor; he spoke of being 'very ill with dysentery and typhoid fever'. Whatever his physiological symptoms, his nerves were completely shattered by the experience of almost losing the entire Guards Brigade. He was no coward, in the sense that he willingly exposed himself to the most tumultuous fire and, as Henry Percy (who was not one to mince his words on the subject of a general's conduct) observed, he was quite cool throughout the action. There are in existence numerous and heartfelt tributes to his bravery from both men and officers. That said, however, Prince George was desperately worried by the burden of responsibility that came with commanding a Division and was reluctant to risk his men. He was also personally of too sentimental a nature to be effective in times of crisis in the field. His grief after a battle overwhelmed him: 'We went over the field of battle to behold a field of blood and destruction, and misery, which nothing in this world can possibly surpass. After dinner I had to ride with Lord Raglan to consult with him, and on my return I was so overpowered by all I had gone through, that I felt perfectly broken down.'

Captain Tipping, who had a severe gunshot wound to the thigh, just below his groin, recalled how he had lain on a stretcher next to Neville on the night of the 5th. Neville had just died:

> The night was bitterly cold and damp, so I thought he had better remain where he was, lying close to me, till morning, rather than allow the tent to be opened, for the purpose of removing him. However, about half an hour afterwards, I heard someone pulling at the string which fastens the door of the tent, so I hollowed to ask who it was, and found it to be the Duke of Cambridge, who was walking about the camp everywhere, trying to do whatever he could for the wounded fellows, who were lying about in all directions, undergoing operations etc. He asked me how I was going on etc., and then, turning his lanthorn upon poor Neville's face which was pale and motionless, he asked me who it was. I told him, and he appeared most shocked, and went out, sending a fatigue party to carry poor Neville away.[14]

HRH's fragility and his personal kindness had made him universally popular, but his breakdown after Inkerman was ill-received. Everybody was depressed; they had all lost friends; of course they wanted to return to their wives and children at home. But the vast majority of the troops chose to bear these hardships with fortitude, even though, at any rate among the officers, a few of them at least had the option of taking a period of leave, or, if really desperate, resigning their commissions.

Queen Victoria was concerned about her cousin George's desertion from duty. She had seen plenty of accounts of what was going on in the Crimea. Prince Edward of Saxe-Weimar, whom she had known since childhood, was a regular correspondent:

I last wrote to Prince Albert on the 7th or 8th of this month. I wrote to him soon after the battle of Inkerman, when I was still under the excitement of that fearful scene, and I am afraid that I made use of expressions that I was afterwards sorry that I had done. I believe I made reflections on our commanders, which are at all times wrong . . . .

Never shall I forget the sight of the dead and dying Russians on the field. Some of these poor wretches had to lie on the field for at least sixty hours before they were removed to the hospital tents; the majority of course died. I am afraid this is one of the necessities of war, for we had to remove our own people first. I went round the hospitals the next morning. It was a horrid sight to see the bodies of the men who had died during the night stretched before the tents, and to see the heaps of arms and legs, with the trousers and boots still on, that had been cut off by the surgeons.

The Russians were so near that most of the officers had to use their swords and revolvers. Many single acts of daring took place; among others, Colonel Percy of our Regiment rushed in front of his company, sword in hand, into a dense body of Russians who were in a battery. I was not in the thick of it, but was engaged with an outlying picquet in the left of the attack. George was in the very thick of it, and not seeing me, kept asking some of our men where I was. They did not know. He tells me that he thought for a long time I was killed, and even fancied that he had seen me lying on the ground; it turned out later to have been poor Colonel Dawson's body which he mistook for me.[15]

After visiting the Duke while he was convalescing as guest of Captain Drummond on board HMS *Retribution* (possibly in the same cabin that Percy had rested in after Alma, for it was a small ship), Prince Edward again reported to the Queen:

He has now gone to Constantinople. There are plenty of ill natured people who make remarks about his going, although I firmly believe it was necessary for his health, but he was indiscreet in not disguising his joy at going away from this in no way enviable abode. George showed a great deal of courage and sangfroid, but he lost his head, he did not know what to do at the critical moment and the responsibility was too much for him; he is popular, amiable and kind, but has no decision whatever, and has certainly not shown the talents of a general which had been expected of him.[16]

The Queen was fond of George Cambridge and showed him kindness on his return from the Crimea, but she took a dim view of his flight from the war.

Those who were still doing duty had their work cut out in the sad business of organizing the collection and burial of the dead. Immediately after the end of the action, late on the afternoon of the 5th, Percy had taken volunteers from his depleted company to pick up wounded. They found 'piles of Russians at the sandbag area more than breast high, in ridges. Though the action was over, the Russian fleet kept up their fire with disagreeable accuracy.' An invitation had been sent to Prince Mentschikoff to agree to a truce and send out parties of his own men to assist in the operation; it was refused and, whether by accident or design, these burial parties were periodically harassed during the course of the next few days by artillery fire from below.

Each bush seemed to hide a body, and dying and wounded men were found in every nook and cranny of Inkerman's ravines. The area around the Sandbag Battery was a scene of the utmost horror, with the sides of the hill up to and around the work not just strewn with bodies, but piled up against the parapet, sometimes three or four deep, guardsmen intertwined with Russian infantry. Within the confines of the sandbag walls, the dead were contorted into the most extraordinary positions, occasionally with arms extended, as if warding off some blow; others apparently kneeling or half-standing, clutching weapons or in the act of drawing a cartridge. The agonies of those who fell at the point of a bayonet caused them literally to 'bite the dust'.[17]

The day after Inkerman, Henry Clifford, the ADC who had so distinguished himself on the other side of the Wellway from Prince Edward, chanced upon a party of Russian prisoners:

A man amongst them ran up and called out to me and pointed to his shoulder bound up. It was the poor fellow whose arm I had cut off yesterday; he laughed and said, 'Bono Johnny'. I took his hand and shook it heartily and the tears came in my eyes. I had not a shilling in my pocket; had I a bag of gold he should have had it. I enquired if he had been cared for and the Doctor told me he had and was doing well.[18]

While the grisly work of collecting the dead and rescuing the wounded continued, Percy took the time to recover from his concussion and have his injuries cleaned up. He wrote his first account of the action:

<u>Camp before Sebastopol Nov 6</u>

My dear Father,

We had a most severe fight with the Russians yesterday, who attempted to force our right in great force and of which we bore the brunt presently getting very much cut up but inflicting at least a terrible loss on the Russians. They behaved scandalously, bayoneting our wounded with the savagery of pagans. You will be glad to hear that I led the way to take a redoubt, being the first in, at a moment when our men were out of ammunition and tired. I received sundry congratulations on my Bearskins' loin. I was wounded in the eye by a stone which was flung with great anger over the parapet, about 5 pounds weight, which caused me intense pain and I feared that my eye was split in half. And a large stone stove into my back as I was holloaing the men on. The fight was severer than Alma, and the Russians lay like flies about the parapet. We had to contend with little support and lost many men and officers. We [had] 3 officers killed and 5 wounded. Don't be alarmed at mine – they are mere scratches and bruises. Part of our men were surrounded by Russians, fought their way through, with them alone, and took fifty prisoners, but our loss is fearful. The Coldstreams have 8 officers dead. Young Amherst wounded, but nothing serious. I have written to his father.*

We had broken ground, mist and every disadvantage, but retained our position, the French coming up in support pretty quickly. They estimate the loss of the Russians at 10,000 men. It is said Archduke Constantine is here with 40,000, but they say they are much reduced now. I was forced to lay down for some minutes after I was hit, but got some Brandy and went on.

I have received your letter of the 18th and I acknowledge Mr. and Mrs. Charles's – thank them for their kindness. I have little time to write, and my hand is sore, <u>only sore.</u> You must have received many letters from me about my wound [received at Alma] *ad nauseam*, but I get your letters asking me questions about it, and forget to mention I have already written about it. My servant was

---

* Amherst had been struck by a musket ball just under the shoulder blade, as he was raising his arm. The ball exited his neck, though luckily not leaving any broken bones in its path.

wounded, and 34 of my company. Poor Neville, Lord Braybrooke's son and my senior subaltern, was killed. If you think it proper, you might write to say how useful and cool he was, and how I regret him.

I think I can say no more at present, as I require time to collect my ideas so as to give you a clear description. We bury 11 officers of the Guards at 3 today. There never were such brutes as the Russians: they bayonet every man who has the appearance of life, and our men treated them like naughty children after they were done. I believe that everyone applauded the Guards' conduct. Poor General Cathcart killed. Charles Seymour (Horace's son) also. [General] Brown wounded. [Generals] Adams, Torrens, Goldie and Bentinck the same. I will say the Duke of Cambridge behaved very well and was exceptionally kind afterwards; he was, as I said, as cool as possible. It is impossible to disguise from oneself the faults and errors caused by poor execution. [General] Evans, who I believe to be very good indeed, and Prince George had begged this place to be strengthened, but it was never done. Who is to blame, I know not. I don't believe Estcourt* is worth much. At least it is his business to make Lord Raglan acquainted with everything and I cannot believe Lord Raglan is.

I hope you are still all well. Give my love to Louisa and everybody, and believe me your most affectionate son,
　　　H. Percy

Tucked into the envelope containing this letter was a further missive, penned in another hand, anonymously, and headed simply, 'P.S.' It was a message from Henry's servant, George Jackett, who was also a private in his company:

The colonel's servant called here today poor man he is very badly wounded. I fear that he will never be fit for much. He is wounded in his L. arm and his chest. The description that he gives of the battles are dreadful. He was at the battle of Alma and Inkermann likewise at Balaklava.

He says that the colonel is very happy and in good spirits and very kind to his men. He was with the colonel when he made the grand charge, sword in hand, on the Russians. He told his men 'now my boys, come on if we don't do our duty now it will be a stain on our

* Major General Estcourt, Adjutant General, and Lord Raglan's right-hand man. He, along with General Airey, the Quartermaster General, incurred most of the criticism for the army's failures.

characters as long as we live,' and bravely they followed him and death staring them in the face. And every one of them done their duty.

The servant saw his master falling and he was in the act of going to assist him when he was nock down with a musket ball. He says that the colonel was struck in the eye, he had a black eye. When he left him, he left on the 6th November.

He says the colonel is a very man.

During the course of the following days and weeks, Henry would reveal further details of the action in his letters home:

We went 430 men into action; 207 returned, but the Russians have lost 15,000 at the very lowest. I was engaged hand to hand, and most other Grenadiers [were] too. I encountered an unprotected Russian, meaning to take him prisoner, but he was too big for me and I was forced to run him through to save myself. The shriek the poor wretch gave still rings in my ears. I hope I shall never do it again . . . .

I got my wound on my head by running forward to a parapet and craning over to shoot the first Russian who tried to climb up when a very large stone was sent bang in to my eye. But the wound is trivial, and I do duty. I have a sore hand also from some blow or other . . . .

The barbarity of the 'civilized Russians' was excessive. Charging and retreating, they bayoneted every wounded man and one major has been convicted of having (though wounded himself) crept about stabbing our wounded. He is to be tried, I believe. Speaking English, he gave a corporal a gold piece to say nothing about it, but the evidence against him is numerous. Such is Russian civilisation. The prisoners all write in saying that the General Order was given right before the battle stating that the positions were occupied by the Turks, which doubtless gave them courage, and they were not disabused, as we fought unluckily in our great coats, to our great disadvantage. A line of red is extremely modifying to the valour of these gentlemen. In those great coats on that day we might have been Turks or anything . . . .

The Russians make a most foul howling when they advance, which makes our men laugh, and when they are wounded they moan, which if it were not for knowing they are in pain, would make an innocent bystander laugh. 'Hubber bubber bubber', more like some animal. They are always fired up to attack us with drink

which may account for their brutal cruelty. I think even Suvoroff*
spared the wounded. They frequently sham wounded for hours
after the battle and then get up: I suppose they are the poltroons of
their army. I shall always stop any butchering _if_ I see my men
inclined to do it, as I consider it unchristian, but I don't think our
men do it unless very much excited, but they are very angry at the
conduct of the Russians, naturally. I tell them they are savages, and
murdering them will do us [no] good, whereas if we don't, the
difference will be too apparent. It does gall one to see one's Guards
Officers and one's poor men, who share their water and tobacco
with the Russian wounded brought in, saying, 'All I had was a slight
wound, but they bayoneted me on the ground several times.' I could
pardon one bayonet wound in the excitement, but there is a
deliberate fiendish murderous feeling in these fellows. One officer
was so hacked that his body would hardly hang together on a mule.
Gah! A Captain prisoner of ours was found kneeling on a wounded
Guards officer of his own, robbing him. Our sentry saw him and
hit him a clip on the head with a musket; he complained, but the
brother officer corroborated the sentry's statement. I respect
the Kaffirs & Indians infinitely more.

In one letter, written more than a week after the battle, he
mentioned that the swivel of his cap chain had been shot off.
Considering it merely one of a host of lucky escapes that day,
which were really too numerous to detail, he hadn't thought to
mention it previously; however, a curious thing happened,
reminding him of the incident: 'I perceived a sore spot on my eyelid,
which I thought was just a scratch. One day, something came out
– a piece of brass from the swivel that had been shot off, and had
lodged below the skin.'

Despite constant and vociferous complaints about the inefficiency of the Army's postal service, letters from Henry's family
continued to arrive in the Crimea, generally between two and three
weeks after they had been posted. As the following example shows,
on occasion letters could make the 2,000 mile journey from
Balaklava to London in under a fortnight, but in the emerging age

* Alexander Suvoroff (1729–1800), Field Marshal and Governor of the Crimea.
He was noted for his ruthlessness in the Russo-Turkish Wars, and his use of
bayonet charges to storm prepared positions was widely emulated in Napoleonic
times.

84

of the electric telegraph, Henry's sister Louisa found this painfully slow:

Friday 17th Nov

My dear Henry,

I am very much obliged to you for taking the trouble of writing me a few lines. I am afraid you would be angry if you knew how it vexed me to find by your letter of the 23rd that you were <u>well enough</u> to return to duty. However, as you are sufficiently recovered one can only say, God keep you.

Your letter of the 4th is just arrived. Alas! The Telegraph has been beforehand with you and we know that a bloody battle took place on the 5th and are wholly ignorant of all details. I won't plague you by describing the horror and anxiety of the interval that elapses between the electric communication and the full official despatch. My father's nerves are dreadfully shaken by all this suspense.

Finding from Sir P. Hunter that packages are made up at Fortnum and Mason's for the East, Lovaine and I have been there, and I hope you won't be provoked at me despatching a box of small creature comforts, in case you are again ill. Also, I send an underclothing of wash leather, which Algernon says is the best preservative against rheumatism. I wish it could reach you by electric Telegraph while you are in those wretched outposts. If you hate these gifts, you can give them away, but I recommend you to keep them in case of need. You will find in the box 2 bottles of salinated solution of Camphor and of a preparation of opium – the latter one third stronger than laudanum. Jones declares that you ought to take 10 drops of laudanum every night as your sleepnessness proves your nerves are shaken by your wound. This quantity would do you no harm with the hard work you have to do, and would sustain and compose you, but, he said, that of course you must first consult your doctor. He said it is a preservative against miasmata, and that a little opium given every morning to the men would preserve them from fever and cholera. A few drops of the Camphor in sugar has sometimes succeeded with diarrhoea wonderfully.

Don't think that I write like an old twaddle about medicines, that my blood does not thicken at the accounts of English heroism; the Guards at Alma, and the Cavalry at Balalkava seem to restore the age of chivalry. We all grieve over the strange confusion which produced that glorious but sad charge – many stories are of course propagated concerning a regular quarrel between Lords R. and L. on the subject. I will not fail to vindicate the claim of the

Guards to the gun [at Alma] whenever I have an opportunity.

I am going to add some warm stockings and a new kind of woollen shirt to Fortnum's packet. Pray say a kind word to young Arthur Gregory, poor Colonel Hood's nephew. His mother is very anxious for him to make your acquaintance. He is just going out (in the Scots Fusiliers). She is a widow, and has been widowed in a manner a second time by her brother's death. God bless you, my dear Henry. We really hardly breathe for anxiety for the next despatch.

Yours affectionately,
L.P.

The casualty list was published in *The London Gazette* on 22 November and the family at last discovered that Henry was saved, though wounded. After expressing relief at his brother's name not being among the dead, Lovaine went on to express the many anxieties and frustrations which were already creeping into the minds of those at home. His lugubrious tone elicited the slightly hypocritical comment from his brother that he wished Lovaine 'would not croak in his letters, for we don't lack for croaking ravens and crows of every description [here in the Crimea].' In any event, so many of Lovaine's forebodings would come true.

Albury Park,
Nov 22nd/54

My dear Henry,

I should not have been so long without writing to you if I had anything on earth to write about. The fact is you and your comrades are the sole and only topic of conversation, and all the news I could tell you would be the lies invented concerning yourselves. I see you have been wounded again, and with such an awful list of killed and wounded, I hardly know whether I ought not to congratulate instead of condoling with you. I can gather nothing from Lord Raglan's despatch but that you were overpowered by numbers, against which you seem to have struggled, as became the men of the Alma – though not with the same fortune as in that action; but we are left in the most tantalising state of uncertainty about everything. For nearly a week all that we have known was that the loss was immense, especially in the superior officers; four days after, comes the news that your Brigade suffered immensely, and for three or four we are left in doubt as to the names of the suffering. This is very hard.

You will be attacked again, I suppose, before long – and then the same thing will happen. However, we must, I suppose, make up our minds to this for many a long year to come. The Ministry seem to me to have been very culpably backwards in taking a true view of your condition, under which they ought at once to have put the country on a war footing. As it is, you can hardly have reinforcements out as far as they will be required, unless, as I hardly suspect, they are going to leave it to the French and to allow you to be reduced to the condition of mere auxiliaries. The former seem always to leave you to do the work and to help you only *in extremis*.

Before my letter arrives you will see that we have been repulsed in an attack on the Kamschatckan capital. I think the Navy wanted taking down a little, but not to the extent they have suffered there. It seems that the Admiral shot himself.* I see Lord Forth, that Scots Gallic *mestizo*, has disgraced the Drummond blood, and has left the army; was his refusal to go into the trenches (the reason alleged) cowardice or mutiny?

As you seem to be bound for a winter campaign, or at least winter quarters where you are, we have sent you out some furs, but I am at a loss to know what to order in the way of boots. There must be lots of sheepskins where you are, but no one to make them up. If you don't use the things yourself, there will be plenty of people to give them to. We are all in *status quo*, my father pretty well, but very nervous about you. He told me the other day that he never, asleep or awake, had the cannon of Sebastopol out of his ears. I fear Pec [Louisa]'s eyes will hardly recover, though she was somewhat better latterly.

Since writing the above, which was too late to be finished by the last post, we have received the account of your [great deeds]. Wood sent my father a letter of congratulations and the information that reports made on your conduct had been forwarded to Prince Albert. I cannot express to you the satisfaction it gave my father (who is here). I really do not think that anything could have given him more,

---

* A friend of Henry's wrote to him in the Crimea with a description of this incident: 'What a curious case that was of Admiral Price in the Pacific. He had with considerable difficulty induced the French Admiral to join him in an attack on Petropaulovsk and likewise to adopt his plan for attacking. The moment he arrived on the spot his nerves failed him, and he retired to his cabin and shot himself through the body. He lived for three hours afterwards, prayed with the chaplain, said he was sorry for what he had done and could not account for it. He was a gay light-hearted little man with no appearance of insanity.'

and you may imagine that <u>we</u> had little less. I recollect that when you were so anxious about that sword of Wilkinson's, I thought you were taking a world of useless thoughts on the matter, seeing it was never likely to be really used. <u>Now</u> it is a consolation to think that your getting it may really have been the means of saving your life. You must have been engaged in downright cut and thrust by the account in the papers most of the time, and my respect for the Russians is greater than I ever expected to feel, though they ought to have eaten you all up. I fear you have still very hard work before you.

They are sending out wood huts and sheepskin coats as I hear, which will probably arrive after one half of the men have died of cold. However, the remainder will be the better for them, and the government will bray as loud as if all the success which you have brought by your superhuman exertions and courage was owing to the tardiness with which they did not supply your wants. This bragging has, however, been brought down a little. They are getting bullied by *The Times* about reinforcements . . . . I believe their power, and not the will is wanting – owing to the original delay and dawdling and the total absence of head at the Horse Guards. You will only get recruits, of course, but they are the same stuff, and will soon be as good as the few you have left, and I would rather have them than your allies, who if all accounts speak truth, are not quite as rapid in their reinforcement as could be wished by your friends. They seem to have been 3 hours before they came to your assistance.

Adieu, my dear Henry. God shield and protect you, and give you all that can be reaped from the harvest of war. Louisa sends you her love, good wishes and congratulations. I do not expect to hear much from you because I know you keep my father *comme de devoir, au courant* and of course you cannot have much time for correspondence.

Yours affectionately,
　　　L.

Shall I send you out some more shoes from Cotterells? Parliament meets on this day fortnight, for what swindle of the government I know not. Some say to get money, others to cheat Militia Regiments into being compelled to take foreign service, when they volunteered only for home. God forbid that getting in the way of giving you assistance, but it is revolting to do that . . . which ought long ago to have been done openly, if the Ministry had been anything but the cheats and incapables they are. I see your deeds related in *The Morning Herald*, but I cannot say that you are fortunate in your historian.

A letter was published in *The Morning Herald* on 27 November (the date on which Lovaine finished the above letter) describing the Grenadiers' charge at Inkerman, as led by Percy. Despite Lovaine's closing comment, the letter was entirely complimentary about his brother and concluded that he 'seems to have shown not only bravery, but ability'. Both Algernon and Henry were deeply reserved by nature, and apt to be suspicious of anything that appeared in the press about their family, not really liking to see their names in print unless in an official capacity. Lovaine's reputation was not helped by the fact that 'nature had chosen perversely to mask his real qualities under a somewhat grim countenance and chilling manner', a handicap which inspired Lord Clarendon (who was Foreign Secretary at the time of the Crimean War) to write some years later, 'I have always felt that, if I was a jug of cream and was looked at by the Duke of Northumberland,* I should instantly turn sour.'[19] However, those who knew him well, like the author, naturalist and historian Sir Herbert Maxwell (one of whose works, incidentally, was helping his friend George Higginson in editing his letters and memoirs for publication in 1916) saw a different side to him: 'Strangers would never suspect the store of kindliness and genial humour that was masked by a demeanour so frigid . . . . I soon learnt to penetrate this disguise and to warm to the gleam of fun and sympathy that smouldered in a pair of rather small eyes.'[20] As it happened, Lord Clarendon changed his mind about Lovaine when in 1868 he showed great kindness to Lady Salisbury after she had been widowed: 'I shall never again even think that he looks peevish, but shall always regard him as a rare exception to that hideous selfishness which wealth generates.'[21]

Henry responded to his brother that he did not mind the mention of him in *The Morning Herald* letter, though he wasn't quite sure that the description of him 'yelling' as he charged into the battery was entirely fitting for an officer and he couldn't remember doing so. In fact, he appears to have been amused and even quietly flattered by the account; but he couldn't think who wrote it. It purported to be from 'An Old Grenadier' and, being published so soon after the action and accurate in its description, it seems possible that it was indeed a first-hand account,

* Lovaine became 6th Duke of Northumberland in 1867.

perhaps even from a Staff or General officer who had been a Grenadier.

The family learnt more details of their warrior's deeds at Inkerman from Colonel Wood, commanding the Regiment at Horse Guards. Wood described a 'beautiful letter' from Higginson to Hatton (quoted in the previous chapter), as well as another from the 3rd Battalion's commanding officer, Colonel Reynardson, describing the action of the 5 November. These letters were forwarded to Prince Albert, Colonel of the Regiment, for his perusal, and then on to Henry's father. The passage in Colonel Reynardson's letter which gave Lord Beverley so much pleasure reads: 'I told Percy I should not forget to mention the gallant manner [in which] he tried to rally our men, and did rush up almost unbacked – single-handed – to the redoubt, and was the cause of returning them to the assault.'

Lord Hardinge, Commander-in-Chief of the Army, also saw these accounts and inspired in Lord Beverley an even greater degree of father's pride. Hardinge wrote: 'My nephew, Colonel Wood, commanding the Grenadier Guards, has sent at my desire the enclosed account of your son's gallant conduct at Inkermann – proving that the Percy blood in battle is as ardent as in Hotspur's time. Everyone in the Guards is loud in his praises. Allow me to congratulate you very sincerely – I never cease to feel a deep interest in your family.'

Colonel Wood's letters and the letter from Henry's servant were clearly passed around the family as treasured possessions. Uncle Charles, Aunt Caroline and their twenty-year-old daughter Isabel, whose handkerchief had been so valuable to Henry at Alma, were among the recipients:

Guy's Cliffe. Sunday 26th Nov 54

My dear Henry,

You must be wounded to extract a letter from me! Most hastily do we thank God that you are safe for the present at least, and that you have deserved and gained consideration and honour; but how intensely do we wish this terrible siege was over, and that you and your gallant and heroic companions were in comfort again, and safety. The anxiety here about you is immense, and extends to all classes. And as glory succeeds to glory, we ask how long can our small band of heroes afford such victories? The electric telegraph may be of great benefit to the Government and the army, while to private individuals it is a curse. We think, talk and dream of nothing but our army in the Crimea, but to you I must write something else. Is it true that the point attacked <u>ought</u> to have been fortified, and if so, who is in fault? Do you believe an attack on Sebastopol <u>immediately</u> after Alma was possible – and if so, do you <u>now</u> think it would have been advisable? If you think these questions worth a reply, send me one through your father, in any letter you write to him.

Our poor neighbours, the wife, mother and sister of Grosvenor Hood are very miserable, but have born their sorrow like Christians with calmness and resignation. There never was so happy a home so sadly broken up. I hear also that Lt. Gen. Cathcart* is calm and thoughtful for others. The Cathcarts live at Leamington, and they are very miserable. Gaddy Seymour mourns deeply for her favourite brother. It was very kind of you to write to the Holmesdales – a letter at such a moment is so valuable and everyone knows how great an act of unselfish kindness it must be. Your father will have told you that he wrote your message to Lord Braybrooke.† I am sure for poor Hood's sake you will be kind to his nephew, young Gregory, who has lost in his uncle his legal guardian and his most valued friend. The boy is a good boy, but very young and little fitted, I fear, to bear all he will have to undergo.‡ He has not, I believe, yet sailed, but is on the point of doing so . . . .

Sadly Lady S. Meade was married on the very day the Gazette of the Battle of Inkerman was published – you may guess if it was a merry wedding – half of those invited could not come, and even the family itself had lost a relation in Vesey Dawson. Perhaps you do not know that she is married to young Vernon Granville, Vernon's eldest son. The parents did not like <u>him</u>, and there were difficulties, but all came right at last. He is a good match as his prospects are excellent. We rather wonder how she will get on with my old friend, Mr. Granville – Vernon the elder.

With every kind wish for your health and safety, and in warm congratulations on your escape, and the credit you have gained,

Ever yours affectionately,

Charles

* General Sir George Cathcart's brother, 2nd Earl Cathcart.
† Henry Neville's father.
‡ Arthur Gregory survived the Crimean winter of 1854–55, but the Bertie-Percies were right in thinking that he was ill-suited the rigours of army life, as he resigned his commission late in 1855.

From Caroline and Isabel:

Monday 25th. We have got today Colonel Wood's letter, and poor Joseph's triumphant note of your honour and glories. God send that you may come safe home and sit on your laurels by a good fire.

To return to Lady S. Meade. We hear today that the marriage had not the usual accompaniments of favours, luncheon etc. It was all arranged with the greatest privacy as suitable to the sad moment in which it was enacted . . . .

The servants here take the deepest interest in your welfare, particularly Mrs Laker, who talks of you with tears in her eyes, and Dunn, the gardener, who 'remembers you so young a gentleman'. Uncle William comes today. He will have a rare cold journey from Rose Castle, and will not arrive till 9 at night. We pray heartily that the same coldness, which set in suddenly yesterday, be confined to the North of Europe. Captain Wodehouse has returned safe and well to the great joy of his wife. He is a very kind creature, as we have experienced in his great good nature and attention to a little son of the Newton Janes, who began his short career last summer in the Baltic, and died on his passage home invalided – such a nice quiet, yet spirited boy! . . .

I wonder what your version is of the grand but fatal cavalry charge on the 25th, and what you think of Miss Nightingale and the nurses? If, which God forbid, you should be at any time obliged to go to Scutari, you will I am sure find our neighbours, the Bracebridges,* who are very kind. Mr B is clever and agreeable and very ugly.

The little girl you and Dundas used to play with here, now Mrs Marshall in New Zealand, never fails to inquire after you and him. In her last letter, she hoped neither of her military friends were likely to take part in the rumoured war.

Caroline and Isabel

During November Henry wrote letters of condolence to the families of friends who had been killed or wounded at Inkerman; these acts of kindness were all the more appreciated by the recipients when they came to understand the conditions of privation under which they had been sent. The story of the two Neville brothers in the Crimea is an especially tragic one. We have already seen how

* Mr and Mrs Bracebridge were Florence Nightingale's mentors, and took care of her finances in Scutari.

Henry was killed at Inkerman, only a few days after Grey had been badly wounded in the cavalry charge at Balaklava. Grey, however, made it to Scutari hospital and on 10 November, more than two weeks after he had received his injuries and ignorant of his brother's fall, he was able to write a short, but cheerful letter to his mother:

My Dearest Mother,

I am able to write and tell you, by the doctor's authority, that I am doing very well indeed. I have been wounded very severely in the side a good many times. I had the bad luck to get knocked off my horse, and then those ruffian Russians stuck their lances into me: the wounds, however, are doing beautifully. I have a bad cough, which the doctors say, will go away soon. Do not fret about me, as I feel already better in myself; and I trust that before long a Medical Board will send me back once more to rejoin those whom I love so well. There has been more fighting round Sebastopol, but nothing as yet clear. Lady Stratford de Redcliffe* and forty other ladies are doing wonders here in the hospitals. With best love to all,

I am your very affectionate Son,
G.N.[22]

Within twenty-four hours he was dead, though the news would take some time to reach England. In the meantime the family learnt of Henry's death and the following letter from a grief stricken Lord Braybrooke is one that was penned to Grey in Scutari a few days after the official returns from Inkerman were published:

Overwhelmed as we are with the affliction with the irreparable loss of poor dear Henry, we have been very much cheered by receiving so good an account of your progress to recovery, under your own hand, and we sincerely hope that the fatal news, which must have reached you soon after you wrote, may not have had the effect of injuring your health. The shock must, indeed, have been most severe, considering how recently you had seen your brother in good health and spirits, doing all in his power to alleviate your sufferings, and to be enabled to report as favourably as possible of your wounds to the family, who, he felt certain, would be deeply interested to learn every particular . . . . I doubt not that the

* The wife of Lord Stratford de Redcliffe (1786–1880), who was probably the most influential diplomat of his age and was British ambassador to Turkey.

circumstances of that last interview will never be effaced from your recollection.

You will like to hear that your poor mother has been wonderfully supported in the heavy trial, and sets the best example of firmness to the children . . . . Though gradually losing strength, I am in good health, God be praised for it, and I was not wholly unprepared for the fatal result; perhaps from some foreboding that, in a series of sanguinary conflicts, few, if any, persons could long escape; or some melancholy presentiment might be mercifully encouraged from on high, so inscrutable are the ways of Providence, to school the mind and shadow out evil to come. And, indeed, the long and painful suspense that intervened before the 'Gazette' came forth, depressed every one's spirits, and led to the anticipation of bad tidings. In such a case, all human consolation is in vain; and we can only hope for support from that Almighty Being who inflicted the blow for reasons which we are not permitted to question . . . . Without his divine aid, I might have lost two sons in less than a fortnight.*

Poor dear Henry! It is soothing to record how deeply he is regretted. We receive daily the most touching tributes to his memory, not only from relations and friends, but from many public bodies, and our misfortunes have excited general sympathy and compassions. We have also most kind testimonies from brother-officers, in which our poor sufferer is spoken of in the highest terms. All these papers will be preserved against your return.[23]

Lord Braybrooke signed this letter before lunch on the 28 November; it was never sent, for that afternoon came the second blow in the form of news of Grey's death:

My Lord,

It is with feelings of the deepest sorrow and most poignant regret, I have to communicate my ever late lamented master's death – your lordship's son, the Hon G. Neville. I am just after returning from his funeral; he was buried here, a few moments since, with the honours of war. He died on Saturday morning, about eight o'clock, from wounds he received at the fatal engagement we had at Balaklava on the twenty-fifth of last month. He was ten days on board attended by a head doctor, who waited on him as a parent; and since he arrived in hospital, no person could be better attended;

---

* Both *had* died in less than a week; Henry on the night of the 5th and Grey on the morning of the 11th.

94

but the Almighty was pleased to take him to himself, and I hope he is now happy in heaven. My Lord, so gently did he – so calmly did he – breathe his last that a casual observer would consider him sleeping. He always hoped to go home; the night before he died, he was talking of the happiness of meeting his family, and of his application for me to return with him to England. He never allowed death near him at all, but God willed it otherwise. Doubtless your Lordship will receive letters from the officers of the Regiment, relative to the sad affair; to them, and with them, he was as a brother. To the men of his troop, he was indulgent, kind, and courteous – popular with all, he was too good to live on earth, and now he is, I hope, an angel in heaven. I enclose a lock of his hair – sad memorial of the once happy, cheerful, noble-minded youth; it is all I could send. Your Lordship will excuse my writing; but, exclusive of its being my duty, I feel as a parent, having a wife and children now at present in Newbridge, Ireland, whose every prayer is for my safe return. That is my excuse for writing, and I feel sure your Lordship will pardon me the liberty I take.

    Your Lordship's humble, obedient servant,
        James Orr
        5th Dragoon Guards[24]

Of the acknowledgements Henry Percy received in return for his letters of condolence, most moving is the following missive from the remaining Neville brother, Richard, who had been a contemporary of his in the Grenadiers.

                      Audley End
                    December 17th

My dear Percy,

    I cannot thank you sufficiently on my own part, as well as for all my family, for your very great kindness in writing to me about poor Henry. The least account, however trifling, as you justly said, is of immense value in our sight – although it cannot be of any assistance in alleviating our sorrow. Although I was sorry to see you were again wounded at Inkerman, I felt sure you would, as so old a friend, if possible let me hear what you knew about my brother's death. I was glad to see in your handwriting a confirmation of what we had heard in a very kind letter from your father to mine – *viz.* that your wound was not of a serious character enough to lay you up entirely. Not, however, that this evidence is infallible, for alas we had a letter written by my youngest brother, who was wounded in the charge of the <u>Heavies</u> on the 25th October, from Scutari Hospital the day before he died; yet giving a most favourable report of himself and talking of a medical board to send him home. By the time this reaches you, you will have heard by this fatal catastrophe we are doubly mourners, and able to form some idea of the fearful shock these combined losses have given us all, especially my father. On hearing of poor Henry's fall, Prince Albert kindly gave an ensigncy to poor Grey in the Grenadiers, so I should still, if he had survived, have had a link to bind me more closely to those amongst whom my happiest days were spent.

Dennis Wright will be gazetted out next week. Lord Rokeby* and Barnard are going out to the Crimea. We are to have a Foreign Legion, much to our disgust, and more as it is to be drilled in England. With many thanks for your kindness and sincere wishes both for the satisfactory progress of your hurt and future career. I am, dear Percy, ever yours sincerely,

R. C. Neville

P.S. We have heard from Sturt and Tipping some more particulars of the Inkerman fight.[25]

---

* Henry Robinson-Montagu, 6th and last Baron Rokeby (1798–1883), was sent out to the Crimea to replace Bentinck in command of the Brigade of Guards. He arrived on 1 February 1855.

Chapter 5

Winter Siege

Although the Guards were relieved from duty in the trenches for six days after Inkerman, they still had to continue manning the outposts for which they had been responsible before Inkerman, and by mid-November they were very much back in the old routine to which they had been accustomed before the 5th. The privations endured by the men were becoming increasingly severe thanks to the onset of winter, quite apart from the fact that their depleted ranks meant that there were fewer of them to do the same work as before.

On 14 November a hurricane visited the Black Sea. It struck early in the morning, and such was its violence that every single tent in the Guards' Camp was blown down. All the bearskin caps, which customarily stood outside on pegs, were blown into a ravine nearly a quarter of a mile away.[1] Kettles and drums from the Light Division camp, upwind of the Guards, flew over the Grenadiers' heads as they crouched wherever they could find temporary shelter, and ended up in the same bush scrub as the bearskins. Every sort of camp accoutrement became a missile; even 'great barrels bounded along like cricket balls' and heavy wagons were blown through the camp 'dragging bullocks after them as if they were mere kittens.'[2] The storm was no respecter of seniority: General Estcourt, the Adjutant General, clung for dear life to one of the shrouds of his marquee, while a junior officer, in drawers and shirt, tore through the rain and dirt like a maniac after (as he thought) his cap, but which he found after a desperate run to be a sergeant's.[3] The mayhem lasted all day, and it was not until dusk that the weather had abated sufficiently for fires to be lit.

The situation up at camp may have seemed comical, though anyone who witnessed the distressing scene at the hospital, which was uprooted along with everything else, would soon have stopped laughing. Down at Balaklava harbour, it was a disaster. William Howard Russell, writing for *The Times*, called it 'the most appalling chapter in the history of maritime disasters'. He visited the scene the following day:

> I worked, through ammunition mules and straggling artillery-wagons, towards the town. Balaklava lay below us – its waters thronged with shipping – not a ruffle on their surface. It was almost impossible to believe that but twelve hours before ships were dragging their anchors, drifting, running aground, and smashing each other to pieces in that placid loch. The whitewashed houses in the distance were as clean-looking as ever, and the old ruined fortress on the crags above still frowned upon the sea, and reared its walls and towers aloft, uninjured by the storm.
>
> On approaching the town, however, the signs of the tempest of yesterday grew on one, and increased at every step. At the narrow neck of the harbour two or three large boats were lying, driven inland several yards from the water; the shores were lined with trusses of compressed hay which had floated out of the wrecks outside the harbour, and pieces of timber, large beams of wood, masts and spars of all sizes formed large natural rafts, which lay stranded by the beach or floated about among the shipping. The old tree which stood at the guard-house at the entrance to the town was torn up, and in its fall it had crushed the house so as to make it a mass of ruins. The fall of this tree, which had seen many winters, coupled with the fact that the verandahs and balconies of the houses and a row of very fine acacia trees on the beach were blown down, corroborates the statement so generally made by the inhabitants that they had never seen or heard of such a hurricane in their lifetime, although there is a tradition among some that once in thirty or forty years such visitations occur along this coast. In its present condition Balaklava is utterly indescribable. If the main sewers of London were uncovered and the houses placed by their brink, the hardy man who walked down the streets thus formed would be able to realise the condition of the thoroughfares in this delightful spot. The narrow main street is a channel of mud, through which horses, wagons, camels, mules, and soldiers and sailors, and men of all

nations – English, French, Turks, Arabs, Egyptians, Italians, Maltese, Tartars, Greeks, Bulgarians, and Spaniards – scramble, plunge, and jostle, and squatter along . . . . Many of the houses are unroofed, several have been destroyed altogether, and it is quite impossible to find quarters in the place.[4]

Twenty-one transport ships were lost; those which had recently arrived had to wait beneath the cliffs outside the harbour for the opportunity of a berth, and so could hardly avoid being driven on to the rocks. *Resolute* sank with more than ten million Minié rounds. The most painful loss of all was the *Prince*, a fine steamer with a complement of 150 crew, which went down with 60,000 blankets, 40,000 great coats and boots, and copious medical supplies – i.e. 'everything most wanted', according to an official report. Not only that: just six of the *Prince*'s crew survived.[5] Henry Percy visited Balaklava a few days after the storm: 'The harbour was in a horrid state – dead bodies, literally in pieces, being washed up after the late storm. A siege does not give much scope for an agreeable letter.'

His friend and saviour, Captain James Drummond, had exercised great skill in saving his little frigate *Retribution*. She was stationed just off the precipitous cliffs outside the harbour's entrance when the storm struck at five in the morning. Drummond lowered her anchors and got the engines running at full speed. He resolutely stood for four hours on the bridge, while enormous masses of water rolled along the ship's deck from stem to stern, sometimes coming up to his waist.[6] He had more reason than most to be anxious, for he already had one wreck on his hands – a nervous wreck in the form of the Duke of Cambridge, who was still recuperating from Inkerman with him. HRH wrote to his family after the storm:

The morning of the 14th, a most fearful gale set in, and so suddenly that in about an hour's time there was no possibility of getting away. There we lay outside the harbour with quantities of ships all around us, which of course increased the danger. It began about six in the morning, and continued to increase in violence. The other ships and transports were dragging their anchors and passing us in quick succession, some so close that we though they must have been upon us, in which case we must have gone with them. These poor creatures drove on the coast, which was of perpendicular rock, and in a moment all perished, the ships all regularly breaking or blowing up. At ten o'clock our rudder was carried away and there we were perfectly at the mercy of wind and waves. Our Captain, Drummond, a fine fellow, behaved most nobly, and by his coolness, courage and determination, certainly saved us under God's blessing. He threw all his heavy guns overboard, and all his shot, and kept her up to her anchor by the steam. We had three anchors down. At twelve, however, two of these anchors went, and we had then only one left, and this one saved us . . . . At two a thunderbolt came down and struck the ship. We thought at first it was a Russian shell . . . and then there came a tremendous shower of hail . . . . I being unwell at the time lay in my cot all day, it was in fact impossible to sit up, and the decks were streaming with the water which was coming in every moment. The men brought us in accounts every now and then how things were going and by their countenances one could see how ill they thought of it. Tho' I did not give up all hope, I confess I thought all was lost and was fully prepared to die, I prayed for you all and thought much of dear home. Had the anchor gone I had made up my mind to go on deck, prepared to try to swim with the rest, but I suspect that not many of us would have had a chance.[7]

According to one mischievous account, the Duke grasped a steward's hand and, bewailing his fate, moaned, 'Oh! Is it come to this? Oh! We shall be lost.'[8] Needless to say, the experience of the storm did not exactly restore Prince George's nerves.

Apart from the cost in human life, the real tragedy of the hurricane was the loss of so many vital supplies. The army had been waiting for these things – clothes, tents, fodder for the horses, hospital and ambulance equipment, etc. – ever since they had left everything behind at Varna two months previously. At that time it was thought the campaign would be short, but now that it was clear that the Army of the East would be stuck in the Crimea for the winter, those supplies were even more vital. The trouble was that Balaklava was a tiny fishing port, in no way adequate as a supply base for tens of thousands of men. When fully loaded transport ships did arrive, there simply wasn't the physical capacity to unload them; even without the impediment of a gale, perishables habitually rotted, either still on board ship or awaiting distribution on the quayside. It was deeply unfortunate that the storm struck at precisely the moment when Balaklava was most clogged with laden cargo ships.

An additional problem in the distribution of food and materials to the troops was the route out of Balaklava. On 25 October, the Russians had captured the Turkish redoubts commanding the Woronzoff Road leading up to the heights above Sebastopol. As a result, until the Russians relinquished these positions, this route – the only properly metalled one in the area – was not available for the supply of the siege lines. Instead, they had to use the Col Road, which was really little more than a track, very steep in places and apt to become muddy in winter. In the rain, and with the passage of a whole army's worth of transport, it soon became the most awful quagmire. Wagons became irreparably stuck, beasts of burden hopelessly bogged, many already so near death from starvation (to the extent that they frequently tried to eat each others' tails) that they could neither extricate themselves nor be freed by the men who tended them. Increasingly the troops stationed above Sebastopol found that they could only get what they needed by trudging down to Balaklava in person. Officers went too, as they were frequently needed to negotiate (or more likely railroad) the imbecilic attitude of the Commissariat, who, being a branch of the Treasury rather than the War Office, were more concerned with avoiding any risk to their own careers by sticking rigidly to the regulations than with assisting an army on its knees.

On 22nd November the Grenadiers were ordered to move their camp to the Sapoune Ridge, overlooking the Fedioukine Hills and the Tchernaya Valley. This new ground, instead of being stony as before, was rather like a ploughed field of stiff tenacious clay, and in wet weather its inhabitants frequently found themselves half up to their knees in mud. This further deterioration told on the health of the men, to whose duties was now added the necessity of helping to repair the road to Balaklava. Nevertheless, somehow spirits held up and even the officers, who in peacetime depended upon personal servants answering every beck and call, became masters of improvisation. William Simpson, the accomplished Glaswegian water-colourist who was commissioned by Colnaghi and Sons to record scenes from the war for a book of lithographs, arrived in the Crimea just after the hurricane. He carried a letter of introduction to the Duke of Cambridge, whom he went to see on board the *Retribution*. The General in turn gave him introductions to some Guards officers, and Simpson met a number of Grenadiers at their camp. He recorded in his autobiography: 'It was rather surprising to find the condition in which such officers lived. Mess pork fried, and commissariat biscuits soaked in water, fried with the pork – this was about the full extent of the menu for breakfast, with tea or coffee, I forget which. The menu for dinner I have now no recollection of, but it was not much different from the breakfast. Lieutenant Sir James Fergusson* was looked upon as a good caterer; when he went to Balaklava, he boarded the ships to see what he could buy, and generally returned laden with jam and other delicacies.'[9]

Officers who managed to maintain healthy horses would use their spare time to help carry supplies from Balaklava. On the last day of November Percy and Higginson both went down to Balaklava. The latter described the fruits of their foraging:

> As for me and our mess, I am indebted to my Russian horse for all our 'wittles'; as he yesterday, notwithstanding the rain, brought up two dozen of wine, about a dozen cases of preserved meat, three chairs, and a bag of potatoes on his back! We made, too, a wonderful haul of chickens, six ducks, two gooses, and a turkey from a newly arrived ship. Young [Lieutenant] Hamilton is today employed in making a hen house and pen for our live stock, which quack and cackle like good old English poultry. So you see we cannot be said to be starving; but as we live almost perpetually in a state of swamp, I believe eating and drinking in moderation is the best antidote to any ill effects.

As Fergusson pointed out after the war in a letter to *The Times*, the Guards officers soon worked out a more efficient way of moving the Brigade's supplies up to the new camp site, which was

---

* Simpson was incidentally also highly impressed that Fergusson was standing as MP in place of Lieutenant Colonel James Hunter Blair, Scots Fusilier Guards, who had been killed at Inkerman. His letter to the electorate was addressed from 'the fields of Inkerman'; he was, of course, elected. Fergusson retired from the army in July 1855 and stood as MP for Ayrshire 1854–57 and 1859–58. In later life he became Governor of New Zealand. He was killed in the Jamaican earthquake of 1907.

at a greater distance from Balaklava than almost any other part of the army. They simply left the horses which they had devoted to this purpose down at the harbour overnight, instead of taking them back and forth twice each day. Why, he asked, did the Commissariat not follow this practice for their own horses, instead of keeping them up near the camps?

> The horses, being stabled and picketed at Balaklava, would not have had the extra labour of carrying their forage to the front; sheltered by the cliff which overhangs the town, they would not have been exposed to the piercing blast and the driving snow; and, above all, being already on the spot to receive the burdens which awaited them, they would have started in good time on their journey, fresh for their day's work, and arrived in camp in daylight, so that the much required articles they carried might have been available for distribution the same day, whereas the unfortunate animals belonging to the Commissariat, after having fished up some of their pittance of barley out of the mud at their feet, struggled their seven miles through the deep and tenacious clay to Balaklava, hustled, and fought, and waited on the crowded wharf for hours, till, as the short winter's day was ending, they set out on their weary journey home. No wonder that, half fed and wearied, many of them sunk under their burdens, and found their graves where they fell, so that when their comrades with diminished numbers toiled down again on their morning's trip a few more bony carcasses protruding from the soil dotted the line of that fatal road. And in the meantime the parties for the trenches had gone and returned, to find half rations served out to them again, and for them too the overpowering work of bringing up from Balaklava shot and shell, clothing, huts, and stores, for which the Commissariat 'could not find transport' . . . May not the apparently trifling blunder I have pointed out been the real cause of the death of hundreds of soldiers?[10]

As for the food when it arrived, the biscuit was so hard it had to be soaked in water overnight in order to soften it up. Obtaining fuel for a fire was a major problem and the only thing that they could get with reliability was the roots of the oak scrub which grew to a height of three or four feet in the rocky ravines. It need not always have been thus, as Lord Beverley read in one of his son's letters home: 'To give you an idea of Estcourt's composition, there was an immense lot of driftwood, excellent for heating, driven onto the shore. He sent an order that it was not to be taken away, and sentries were placed over it. In the meantime, a different wind sprung up and drove it out to sea. The imbecile forgot to [rescind] the order.'

Higginson wrote: 'Extracted from the half-frozen ground by pick-axe and mattock, the green roots were kindled with difficulty; the result being smouldering embers, rather than the welcome blaze which would have served to dry the drenched and tattered great coats of the working parties, returning from their six-and-thirty hours in the trenches.' One trick was to lay an eighteen-pound shot in the embers after cooking so that, when it had accumulated heat, it could be transferred to the end of the camp bed, under the blankets.

As a career officer on active service, Henry's letters home were much more concerned with the progress of the war than with trivial aspects of their living conditions. In fact, even as late as 19 November, when he had already been down to Balaklava following the storm and seen the chaos with his own eyes, Henry found it in himself to be surprisingly complimentary about the Commissariat: 'It is certainly well managed, but they give the men coffee, who have to roast and grind it, instead of tea, which is easy to carry and make. In the troubles of Canada we sometimes got nothing to eat; here we have our rations regularly, and good. No complaint on that score can be entertained.'

Despite the physical endurance and constant wet, men and officers alike seldom grumbled, and everybody pulled together to help those who were too exhausted to see to their own shelter; off-duty soldiers, overseen by their officers and assisted by Turks, were quite happy building a hospital or mending a road in their spare time. In fact, these activities presented some welcome relief from the interminable boredom of the military stalemate.

We are now far from comfortable, the south-westerly gales contin-uing without interruption with very heavy rain which makes our tents and everything moist and unpleasant, and an utter impossi-bility of going out without being up to one's calf in mud and water. It is, however, not cold, and we are told that in December it will be fine. The sun is all we want. The men, though they are very wet, do not lose their spirits, but they are much to be pitied, as they are wretchedly uncomfortable. The siege, to judge by the firing, has gone on with more vigour, but the Russians will not give in till forced. The rain, at all events, prevents any attack *extra mures*, and the Russians every time they put their heads out of the city catch it, so that I fancy they will not make many attempts. The nights are dull, and make our position insufferably dull.[11]

The bitterness expressed in officers' letters during the winter of 1854–55 was primarily directed against the generals and their staff. Doubts about Lord Raglan's ability to command an army in the field began with his failure to learn the lessons of the surprise attack of 'Little Inkerman' on 26 October and reinforce the defences on the British right, despite practically everybody from the Duke of Cambridge down pointing out the necessity of doing this. Even after Inkerman, the high command were still gripped by sloth and inactivity:

Conceive that the defence of an outpost close to the town was so neglected, that till I made a fierce remonstrance, nothing was done. Now they are beginning to find out it is very weak, and to fortify it. There really is such a want of care, and apathy in the higher branches of the Staff, and such a flippancy in the Engineers that is quite disgusting. Everyone says the same. They will throw the grand principle of war: 'never leave a chance open' aside to save themselves trouble. I attribute, and would so publicly, the redoubts at Balaklava being captured from the Turks to these causes. It now turns out the Turks fought well . . . .

To give you an idea of the authorities: young Ashley Ponsonby, who has just come, makes acquaintance of the Chief Engineer of the *Queen of the South*, by which vessel he sailed here, and found out the man was 11 years employed in the Russian service in the Black Sea, and knows Sebastopol well, and Nikolayeff [too]. He goes to the head of the 2nd Division to report this, and the ADC pooh-poohs. He persists, and sees the Military Secretary, who goes to Sir J. Burgoyne, who says he doesn't want to see the man, that he knows quite enough about Sebastopol. Ponsonby is sent away without thanks for his trouble. If I had gone, I would have seen Lord Raglan, or stopped till I did. Of course, the engineer may or may not have important information, but conceive his throwing the chance away![12]

Percy still admired Lord Raglan himself, and blamed all these ills on his subordinates – chiefly Airey, Estcourt and Burgoyne. It was a pity, though, that his lordship didn't do more to inspire the troops: 'Lord R, they say, is in the highest spirits and health through the hard endeavours of Brownrigg, a Grenadier officer and friend of mine, and Assistant Adjutant General to the Division . . . . [But] the worst thing is that Lord Raglan never shows himself, not even after an action, to the men. During the action he rides around perfectly unconcerned, surrounded by shot and shells, but he does nothing to endear himself to the men. A little more moving about would make the men know him. Now he is a myth to half of them.' By mid-December, Percy was becoming exasperated:

I doubt Lord Raglan's elevation to the dignity of Field Marshal has given the slightest pleasure to anyone. He has so thrown away his opportunities of being known to the troops, he is a myth to half of them. There was a night attack, I think mentioned in my last letter, which was repulsed, it was <u>then</u> discovered that this approach to our lines was utterly defenceless . . . . The French general went to see it and said, '*Je ne conçois pas comme on a pu dormir dans cet état de choses*', and immediately volunteered his men to erect defences. It is the universal opinion of everybody that the ground allotted to us has never been properly reconnoitred by our engineers. Probably that inefficient old twaddle Burgoyne* will be made Field Marshal too. I dare say that you will think that I am very bitter, but it is not unreasonable when our blood, honour and liberty are at stake, to complain that the usual precautions comprehensible to a child are not taken, purely from inefficiency and apathy. Besides, one must reckon the delays that are caused by each of these errors in the siege. Should Inkerman have been defended by proper earthworks, the Russians would have either not dared attack it or would have inflicted considerably less loss upon us, and not have retarded the siege. Had the redoubts at Balaklava been constructed so as to give confidence to raw troops, the Turks would have held them, and would not have been obliged to withdraw. Everything is marked with the same brand – apathy and inefficiency. An engineer officer avowed to me that the Balaklava redoubts were poor things. Why then trust them to untried troops who had never seen fire? They had plenty of time to make them

---

* Percy crossed out 'Burgoyne' many years later.

model. It is all very fine the engineers crowing over the French about the exploded powder magazine, they forget that the English ground is much more difficult to hit than the French . . . .

One might fight and win a battle by oneself now, as the Staff think of nothing but halting and making kitchens for themselves. Lord R. and all the heads of departments are located in a large and comfortable farm villa, whence they emerge occasionally when it is very fine. Canrobert lives in tents boarded over.

The post continues its usual vagaries, thanks to Estcourt and the civilian Postmasters sent here by Lord Stratford for more patronage's sake – when a captain of a Line Regiment or two would have done the business effectively, and for half the pay, and been thankful, as they do in India.

The disarray in the entire British war effort contrasted wildly with French professionalism. Because the British had borne the brunt of Inkerman and the French were not suffering quite the same hardships as the British (partly owing to their much easier supply situation), the French now made up the vast bulk of the allied forces in the Crimea, and indeed they had taken over the 'Right Attack' (i.e. the right hand sector of the trenches) from the British. One day Percy rode over to Kamiesch harbour, where 'the Frenchmen are all civility and kindness and give their attention liberally; they are of course dear, but they will do anything to satisfy you and always insist on giving you a mouthful of something, a *petit verre* & a cigar. It is the only amusement I have going there. They are so friendly – unlike the rascal Greek Maltese, and the few English scoundrels who haunt us [at Balaklava].'

The Zouaves, who had come to the aid of the Guards at Inkerman, came in for particular praise. Three weeks after that battle, he wrote:

The wet does not seem to affect my constitution unfavourably, and my head is nearly healed. If we can get a dry day to wash, dry our blankets and dry the floor of one's tent, it will be pleasant. A colonel of the Zouaves is going to hand me some of his handy good-humoured civic rascals to make a '*petit four*' in my tent, sufficient to boil a pint of water and dry one's floor. They are certainly the handiest fellows. They delight in our biscuit, and used to offer our men money for it. This our men refused, and gave it to them (which

107

they did not want); but their *amour propre* suffered by this, so they always insist on giving them bread in exchange. One cannot help liking them. There is a sort of readiness and complaisance about them which you do not find in the other troops of the French. The French artillery seem a rough lot, and the Line stupid. The officers of the Zouaves, I hear, own that they are obliged to overlook peccadillos, as they are such good soldiers in every way. Someone the other day, overhearing one Zouave talking in perfect English, expressed his surprise. The Zouave replied: 'No wonder, as I was 4 years at Eton'! I was talking to some the other day, and they said this was infinitely worse than Africa. An officer of the Zouaves narrated to me his career in the Zouaves. He is a very distinguished man amongst them. The man who introduced me to this Colonel described me, imprudently I thought, as one of '*les plus nobles familles d'Angleterre*'. I thought he would have sneered, but on the contrary, he said with a sort of sigh, '*notre aristocratie ne veut peu entrer dans l'armée*', and uttered some sort of compliment on the number of officers in our army '*de bon naissance*'.

Two days after the Zouaves had installed a fireplace in Henry's tent, he was able to report that 'it answers pretty well, but its fire has not quite yet *dénoué* the damp; it is cheery, however.' The French officer who had facilitated this was a man named Colonel Cler, soon to be a very distinguished general. Percy and Cler remained lifelong friends, and when after the war Percy was formally appointed to the Légion d'Honneur, General Cler gave to him his own Cross, which he had earned for his conduct in Algeria, saying that he was glad to give it to one whom he knew was '*un brave*'. Percy gave to Cler his Cross in exchange.*

Henry's friendship with Cler made him increasingly annoyed by accusations, which were widespread in Britain, that the French had been slow to assist the British at Inkerman. Both Lord Beverley and Lovaine were ticked off on this count:

Pray contradict any nonsense you may hear from ill-disposed individuals about the slowness of the French in assisting us. They were <u>not</u> slow, but came from a great distance having been deceived by the

* Gustave Cler (1814–1859), whose diaries formed the basis of *Reminiscences of an Officer of Zouaves* (1860). General Cler's life was cut short in its prime during the Austro-Italian War at the Battle of Magenta.

Russians, and their officers were almost in tears at their not coming sooner. I believe that they did not come much after Lord Raglan. Now we have Frenchmen all about us and I shall give a most formal *démenti* to anyone who ever in my presence says that the French are slow to assist us either in fights or in camps. They are admirable comrades, obliging, liberal and good-humoured. They get the best of everything, it is true – why? Because their generals are not effete officials and inactive ignoramuses, but active hawk-eyed soldiers. Their generals don't have attacks of nerves, and are always thinking of their men and not of their own comforts and *douceurs* . . . .

Their [Army System] is not the [product] of nepotism and inefficiency. Their generals are selected from experience, and not because they have got round the ear of some woman – or worse than that – some man degenerated with women. Forgive me for saying <u>degenerated</u>, for from what I now see, men are more like what we choose to predict women as being, and women more like what we fancy men should be. The French officer has a thousand faults, but he <u>is</u> a soldier, and I'll be hanged if above one or two of Lord Raglan's subordinates are anything like one.

Relations between the Guards and the headquarters staff took a dramatic turn for the worse when Lord Raglan's official despatch on Inkerman was published in the Crimea. The officers were unanimous in their condemnation of injustice that had been done to their Brigade. Higginson spoke for all when he wrote on 12 December:

We are all frantic. I can bear being slighted as well as anyone, and heaven knows that in this army anybody in an official position, however humble, must not be too sensitive of snubs; but anything so materially false as the account of our doings at that great battle I never saw. Despatches are reckoned as sound materials for an historian to work upon, and should not be hastily or timidly framed. After the arrival of the Alma despatch, I called together the battalion and read the account with some pride; but on this occasion I could not bring myself to do it, so shamefully were we treated.

Percy, writing at about the same time, was rather more forthright:

Lord Raglan's despatch of Inkerman is very official. Had he recounted the real valour and efforts of the troops, he would have been called upon by the Sovereign Press to explain why the precautions evident to common sense, and which would have saved the energies and blood of the troops being taxed so heavily, were not taken. So his despatch is guarded and unfair to the troops who saved him. We, the Brigade, are very sulky. He represents us as retiring. The fact, and upon which no doubt can be entertained, is that 'unsupported, in want of ammunition, outflanked and surrounded, the Brigade cut their way through the enemy', taking prisoners too . . . . [Afterwards] we formed in line as support in rear of a battery under a heavy fire of shot and shell, laid down, and the shot flew everywhere about us. One shell burst 2 yards from me, and we had men killed there . . . . The returns are wrong too: we have not a man missing, and they put down 30. As for being mentioned in despatches, as long as it is the fashion to mention every staff officer by name, and no regimental officer unless he commands it, it is no use thinking of it. Half of the staff officers mentioned were not under fire but are mentioned as a matter of form . . . . The stand of the Guards, which the French and the Line confess could only have been made by the Guards, is hardly mentioned. This is to avoid jealousy, it is said – but he can praise the Highlanders, the wretched generals of cavalry and the Rifles perfectly well – bulgar!

The natural impulse was to blame Lord Raglan for the mendacious Inkerman despatch but, on reflection a few days later, Henry preferred to blame 'some dirty under stopper', for he still had an enduring fondness for the Commander-in-Chief. Lord Raglan, however, was definitely to blame; as a Grenadier himself, he was very anxious not to be seen to favour the Guards over other regiments in making appointments, even though, deep down, he was intensely proud of his own Regiment and was more than happy to tell his own daughters in private letters how gallant Percy had been. It was a well-intentioned bias, but it grieved greatly that body of men who had lost half their number in the bloody fight around the Sandbag Battery. Indeed, all regimental officers, not just the Guards, had a right to be aggrieved at their being ignored in the Inkerman despatch. As proof of this, of the twenty individuals who were eventually awarded Victoria Crosses either wholly or in part for their actions on that day, not one was mentioned in Lord Raglan's official despatch. Staff officers, on the other hand, received liberal recognition. Some, of course, deserved the praise.

Most, however, were just ordinary regimental officers, be-plumed and on horseback, but with less technical knowledge than their contemporaries in the front line. *The Times* of 22 February 1856 observed that out of 291 British Army staff officers in May 1854 (i.e. two months after the declaration of war on Russia), only fifteen had been trained at the senior department of Sandhurst.[13] The book *Our Veterans of 1854*, published in 1855 by 'A Regimental Officer', who was in fact an officer of the Coldstream Guards, Lieutenant Colonel Wilson, posed the question: 'How shall we describe the staff?' The response was that 'to serve on the staff is the legitimate ambition of every officer. The pay is double that of regimental officers, the chances of promotion and distinction more than double, the life pleasanter and easier. These advantages and privileges are most reasonably assigned to staff officers, in order to secure for that important branch of the military profession the very best men in the service. But was the staff of 1854 composed of the very best men in the army? Without intending any disrespect, we may answer – Hardly.'

Edward Barrington de Fonblanque, the Commissariat friend of Henry Percy who wrote so much about the Army's organization after the war, explained that one absurdity of the Purchase System was that a regimental officer could only get paid a proper salary if he found a staff appointment: 'We unfortunately pay our Staff Officers one rate of pay for what they do, and another for what they do not do, and we occasionally add a third rate for what they are supposed to have done, and frequently never did.' Since officers saw their regimental pay only as the interest on their capital investment, they felt they should be paid separately for staff duties.

Henry Percy's ambition in this regard was no exception. He was beside himself with frustration at not getting anything after Inkerman, particularly as he had been personally congratulated on the spot by the general commanding his Division (namely the Duke of Cambridge), and as his own commanding officer, Colonel Reynardson, had promised to report him. Percy's hopes were also up because, back in Varna, Lord Burghersh, Lord Raglan's nephew, had privately told him that his uncle was very impressed with him and was looking for an excuse to give him something. The problem was that in the aftermath of Inkerman the usual channels that might have facilitated an appointment did not function. Reynardson failed to make a timely report; his superior commanding the Brigade of Guards, Brigadier General Bentinck, was wounded and *his* superior's nerves were too shattered to do anything much; all the Duke of Cambridge could say on the subject was, 'Oh, they all behaved admirably'. In his private letters at this time to his father, Henry poured a lot of vitriol on the name of Reynardson. The Colonel had 'blubbered' after Inkerman, a clear indication, he thought, of his lack of moral fibre; he related to Lord Beverley another example of Reynardson's weakness: one day when Henry was on outpost, he arranged for Reynardson to come down that he might press for the strengthening of its defence, the staff being 'utterly useless, naturally, being all men selected for their political or other connexions . . . . [Reynardson] fixed 8 am, and never came till the afternoon. Why? Because of the rain.' No wonder he failed to keep his promise of putting in a good word for him.

Percy's conduct at Inkerman did eventually get reported to Lord Raglan, but it was too late for the official despatch and he would have to wait before any official recognition came his way. Unofficial praise, however, poured in, both for the Guards in general and for Colonel Percy specifically. Everybody at home, including the Queen, who knew from both Prince Edward's and the Duke of Cambridge's letters how well the Guards had done, soon realized that Lord Raglan's despatch did not do the Brigade justice. Colonel Wood at Horse Guards was also sympathetic:

Orderly Room
Horse Guards

My dear Percy,

I am very glad that you sent me the particulars of the capture of the gun at the Battle of Alma. It seems to me that the French had as much to do with the capture as the Highlanders. Poor Pakenham! The affair derives an additional interest from being connected with his name. We are putting up a tablet to his memory, and the other officers who have fallen, in the Military Chapel. God grant that there may not be many more names to be inscribed.

I had great satisfaction in writing to Lord Beverley, and transcribing that part of Reynardson's and Higginson's [letters]*

---

* Wood later sent to Lord Beverley the original manuscripts of these letters.

relating to your gallant conduct at Inkerman. Lord Beverley was very much gratified, as well he might be with such honourable mention of your very gallant conduct – 'not the less honourable' as he observed, 'coming from his brother officers'. Ours is such a system of routine, or I should have expected to see you mentioned in Lord Raglan's Despatch.

I tremble when I think of what you have to [go through] this winter; and how difficult it will be to keep up the drooping spirits of the men . . . .

Let me hear when I can be of any use,

Sincerely yours,

Thomas Wood

Wood, as commanding officer of the Regiment, and senior to Reynardson (who was only temporarily commanding the Battalion in the Crimea, by virtue of Colonel Hood's death) was already trying to help Percy, and he had the full backing of his adjutant, Captain Hatton, who, it seems, rather agreed with Percy about Reynardson:

Horse Guards

15 December 1854

My dear Percy,

Thanks for your letter of the 20th, which I received two or three days ago. I quite [sympathize] with your feelings about the injustice that has been done you, but I am in hope the matter may yet be remedied.

I never saw anyone take up your cause so warmly as Wood. He has taken up the matter with Lord Hardinge stating the way in which you behaved and hopes your heroics will be rewarded, and mind you he did this entirely from himself, and not in consequence of anything said by me. He is a good fellow after all, I really believe, but certainly requires a little management. Reynardson's conduct is precisely what one would have expected from him. Long ere this [reaches you], your eyes [will] have been gladdened by the sight of old Ridley,* who if he keeps his health is sure to do well. Rokeby is to have him as his guide, and starts in a few days . . . .

* Colonel Ridley was sent out to fill Colonel Hood's place and arrived in the Crimea on 1 December. However, owing to the fact that Bentinck's designated replacement, Major General Lord Rokeby, was still on his way, Ridley temporarily took command of the entire Guards Brigade. This left Reynardson still in command of the Grenadiers for a further six weeks.

I sent all the letters you enclosed to me as soon as I received them.

Excuse this short note, and with my best wishes, believe me, my dear Percy, very sincerely yours,
V.L. Hatton.

There was a most astonishing! (in my opinion) motion made in the House of Lords last night to bring in a Bill to enable the Government to raise 15,000 foreign troops!!

Henry's correspondence with his family throughout November and December was chiefly concerned with discussion of the progress of the war. Was there any 'rascally political intrigue' going on? What was that weak Prime Minister, Aberdeen up to? What did people at home think of Admiral Dundas, who everybody in the Crimea from Lord Raglan downwards considered to be a snob and a coward? 'Damn'd Ass', he was nicknamed, in contrast to his naval and social inferior Admiral Lyons, who was universally admired.

Sir E. Lyons has done remarkably well and has some Nelson in him, which Dundas has not . . . . The crews of the *Britannic*, Dundas's ship, are jeered by every other; if a boat from one ship goes to her, that boat's crew will not go on board her. In fact she is but in Coventry. If a boat from *Britannic* comes alongside another ship, it is ordered to keep off at a distance, and the boat's crew ask how far, the answer is '2,500 yards out of fire . . . ' and numberless other professional jibes. I wish Dundas would come to our lines – we would all turn our backs on him. The Navy are quite furious, but I have no doubt he will be protected by Aberdeenovitch and prove that he has acted up to instructions . . . . If he had gone and battered the forts [of Sebastopol] after Alma directly, the Russians would have not known what to do – and if he <u>had</u> lost a ship, what then?

With regard to the progress of the siege, there was very little to report. There was occasional cannon and mortar fire from both sides; there were frequent night alarms (usually false), and there were interminable hours doing duty in waterlogged trenches or on outpost. This monotony was only broken by a prisoner exchange, or the appearance of Russian deserters, who provided some intelligence on the state of Sebastopol. One prisoner exchange occurred in early December, involving a Coldstream Guards officer, Lord

Dunkellin, who had been taken very early on in the siege, a few days before the Battle of Balaklava. He had been out with a working party, got rather off course and observed another party of men ahead of them in the gloaming. William Howard Russell of *The Times* described the manner in which this officer was taken: ' "There are the Russians," exclaimed one of the men. "Nonsense, they're our fellows," said his lordship, and off he went towards them, asking in a high tone as he got near, "who is in command of this party?" His men saw him no more.'[14] When he was exchanged for a Russian artillery officer six weeks later, Henry wryly commented that, given the circumstances in which Dunkellin had been taken, he did not think the British army would gain a great deal from having such a short-sighted man back on its side! There were some other faintly comical scenes when it came to prisoners:

> Don't believe any of the stories of the town being ruined. It is not, it has been spared. Chivalry versus barbarism, but I hope chivalry will get house room thereby . . . . The deserters say they have all been told the English hang their prisoners. It proves how badly off they must be to come over. The men stuff them with biscuit and more, to their great surprise. The other day 3 came who were well treated, and an escort of cavalry was ordered to take them to Headquarters. The commander of the escort gave the word 'Draw swords', whereupon the poor Russians let up a shriek, thinking they were going to be decapitated on the spot! I believe there have been 3 deserters from the allied army – one English, and two Frenchmen. Our paymaster has not yet deserted us.[15]

Meanwhile, those at home busied themselves with raising money for the Patriotic Fund, launched by *The Times*, and in collecting up clothing to send out to the troops. Isabel wrote:

> The whole country seems to share the same feeling. Lady Hunter, (who shall duly have your message, and who is always anxious to hear about you) told me that when she and her husband went the round of their parish to collect subscriptions for the Patriotic Fund, in many places where they expected to get a halfpenny, or at most a penny, they received sixpence with a 'God Bless them, they want it more than we do', and now all that can are knitting things to send out. The maids are hard at work at socks and stockings – those like your humble servant whose education has been neglected in that

point do what they can – mitts, comforters. I try my hand at fleecy boots, which may do to sleep in (I shall send you a pair at the first opportunity; I hope you may find some use for them) and this at least gives us a [sense] that we are doing something that may be of a little use. I am rather amused at the petition addressed by the Government to Oxford and Cambridge, appealing to the young men to give warm clothing, and going on to list as acceptable every article of clothing that was <u>ever</u> worn. I expect the next thing will be an appeal to the 'Women of England' for a subscription to refit the undergraduates, who in their enthusiasm will have given away every article of clothes they possess, and will have <u>nothing</u> left to wear but their college gowns – the only thing I can see Sidney Herbert* does not ask for! . . .

Archer Amherst is in London. Mamma saw [his mother] Gertrude yesterday. She thinks he would perhaps have done better to stay at Malta, as he has suffered much from the tossing about on his passage home. He can hardly walk across the room now – yet, poor boy, he tortured himself to sit down to dinner daily with the rest of the passengers, though sometimes obliged to go away, and rest his head. The surgeon who dresses his wound twice a day desires he should be kept quiet, and see no one but his father and mother. Gertrude was so touched and grateful for your kindness in writing when you yourself were wounded and worn out; and Archer was not even in your regiment.

There is really no private intelligence of any sort to give you, for the war absorbs everything – no one thinks of anything else. Mamma and I are going to try and give our attention to a poultry show, which we mean to go and see one day next week. Never having been to one, and being curious to see and <u>hear</u> it, I suspect to come back stone deaf, as they say the noise is indescribable. The Warwickshire hunt have the good feeling not to give a ball this winter, and to hand over the money it would have cost to the 'Patriotic Fund'. The week after next Mamma and I have the agreeable prospect of slaving for 2 days at a charitable bazaar to force down the throats of reluctant customers the handiwork of distressed gentlewomen – whose distress apparently is too profound to admit their making anything that anybody can wish to possess – and besides as nobody will have any money this year, I think our tasks as saleswomen will be particularly dreary . . . .

Pray don't think about owing a letter either to me or to any of

* Sidney Herbert, the Secretary at War.

116

us who may write to you. Of course a letter from you is most welcome when you have leisure and inclination for it, but as I fancy letters may be some amusement to you out there, we should write just the same without expecting them to be answered, and when we ask any questions, you can always reply to them through Uncle B, who is most kind about writing to us. This time I have none to ask, as of those who I know amongst the wounded I can ask through their friends at home. I only know besides Archer, 3 severely wounded – Percy Fielding, Major Maitland and Hugh Drummond. Poor Major M's especially <u>sounds</u> very severe. I am afraid this is a very dull letter in return for your interesting one, but you must excuse it, and with Papa's best love, believe me, my dear Henry, your very affectionate

   Isabel Percy

His unmarried sister Louisa, much older than Isabel, was, in her good-natured way, equally busy:

Portman Square
9 Dec.

My dear Henry,

 Don't be provoked – I have sent to you half a dozen knit long waistcoats, which appear to me to be better than jerseys, particularly if a man is wounded as they can be got off and on easily. The poor people here to whom I have given jerseys dislike them extremely. With them you will find 2 dozen knit stockings (coarse) and three pairs like those I sent by the *Royal Albert*, and some gloves. What you don't like or want, give away to any of your poor dear men – who are, I am told, in absolute rags. I shall forward these by a ship that goes next week for the offices of Hayter and Howell. The boxes are left at the Commissariat at Balaklava and must be sent for by the owners. You will judge for yourself whether mine is worth sending for. You have all a long and severe winter before you, so don't despise a superfluity for yourself or others and I have no doubt the Government sends rubbish to the men and so much has been lost in that horrible storm! I should have sent more, but the agents particularly enforce <u>small</u> boxes.

 I could have cried over your disappointment, but not over my own, for I am more than satisfied with hearing the name of Percy once more coupled with the epithet 'heroic' – and that on all sides. You who are a Squire of Dames would be pleased with the many fair ladies who come to talk over your feats with me. Lady Canning and Sarah Lindsay, amongst others. Poor Lady St. Germans* wrote a touching answer to my letter of condolence, 'praying', she ends, 'that your dear brother may be preserved.' Nothing pleased me more than dear Joseph, who almost cried when he told me of when he went to the Horse Guards to ask if there was any news. Captain Hatton called him in, and bade him congratulate Lord B. 'on the magnificent gallantry of his son', and how the sergeants told him Colonel Reynardson's letters had been read to the detachment that started that Monday, and how one added, 'I always knew Colonel Percy would do something.'

We have just heard from Margaret who sends her kindest love to you and is full of enquiries about your fate. If you know what is become of a soldier of yours called Stacey – pray tell me. I get a visit from his poor wife sometimes, who is in agonies of anxiety about him.[†] Does that blow on the eye not affect you in any way? I wanted to send you cigars, but Papa will not hear of it and says they are plentiful in the Crimea. Amherst is arrived – quite clipped, poor boy, but in high spirits and with good hope of in time recovering. All that family are *penetré* with your kindness in writing to the mother. God bless you – we go to Torquay in a week.

Poor Louisa was still fussing a week later:

15 Dec.

My dear Henry,

I must thank you for your short letter to myself, and your long one to my father. Never trouble yourself to write to <u>me,</u> unless you feel inclined. In spite of what you say, I fear you suffer a good deal from your <u>scratches,</u> as you call them. I will send no more <u>fine linen,</u> though [it must] be pleasant for your poor bruised skin. Don't be furious at what we send you. Algernon, who always croaks, declares our presents will only bother you. If so give them away. Everybody is working at dispatching mountains of clothing and food by the yachts. I must add my mite to the <u>Hero-Fund,</u> but distrusting all associations, I have transmitted them to you, in the shape of half a dozen long knit waistcoats, a dozen knit stockings and a dozen mitts . . . . Pray give them to any of your special favourites among your

---

* Her son, Captain the Hon Granville Charles Cornwallis, Coldstream Guards, was killed at Inkerman.
[†] Private Thomas Stacey died of dysentery aboard the hospital ship *Kangaroo* in the Crimea, 23 November 1854.

men, keeping what you like for yourself. In this same box you will find 3 pairs of lambs' wool hose for yourself, and Papa has added 2 pairs of boots, 1 pair of trousers, a box of cigars, candles, soap and a cheese, and portable soup. The box is forwarded to Balaklava by Messrs. Hayter and Howell, and I trust will be sent in the *Adelaide* early next week and reach you long before the yachts arrive. It is directed to the care of the Commissary General – and if you like this list of contents, you must send for it: these are the directions given at the office. The cheese and cigars were suggested to me as very acceptable presents, by General Bentinck. I met him and was introduced to him at Lady Ch. Greville's. He said immediately we 'must enquire after my brother's wound and congratulate me on his having so greatly distinguished himself'. I replied; 'I am very proud to hear <u>you</u> say so'. 'Yes, very distinguished indeed,' he repeated.

I am sorry to see that the monster who stabbed the wounded is not yet hanged. Everybody knows that the mass of the Russian nation is half civilized – but that will not account for such atrocities, for our beloved and highly civilized allies did just the same at Waterloo – often I have heard Uncle Henry tell it – and in later times their <u>Generals</u> boasted in their despatches of the number of <u>heads of Arabs</u> brought in by their troops.

Don't suppose now that the war is begun that Lord Aberdeen is not as anxious as everybody <u>for victory</u> – his <u>place</u> depends on it – but they wish to boast to their radical friends of the <u>cheapness</u> of their war – and so have sacrificed your precious lives to that Moloch. May that blood fall upon their heads! I dare not, however, touch upon the subject – I feel so bitterly.

I have just heard a very good account from Margaret, and enclose a note which she begs you will not trouble yourself to answer – only she says she cannot bear to have no communication with you in the midst of danger.

I think it would be well for you to write a line or send a message to Algernon. He has always a notion his family don't <u>like</u> him, and his great wish is to be <u>liked</u> by them. He has been very eager about you and your fame.

My eyes stop me. God bless you. Yours affectionately,
  Louisa Percy

In spite of the family's obvious pride at Henry's deeds, in some circles at home there was disquiet about the army having to fight under what Sir William Napier had termed in his *History of the Peninsular War* (1851) as 'the cold shade of Aristocracy'. Not surprisingly, blue-blooded officers serving in the Crimea were grieved by this attitude, and it particularly vexed them if this type of criticism came from one of their own kind. They did not like being tarred with the same brush as the unpopular Lord Cardigan, who berthed in his own private yacht in Balaklava, or Lord George Paget, who resigned his commission after the charge of the Light Brigade.

Colonel Harcourt, Member of Parliament for the Isle of Wight, was one of those who defended in the House of Commons the charge that the aristocracy were to blame for the woes of the expeditionary force. Percy must have been highly flattered when he found out that he himself was cited as a model example. Hansard reports how on a former evening an observation had been made in the House of Lords about our soldiers 'fighting under the cold shade of the Aristocracy'. Colonel Harcourt denied that that was so. Could they forget the brilliant charge led by Lord Cardigan at Balaklava? Did they not all remember how a gallant scion of the House of Percy distinguished himself at Inkerman, when, fifty or sixty of his men becoming enveloped in a host of Russians, he rushed down the hill over which the enthusiasm of his soldiers had led them too far, and succeeded in rescuing them and bringing them back? The owner of another aristocratic name, Colonel Cadogan, on the same occasion acted in a precisely similar manner. In the face of such facts as these, then, was it to be said 'that the soldier was fighting under the cold shade of aristocracy?' He wondered that the blood of the noble Viscount had not mantled in his cheek with shame when he indulged in such an attack upon his own order.[16]

Percy rightly blamed officialdom for the woes of the army, but that was not to say that there weren't a few titled gentlemen who had let the side down:

> If Napier had stated instead of 'the cold shade of Aristocracy', 'the cold shade of Officiality', he would have been right, but not a thing is done to give an *élan*, or excite the troops, not even announcing that Alma was to be on the colours. The French have done this long ago, being anxious to reward people that live .... HRH stated, but I don't believe it the more for that, that the Sultan had written to Lord Raglan to offer the officers present at Alma a gold medal and

the men a silver one, which Lord Raglan refused – for which, if true, I don't thank him. Covered with orders as he is, he might let us have some too. And as we have done the Sultan's work pretty effectively he might have been allowed to show us honour. However, one must not complain of anything Lord Raglan does – he is the only <u>man</u> we have got . . . . There is a report that Cardigan has sent in his resignation. If so, he and Lord George Paget deserve kicks from the Aristocracy.

Lord Cardigan was deeply unpopular with his own kind, and Lord George Paget was shunned in his club when he returned from the Crimea after resigning his commission. He soon got the message, however, and returned to the front.

Shortly before Christmas, in spite of all the adulation, Henry was still disappointed that there was no sign of a staff appointment. Competition was hot and it didn't do to be seen to be trying too hard or fighting one's own corner publicly. He told his father that he had boasted quite sufficiently to his family already. 'All I shall say further is that I had one pleasant moment – *viz.* when I returned from the fight [after Inkerman], an officer* lying sick in his tent said to me, "Percy, what have you been doing? The men have been talking of nothing but Colonel Percy." Another moment also, your praise.'

---

*Lieutenant Colonel Bradford had only been slightly wounded, but was laid up with acute rheumatism and was soon invalided home.

Chapter 6

Nurses and Hospitals

In the middle of December Henry received word from his father that his elder brother Josceline was coming to the East with a party of nurses, at the solicitation of Sidney Herbert, the Secretary at War, and his wife. Newspaper reports of the situation at the hospitals in Scutari had caused uproar in England, and Josceline, an MP who had an interest in health matters, was keen to be of some practical assistance.

Sidney Herbert had already enlisted his friend, Florence Nightingale, to take charge of a party of nurses to go to Scutari. He and his wife Liz had always been interested in providing hospitals for the poor, but, given the widespread suspicion of female nursing at that time, Miss Nightingale had until now never really found the role that she longed for. Herbert, though he was in the Cabinet, was junior to the Secretary of State for War, the Duke of Newcastle, who ran all the operational aspects of the conflict. He was merely in charge of finance and administration, and as such received all the blame for the appalling muddle that prevailed. But he found it deeply distressing that no matter how many instructions he issued for medical supplies to be sent out to the Crimea, they simply did not reach their destination. Most ended up at Varna; some ended up at the bottom of the Black Sea outside Balaklava; some even were returned home. As a result, men were dying in their droves and the rate of sickness was accelerating, leading to overloaded hospitals and overworked medical staff, and so was created a vicious spiral of disease, overcrowding, more diseases, universal suffering and a rising death toll – and all this before Inkerman and before the winter added cases of severe frost-bite to the army's list of woes. Towards the end of October, therefore, Sidney Herbert despatched Florence Nightingale and thirty-eight nurses to Scutari with *carte blanche,* and effectively a blank cheque, to sort out the mess.

Montague Burgoyne, the young Lieutenant who had been wounded in the leg at Alma, was one of those laid up in hospital at Scutari when Florence Nightingale and her nurses arrived in early November. He described the state of affairs in a letter to his mother:

> I am glad to see *The Times* is 'hustling' the Medical Authorities – indeed they want it. 40 females have now arrived and are now a regular subject of ridicule. The very commonest medicines and appliances are wanting, and men are dying by scores for want of them. I wonder no one has written about the absurd system of 'requisition' in the hospital. That is the thing that causes <u>all</u> the mischief; instead of <u>one</u> doctor signing an order for any 'necessary', or 'comfort' and being able to draw it at once, it has to go through all sorts of 'hands', 'delay' and bother. Suppose a sick or wounded man arrives, he is laid upon the stones as he is, till some one notices him; then a medical officer has to be found to sign a 'requisition' for bed, bedding and blankets, then it has to go to the Principal Medical Officer to be countersigned, then to be taken to the stores, where the storekeeper is sure to be out, or past the hour of delivery – and the consequence is one gets nothing, although there are tons and tons of all sorts. An intelligent (not a fool like the present) Commandant is required to be <u>over all </u>doctors in the first place – no one can be more attentive and kind and aware of the abuses of the system than Dr Menzies, but he is tied down by his immediate superiors. The Commandant is a perfect fool, and although he had a certificate sent him by the P.M.O. he would not sign it, <u>unless I came myself</u>! When the impossibility of that was explained . . . he <u>grinned like an idiot </u>and signed it.[1]

Soon after this, thousands more casualties from Inkerman appeared, and still there was no sign of even the basics of sanitation – towels, chamber pots, soap etc., let alone proper bandages or chloroform. Only thirty patients a day could be cleaned in the few hip baths available.[2] The scene was one of almost unimaginable suffering. Amputations were frequently performed without a screen in crowded corridors, amid dirt, filth and diarrhoea.

It was against this background that, a few weeks later, Sidney and Liz Herbert sent out a further party of forty-six women, under Miss Mary Stanley, a friend of Miss Nightingale who was also interested in nursing, and Dr Meyer, a physician. They persuaded Josceline Percy, MP for Launceston, to accompany them, as he knew Florence Nightingale from his previous experience with hospitals. It has occasionally been hinted that there was a degree of impropriety in Josceline's admiration for Miss Nightingale, though there is no evidence for this and he had been happily married since 1848.

In his letters to Henry Lord Beverley declared that he had tried to dissuade Josceline from getting involved with this new enterprise; he thought that he had been 'wheedled' into it by Mrs Herbert. The problem was, explained their father, that Josceline was not going out to Turkey in an official capacity, for example as part of a commission of enquiry into the state of the hospitals: 'They have commissionaires there already. So, he goes with a letter of recommendation from S. Herbert. He refused to <u>take charge</u> of the nurses in any way – yet consented to go with them. Without authority, nobody will care about S. Herbert's recommendation, and of course all the departments will consider him an interloper . . . . The only part of the arrangement of which I approve is that he won't take a farthing, nor have his expenses paid.'

Henry, while commending his brother's admirable motives, agreed that he was likely to find the reality less romantic than the idea. He told Lovaine, 'Don't let Josceline go to Scutari. He will lose his health. He is too honest and hardworking, uncompromising and severe to do any good . . . . The surgeons will lie about him, the clergymen will abuse him (in secret) and the women will be furious, as he will detect many little private errors which <u>will</u> take place. Besides, [consider] his health.' He went on to say that Sidney Herbert, who he felt bore much of the responsibility for the army's woes, would probably stitch up Josceline for his own political advantage.

Nevertheless, he soon got word that, in spite of the family's pleas, he was definitely on his way:

Andros Passage
Dec 15th '54

My dear Henry,

At the solicitations of Sidney Herbert, I am now on my way to Scutari conveying 47 nurses for the hospital, also with a view to the possibility of my hospital experience being of use there. The ladies of our company have behaved like angels and the paid nurses, though somewhat [keen on] cognac (some few of them I ought to say) have likewise conducted themselves admirably, so that the journey has been without any difficulty, or disagreements on their part. We have had two short but sharp gales of wind on the passage from Marseilles, amply repaid by beautiful weather as we approached that most lovely of all regions, the Straits of Messina and the Piraeus, and we now hope to reach Constantinople on Sunday morning. I was in [a steamer] with 250 French soldiers, treated like dogs, but behaving like lambs . . . .

We left England at 4 am on the 2nd December. All the family well . . . and the children generally thriving. I long to hear how you really are after your glorious action which the French say makes them *pleurer* with emotion to read of. They say that together we are invincible . . . .

Louisa sent you a bag of all sorts of good things. I hope you have got them by this time. A fur coat was among the clothes. Let me know <u>quickly</u> whether you are in possession of her stores and whether there is anything I can get for you in Constantinople. I could bring nothing, being limited in baggage as one of 52; however, some of my things may do you – another fur coat, for instance.

I may <u>possibly</u> be some time in the hospital in Scutari; if not I return *quanto prima*, for I pay my own expenses, and they are many. Still, I have a hankering after a visit to you at Sebastopol (without any military ardour or curiosity to smell fire) and if I can get a passage to the Crimea, tell me if I should be a fool for my pains, and only in the way and a nuisance there. I hear the *Retribution* is gone, or Drummond could have given me a helping hand. I know nobody else, though no doubt through Lord Stratford de Redcliffe or others I could find some other way. I care nothing for roughing it as you know for a day or two, which would be the amount of my stay if I went. Tell me what you want, for my father has given to me handsomely, and would be pained to think that you wanted anything that could be got – as we all should, including my wife.

Do answer immediately if you can. I have written 3 or 4 times without knowing whether my letters reached you. This I send by a

125

most invaluable courier, who is going as servant to Captain Mitchell, Grenadier Guards. Direct to the 'British General Hospital Scutari'. I shall send a digest of this by the post in case the courier be delayed.

Yours affectionately,

J.P.

Henry was quite prepared to give his brother every assistance if he really wanted to come as far as the Crimea. It was relatively common for travelling gentlemen to make a short trip to the theatre of operations, and sometimes groups of them would go together in private yachts.

> Sebastopol Camp
> Dec 23rd

Dear Josceline,

I cannot say how sorry I am nor how much I admire your virtue in coming out, for I pity you being under . . . such a newt as S. Herbert. If you come here for two or three days it will repay you, but you had better make arrangements (if you cannot with a man of war, which would be easiest) with the Captain of some merchant steamer in government service to bring you, and keep you on board whilst here – as the result of my hospitality would probably give you rheumatism and diarrhoea, as all newcomers who live in tents do suffer. I could get you perhaps a *bouge* in Balaklava, but if you slept and dined in your steamer, you would have the day to wander about. Wait, however, till the weather gets better, for the state of wet and slush we are in is quite dreadful. I am sorry you cannot get at Drummond: he is an excellent man – kindness itself. Surely [our uncles, the Admirals] William and Josceline might have had the prevoyance to give you letters to their Naval friends in case of necessity, particularly as you come out on a work of mercy. If it had not been for Drummond's kindness, I should have lingered on a Hospital Ship, which under the best circumstances is unpleasant, and <u>then</u> dreadful, though no blame could be attached to the authorities here – but much to those at home, on account of the fewness of Medical Officers.

There is ten chances to one of this letter reaching you, the postal service is so badly conducted. I don't want anything that is feasibly to be got. My father's and Louisa's presents may come or may not, as it is all *kismet* here. Bring me only as good a lanthorn as can be

Colonel Percy in civilian clothes, c. 1855.
(Duke of Northumberland)

2. Field Marshal Lord Raglan.
(Fenton, National Army Museum)

Colonel Grosvenor Hood.
(Grenadier Guards)

4. The Earl of Beverley.   *(Author)*

5. Lord Lovaine. *(Author)*

6. Colonel Henry Percy VC in 1862.
(Grenadier Guards)

7. Captain George Higginson.
(Grenadier Guards)

8. Captain Henry Neville, from an oil painti
by E. U. Eddis. *(Lord Braybrooke/Eng.
Heritage)*

Lieutenant Colonel Prince Edward of Saxe-Weimar.

(Fenton, Gernsheim Collection)

10. Captain Robert Lindsay VC. *(Author)*

. Major General Lord Rokeby, from a drawing by George Cadogan.

(National Army Museum)

12. Lieutenant General HRH the Duke of Cambridge.

(Fenton, Gernsheim Collection)

13. General Cler in Zouave costume, from a watercolour by George Cadogan. He gave the cross of the Légion d'Honneur that he is shown wearing on his chest to Henry Percy.

(National Army Museum)

14. Lieutenant Colonel Studholme Brownrigg with two Russian boys.

(Fenton, National Army Museum)

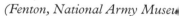

15. The Grenadier Guards at Scutari, May 1854. The Barrack Hospital is in the background. Colonel Hood is standing in front wearing a bearskin; Captain Higginson is on his right. *(Robertson, National Army Museum)*

16. Officers of the Grenadier Guards in the Cypress Grove, Scutari, May 1854. Within six months six of the men in this photograph were dead; four were killed in action, one died of wounds and one of disease. *(Robertson, National Army Museum)*

17. Balaklava Harbour, looking north.   *(Robertson, National Army Museum)*

18. The Ordnance Wharf at Balaklava.   *(Fenton, National Army Museum)*

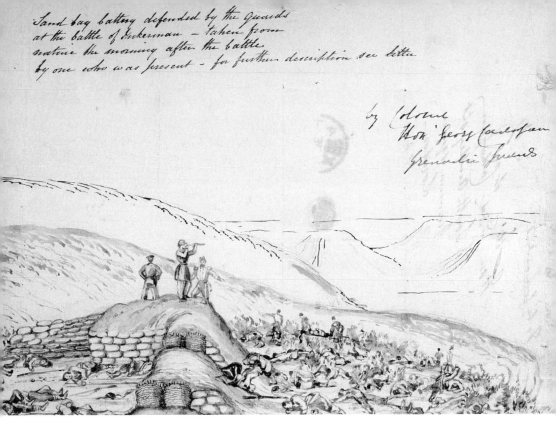

19. The Sandbag Battery, from a drawing by George Cadogan.

(National Army Museum)

20. The charge of the Guards at the Sandbag Battery, after a watercolour by William Simpson.

(Author)

21. The Greenhill Battery. *(Robertson, National Army Museum)*

22. 'The Roll Call', after an oil painting by Elizabeth Thompson, later Lady Butler. The Grenadier Guards after Inkerman were the inspiration behind this picture. There was no snow on 5 November, but the artist wanted to symbolize the winter campaign. *(Author)*

23. Captain E. S.
Burnaby.
*(Fenton, Gernsheim
Collection)*

24. Captain Burnaby dressed for picquet duty.   *(Fenton, National Army Museum,)*

25. The hurricane at Balaklava, after a watercolour by William Simpson. *Retribution* is on the far left. *Prince* is in the centre of the picture, about to founder. (*Author*)

26. Commissariat Difficulties, after a watercolour by William Simpson. (*Author*)

27. The Grenadier Officers' Christmas dinner on the Heights before Sebastopol, after a watercolour by William Simpson. *(Author)*

28. The embarkation of the sick at Balaklava, after a watercolour by William Simpson. *(Author)*

29. Balaklava from the Guards' Camp, summer 1855.   *(Robertson, Gernsheim Collection)*

30. French trenches facing the Malakoff Redoubt.   *(Robertson, National Army Museum)*

31. A quiet day in the Mortar Battery. *(Robertson, Gernsheim Collection)*

32. A group at HQ, with Lord Raglan and General Pélissier in the doorway. Lord Burghersh is on the far left. *(Fenton, National Army Museum)*

33. The dry docks at Sebastopol before demolition.

(Robertson, National Army Museum)

34. The dry docks after demolition. *(Robertson, National Army Museum)*

35. View from the rear of the Redan looking towards the salient point.

(Robertson, National Army Museum)

36. Inkerman today, looking towards St Clement's Ravine from below the Inkerman Ruins.

(Author)

37. General Lord Henry Percy VC, KCB, from an oil painting by A. Pope, 1877-78.
(Duke of Northumberland)

got, small and strong, and a dozen pots of cocoa paste. Those are the only things I can think of – but don't send them except by hand. The cocoa paste being a luxury, it doesn't signify, but the lanthorn would be useful. A pair of high black waterproof boots over the middle of the thigh would be useful. If I had known you were coming, I would have asked you to bring them [from England]. If you find them at Stambool, do . . . .

There is an artist [in Constantinople] named Preziosi,* who [you may] call upon from me. He may be useful to you and is a civil man, and could get a servant for you, and lodgings if necessary. He is a very good artist too.

Don't be uneasy about my health. I had an attack of fever, and afterwards diarrhoea, which latter was cured by a French Colonel giving me an excellent dinner. They live better than we do. Many thanks for your kind offers of despoiling yourself of your furs on my behalf, but don't think of it – I don't want them.

Goodbye, yours most affectionately,
    H. Percy

I hope Mrs. J. was well, and your child.

Though he had done his best to prevent Josceline from coming out on what he perceived as a rather hare-brained scheme, Henry was clearly rather looking forward to seeing him. He wrote to him on Christmas evening. 'It will be worth your coming here . . . . Besides having lots of money, I will pay all your expenses with pleasure – you have paid mine before now . . . . I should have no difficulty in feeding you, as I know any filth does for you – but you must not risk diarrhoea or rheumatism.'

As Christmas approached, old Lord Beverley was thinking of the men in his son's Company. He was confident that the widows and children of those who had been killed would be taken care of by *The Times*' Patriotic Fund, but was concerned that those who were still on active service would be left without any charity. He told his son that he thought they deserved at least a 'Xmas box, in the shape of some little comforts . . . I think your father might not improperly pay this little compliment. If you are passed unnoticed by your superiors, there is no reason why your gallant company should not

* Vittorio Amadeo, 5th Count Preziosi (1816–1882) was a well known Maltese painter of contemporary life in Constantinople.

be congratulated, if this appears reasonable. Perhaps I had better transfer £100 to Cox & Co., which you may give some and use the rest for other purposes. If it won't do to give, keep all for yourself.' In the event, he sent to his son two lots of £100, a substantial amount of money, in total equivalent to some £15,000 in today's money, and theoretically enough for Henry to have given each of his remaining men an extra month or two's wages. A soldier's basic pay was in principle 1s a day, but extra allowances could bring this to more like 2s 6d, though this gross figure was subject to deductions.

On Christmas evening the officers of the Grenadier Guards dined in Higginson's tent. They commissioned William Simpson to record the occasion and the resulting watercolour was reproduced the following year in *The Seat of War in the East*. Simpson's picture presents a colourful scene, for the tent was specially fitted up for the occasion, a chandelier being made from upturned bayonets lashed to the tent pole, the backdrop decorated with the Colours, and drapes displaying the names 'Alma' and 'Inkerman', two brand new battle honours for which authority had opportunely just been received that very morning. They consumed, Higginson said, 'some fearful effervescing stuff which was called champagne, some scraggy fowls and a ham'. F.W. Hamilton, who was one of those present, recorded in his history of the Regiment: 'They were a small band of twelve, almost all that remained with the Battalion of above thirty who, not three months before, marched with it to Balaklava, all full of spirit and high ambitious hopes of honour to be won by their own deeds. No less than eight of their former comrades had already found a Crimean grave, and others had been invalided.' Also present were Charles Lindsay, Prince Edward of Saxe-Weimar, Edwyn Burnaby, Sir Charles Russell, Lord Balgonie, Sir James Fergusson, Henry Verschoyle, Frederick Bathurst, Charles Turner and Robert W. Hamilton (Frederick Hamilton's nephew). Colonel Reynardson, still commanding the Battalion, celebrated the day with the Brigadier.[3] It is not clear where Henry Percy dined that night: perhaps he drew a short straw, as one presumes some officers had to remain on duty, for Christmas did not entirely silence the guns; or it may be that he had an inkling of the fever that struck him down the following day and remained in his tent. In any case, it would have been difficult for him to have been included in the painting because Simpson did not do his drawing until some days after the occasion, by which time Percy was unavailable for a sitting (although, in Lord Balgonie's view, Simpson did not make good likenesses of people anyway).[4]

Among the letters Henry wrote on Christmas day was one to George Cadogan. As he had previously informed his father, Cadogan had 'gone for a month to Scutari for his health, his old enemy the ichthyosis appearing. He has suffered a good deal, with great patience and courage, but I am glad he is gone – he croaks so.' He had promised to keep Cadogan up to date with all the goings on in the Crimea, but in turn wanted his friend to keep him informed of the situation at Scutari, especially as he knew that Josceline would be there. When Cadogan had departed the previous month, Henry had particularly asked him to find out about his servant Jackett, who had been wounded at Inkerman. He soon discovered that the man made it safely home in January. He was eventually discharged with a disability pension.

Little did he realize when he wrote to Josceline and Cadogan in Scutari that he would soon find out for himself exactly what was going on in that hellhole. After being taken ill on Boxing day, he could write nothing for nearly four weeks, other than, literally, a couple of two-liners. Having read in the press about the awful disaster that was unfolding in Scutari that January, Lord Beverley must have feared the worst when his son's normally voluminous correspondence, often running to dozens of pages of small hand writing in a week, suddenly dried up. Then, towards the end of that month, the old man received the following missives, in an unfamiliar hand – that of Captain Higginson:

Camp before Sebastopol
January 5th 1855

My dear Father,

I have been very unwell and am still weak so that tomorrow I am going on board ship to recover my strength. I am too weak to write myself, as you can see, and so have found a brother officer to acquaint you of this.

Believe me your affectionate son,
H.Percy

My lord,

I have written this at your son's dictation as he is decidedly unequal to the execution of writing himself. At the same time, as his dictation has been somewhat abrupt, I think it right, though without his knowledge, to add a few words to relieve an anxiety which perhaps so short an announcement in a strange handwriting might arouse.

He is suffering from the effects of a feverish attack and as the snow is lying deep on the ground and the cold intense you can well understand that removal to the warm cabin of a ship will be of great advantage to him, for the privations of our camp life would undoubtedly retard his recovery. I am however assured by the surgeons that your Lordship need be under no apprehensions as to your son's speedy restoration to health so long as he finds himself comfortably housed in a place more adapted for a sick man's home than our camp before Sebastopol.

I have the honour of being
   Your Lordship's obedient servant
      George Wentworth Higginson

The following day, a cold one, he was sent down to Balaklava. In one of his last letters to his father he had said: 'There is one thing, by the bye, which might be useful in case of illness or wounds – if Uncles Josceline or William have any particular friend in the Navy out here, to let them know of my existence, as it might save me a residence on a hospital ship, of which I have a bitter recollection.' It was not to be: he remained in Balaklava for a week on board the *Colombo,* destined for Constantinople. It was as good as a death sentence, for an analysis of mortality rates undertaken after the war showed that a hospital case (whether wounded, recovering from an amputation or suffering from disease) had a better chance of surviving if he remained with his unit in the Crimea, in spite of the lack of proper shelter and the incessant cold and wet, than if he went to one of the hospitals at Scutari.

The crisis reached its nadir that January and the sheer quantity of stricken was too great for the few ambulance wagons that were available. William Howard Russell of *The Times* described the endless caravan of horses and carts carrying away the remnants of an army, which already had more of its personnel in hospital than in the Crimea:[5]

130

They formed one of the most ghastly processions that ever poet imagined . . . . With closed eyes, open mouths and ghastly attenuated faces, they were borne along two by two, the thin stream of breath visible in the frosty air alone showing that they were alive. One figure was a horror, a corpse, stone dead, strapped upright in its seat . . . no doubt the man had died on his way down to the harbour . . . . Another man I saw with raw flesh and skin hanging from his fingers, the raw bones of which protruded into the cold, undressed and uncovered.[6]

Too often it happened that, on reaching the beach, insufficient measures had been taken for conveying them on board ship and many died before being laid in the boats, and more still on the passage to Scutari. One can only imagine how torturous a voyage across the stormy sea must have been for men in this condition.

Josceline, on the other hand, had an uneventful voyage out to the East, and he delighted in taking the women under his wing, acting as their interpreter when they went shopping at Marseilles and escorting them to the English chapel there.[7] On arriving at Constantinople on 15 December, however, he found that his family's forebodings were entirely justified. Florence Nightingale received them in a blind fury and immediately wrote a scathing letter to Sidney Herbert accusing him of betraying her and wilfully subverting her authority. She had not asked for any assistance and he had promised not to do anything with respect to the organization of the hospitals without referring to her. As a result, she wrote, 'these unoccupied women would go to the devil'.[8] She pointed out that there was nowhere to house a batch of women and that, in any case, most of them were not trained nurses: 'The ladies come out to get married, and the nurses come out to get drunk.'[9] Privately, also, she was deeply suspicious of the nuns among them, who she believed had come out merely to give religious instruction to vulnerable men. There was a degree of truth in some of this, in that Josceline's party was hastily convened and was not necessarily composed of ideal candidates: only 22 were trained nurses, 15 were nuns and 9 'ladies'. A good number of them did appear to be over-fond of their drink, though they had been vetted as to their suitability beforehand. But these could not be the real reasons why Florence Nightingale was so cross, as she railed

131

at them before she had even met any of them. In truth, she was jealous of her authority: for all her subsequent reputation as the 'Lady of the Lamp', she had essentially been employed by Sidney Herbert as an administrator and a means of advancing the cause of women's nursing – not as an Angel of Mercy.[10]

Miss Stanley, Dr Meyer and Mr Percy all came with the very best of intentions, at the direction of a cabinet minister who was equally devoid of ulterior motive and who never imagined that there could be any misgivings as to their welcome;[11] but they were sent away with their tails between their legs, having been forced to sign a transcript, before witnesses, of their dealings with Miss Nightingale. Josceline described his disappointment on 29 December, not realizing that his brother was now destined to join the very people whom he was trying to help:

> I have come to the conclusion that I had better give up the Crimea and seeing you. In the first place, I am troubled with diarrhoea and my stomach is in an uncomfortable state. I dare not try it and I am altogether out of sorts – no good preparation for the Crimea. Then, I have already been here too long: it would take another month, if I am to go to Balaklava, before I could reach England; an urgent whip has been sent me, and – no doubt business of the first importance will be coming on, from which I should not like – not ought – to be absent. Amongst other things, I look with horror on Lord Palmerston as Minister of War,* an idle insouciant man, who knows that his importance will carry him through any scrape – besides a very stench in the foreign nose. He would prolong this miserable war and would not have the activity and zeal to carry it out effectively – witness his preparations for cholera in London – an instance of utter inefficiency. He would be worse still than the Duke of Newcastle and Sidney Herbert, whose intentions I believe to be the best, at all events. Think of the way their objects are carried out – they have, for one instance, actually found difficulties in the way of receiving our nurses, and only 2 of the 46 have as yet been employed here, though they have sent away 12 of the old batch. It really seems that it will be some time before the others are, if at all, employed, and for reasons I think paltry, beyond imagination. This failure, though I had no part in the scheme of sending them out, has all vexed me beyond measure, owing to the miserable state of the

* In the event Palmerston did not replace Newcastle (Lord Panmure did). Instead, he became Prime Minister in place of Aberdeen.

unfortunate sick. If you had been ill, I should have gone to Balaklava, but as you seem to be in full force, I have no excuse for longer delay or doing what the family begged me not to do – i.e. going to the Crimea.

This hotel has been amusing, though stinking beyond belief . . . . The Duke [of Cambridge] spoke very flatteringly of you, as does everybody else, even if Lord Raglan says nothing. The Duke is boarded to home. He has the fever upon him, but no sign of the mental state assigned him by the civil papers. I have brought the boots with a pair of semi-stockings, worn by the people to stuff them if too large. I could not get the cocoa paste anywhere, but send you my stock of chocolate, together with some more concentrated luncheon, my stock of ½ lb of tea, a tin box of digestive dinner lozenges to help your stomach and a box of wax matches I brought from England. Also a lantern, a desk one to be used for oil or candle by unscrewing the lamp screw. If it does not burn well, you can enlarge the admission of air below. The only other lantern I could see was very large, and surrounded with glass easily broken. A string nicely adjusted round the top with two long one-pounders brought together above it will make it available for the tent. If it does not suit you (and you did not tell me what kind you required) write to our Commissary, who is now going to a Mrs Rose (whose son is at the camp, or coming by the *Royal Albert*). His name is Angelo Ragni, a very old friend of ours, and trustworthy, and desire him to get anything, and Mrs Rose will I have no doubt get it sent on to you. I shall desire him to send you the cocoa paste as soon as he can get hold of it. I served Mrs Rose many good turns in the voyage out and here, so I have no doubt she will be kindly disposed. Write legibly to Ragni in English, French or Italian.

I was very reluctant to give up going to see you, but I really fear that in my present state I might turn out a nuisance to you and I feel so little strength that I should question whether if I could get a berth on board ship [at Balaklava harbour] and whether I could manage without much discomfort the 10 miles march backwards and forwards [to your camp]. I must acknowledge that I will leave this very filthy place with unmitigated delight. My coming here at great expense (i.e. my money), for I would not be paid by the Government, has been fruitless as far as Scutari is concerned – nothing but disappointment and annoyance at seeing our poor gallant men made the victims, killed I believe sometimes by official neglect, and notwithstanding the unlimited ammunition sent out by the Government, most scantily supplied with the common comforts e.g. one chamber pot to about 12 sick men, not without repeated requisitions, but through gross mismanagement or inefficiency. There may be faults at home, but they are legion here – but I will not annoy you with instances, as you must now be too deeply interested in the soldiers. A severe cold and cough has added to my disgust, moving about perpetually, and crossing daily the now odious Bosphorus.

We were met on arrival most coldly, as if we had committed an offence. We, Dr Meyer (my colleague) & I, held a conversation at Scutari Hospital, on our side all openness – no dream of misusing our words. Next day, we were astonished by a request to sign a note of this, as it happened, unimportant conversation, as if we had been in our Atty's chambers. Miss Nightingale has not shone and I suspect Dr Cumming, the Medical Inspector, is an enemy to anything like a new system by which the soldier may be cared for. Dr Menzies of the General Hospital, on the other hand, told me he wished for the nurses. When every available soldier is wanted, it seems strange that they should not grasp an opportunity of relieving men – a few of the orderlies – leaving out all humanitarian views. They talk trash about the dangers to the nurses from soldiers and orderlies. Why, we have old women who would frighten them . . . if there were any danger, of which we have been without an instance. It is a cruel vex. If you are again ill, take sick leave and go to Malta, for this is no place to recover from a wound. The Duke of C. desired me to tell you this. Heaven preserve you in health.
    Yours affectionately,
        J.P.

I enquired at Grace's for your box sent by Louisa, but it was not there. I have some idea that it was sent by the *Royal Albert*, but surely Louisa told you how it was dispatched. Carmé, Captain Mitchell's servant, is a most indomitable courier, I hear, and swore eternal friendship with me. He was to give you some provisions – soup and luncheon – which I hope you got. I shall send you a few more concentrated luncheons with the boots and my India rubber coat, as your greatcoat is wanting, and at all events it will do for the ground to keep out damp. You tell me to wait for fine weather – there seems to be no such thing here: it is now pouring, with a northerly wind, which makes me fear that you have snow. I have today gained an opportunity of sending the things. A friend of Carmé's has kindly agreed to take them on Monday. Our Commissary knows him, so be civil to him; he might turn out useful perhaps.

I have taken a passage on Monday next for England via Marseilles, heartily disgusted with my fruitless journey here, except so far as coming for the comfort of 42 nurses, some of whom, the volunteer ladies especially, are as heartily disgusted as I am. Today I went round to the French Hospital. It is as good as any in France to all appearance – but then it is only one of six, as I am told. With 1,500 beds used they do not appear to have the same proportion of sick as ours have. I conclude, being so many in number, they are not so hard worked as our fellows. I shall propose a sailing <u>Hospital Ship</u> to convey the sick from Balaklava to here, arranged with every possible comfort, as I am sure this would save many a man, for they are necessarily sometimes kept here 2 or 3 days on board. What do you think of sending out an iron hospital or ambulance lined with wood inside for 500 or 1,000 sick to be placed close to the camp with awnings for the summer or spring, with its own horses and vans for the conveyance of stores from Balaklava? The hospital ship to be used on its return voyage to Balaklava to carry in stock for the hospital. If you think this a good idea, or of any other, write instantly to me – to England, which is willing to do anything for the army, snubbed and foiled by people out here as it is. I could do much by application to the authorities at home or the Public in some way or other. Is there no place ashore, or could not a hulk be made use of as a receiving stockhouse? Goodbye again and God bless and prosper you. But please come away if you are sick, and do not linger on with diminished strength and energy.

P.S. As you have plenty of mud, and supposing it to be of a tenacious kind, would it not be possible to make Pisé work huts – mud huts being the warmest? Irishmen ought to know how to make mud huts. The Pisé ones are made, as far as I recollect, by filling and stamping the earth or mud, which is broken up between two boards or more, and so layer upon layer is raised.

I should mix it with the scrub bushes and use them as ties between the layers. The roof is the difficulty without something like timber, but the scrub and mud together might be made available. I should like to turn architect for you, but if the hint is worthless, the paper is soft. If you have got the wooden houses, might not the scrub, with a modicum of mud be placed against the sides & roof with the help of pegs, render them warm? The Irish in the north use the scrapings of the roads for their floors, and very hard they are.

I shall ask Mrs Rose to pay Angelo for everything you desire him to buy, and to write to me to pay it in London. Direct to *Angelo*

Ragni, Poste Restante – Porte aux lettres Françaises – Pera, or *Constantinople* – you know best.

Lady Guernsey tells me Parliament meets on the 14th, so I should be just in time. I am told that the object of the opposition is to refuse supplies if the Duke of Newcastle is not ousted, and of the Whigs to get rid of the Peelites.

Drummond has got the *Tribune*. He will be with you at Balaklava soon. I shall try to send the cocoa paste and a pair of warm gloves. You appear to dislike fur, or I would have sent you a fur cap, so I gave it to Drummond with the fur coat. I have again been very seedy, debauch at the Embassy having set my stomach wrong, which it has been more or less always here. A good dinner is no good to me as to you. It is better to say nothing about the nurses. The authorities may perhaps think better of it, and must not have their dandies set up. Cadogan and Wilson sailed for England the day before yesterday.

Henry arrived at the General Hospital in Scutari three weeks later, on 19 January, but he was too late for Josceline, who Miss Nightingale unkindly described as having 'sneaked home like a commander who has set so many Robinson Crusoes on a desert island'.[12] Henry could already feel that his absence from the Crimea was likely to be more prolonged than he had previously thought and, on the day he arrived at the General Hospital, he penned a short note to his father: 'I shall be invalided home to England as totally unfit for work and shall return a rotten sheep in your hands without wit or constitution. If I had come home with the loss of a limb, I should not have minded, but to return as I am is too dreadful, [though] I ought not to murmur, having escaped by little.'

The fever waxed and waned over the course of the ensuing fortnight, during which time he was virtually incommunicado with his family, as he was too ill to write home, and what few lines he did compose were largely dictated. As an officer, he was more fortunate than most, though that is not to say that officers were necessarily more immune from death in Scutari than ordinary soldiers. He was at least able to send people out to buy provisions for him, the hospital rations being very meagre and largely uneatable. In fact a large part of his sustenance came from Lady Stratford de Redcliffe, wife of the British ambassador, who regu-

136

larly sent him delicacies; it is not clear that she visited his hospital bed in person, as firstly she avoided Scutari like the plague (literally) owing to the appalling stink emanating from the hospitals there, and secondly she was busy with a hospital of her own at Koulali, where she had found employment for some of Josceline's nurses.

In spite of the institutionalized shambles and all its attendant discomforts, Henry had nothing but good to say of the medical officers, who were 'all kindness, and regret the disorganization, having their time fully occupied in doctoring'. His first substantial letter, in his own handwriting, is dated 25 January:

> I am a little better but my strength does not come – but I don't suffer much. I had a few hours' sleep last night for the first time for 29 days. I have applied for a Brevet, and Lord William Paulet* will facilitate everything. He is coming here and being very kind and friendly. Lady Stratford has been increasing in her kindness, sending me delicacies etc, which are much wanted here as the administration is infamous – circumstances confusing, which I will relate to you I hope in person . . . . I shall make my statements before the Highest Authority.
>
> My best friend here is a cook who the Government has sent out here at £100 per annum, and he takes care of my interior well and is very obliging and serviceable. By the greatest good fortune [the new servant I took on], my other one being seized with dysentery whilst I had my fever in camp, has turned out the best and tenderest nurse, and I would rather have him as one than any of poor Josceline's 42 ladies, some of whom send civil messages which I return in the same tone. Mr Bracebridge came to see me, but I was not well enough to see him. From what I hear, the bulbul,† Miss Nightingale, does not inspire as much reverence as one might think, and as I hear this from persons who have no cause for jealousy, and with whom she cannot interfere, there may be some reason. I suspect she is imperious. She won't visit officers – why? I don't know.
>
> I hope you are quite well and not in a state about me, as <u>now</u> there is no cause. Three weeks ago it was not a safe business. Would you order my room to be got ready in about 17 or 18 days in case

---

* Lord William Paulet was the Military Commandant of the hospital.
† A family of Asian songbirds, most commonly a nightingale.

I should get away quickly . . . . I shall have to wait in London some days for a Medical Board.

Henry was premature in his expectation of a quick departure, as he continued to suffer from residual stomach cramps, though by the end of January he was out of danger. He had been fortunate to survive: in the months of January and February 1855, the average number of patients in the Barrack Hospital (which was the largest one, attached to the General Hospital) was 2,349. In the same period 2,315 died – probably an underestimate, given the number of deaths which went unrecorded in the confusion.[13]

Having obtained his discharge on 7 February, the next problem was to secure a passage home, which was no simple matter, given the number of troops coming and going: 'I am so annoyed at the delay here, as every day lost here will make my return to the Crimea later . . . I don't know when I shall embark. You must have an order from one man countersigned by another, and so on, so that I have half a mind to start on my own from this horrible place of misery. Any adjutant of common ordinary qualification could arrange it far better, and yet there is an army of staff officers at Scutari.' After tidying himself up at the British Embassy, courtesy of Lady Stratford, drawing some money to do a bit of shopping (he wanted to find a silk gown to give Louisa), he was able to depart for England by the middle of the month. He would by this time have received Isabel's account of the goings on at home over Christmas; they must have all seemed quite trivial, compared to what he had been through during the past three months, but perhaps, in a way, reassuring:

Guy's Cliffe
January 14th

My dear Henry,

It seems to me that I have been rather remiss in not thanking you more speedily for a long letter of 7th December, when you were so amicable as to write to me, and which I received some time about the 28th. We were all so grieved to hear of your attack of fever (of which as you desired, no mention was made to your father and sister) though not <u>surprised</u> for the wonder is rather that anyone should keep well when exposed to such hardships. You at any rate have frequently given yourself good practise of <u>roughing</u> it in your travels, but think of the numbers of lads whose nannies would never

138

have let them sit in a draught or keep on damp stockings for ½ of an hour.

You reproach me, and I doubt not very justly – with writing a gloomy letter. You are quite right, and I beg pardon and will try to do better in future – but I must just mention in excuse that <u>that</u> particular letter was written after the news of the Battle of Inkerman, and before the despatches when it was impossible for anyone writing a letter to the armies not to be impressed with the utter uncertainty of whether the letter would reach its destination – and another that I wrote to you just after the despatches came when one heard of nothing but grief and misery around one, will I fear have been no better. However, I must mend my ways in future if I can, and now that the papers hold out the best of all prospects – that of a possible <u>peace</u> – but somehow I can't believe it – it seems too good to be true. God grant it may prove so . . . .

The principal thing I have done since I last wrote to you is to spend 10 days with the Dowager Lady Leigh in Gloucestershire. I went there on the 22 December, and returned on 2 January, when they all came to Stoneleigh. A merry Xmas was not a thing to be looked for this year by anybody, but I was very happy in being with such old and kind friends . . . . We got up, for our own diversion, a couple of plays – and fate got up for us an accident which was still more comic than the comedies: Lady Leigh drove me over in her pony carriage to Batsford, which they have modernized and smartened up very successfully, with arabesqued ceilings and French papers and chintzes – and it being 7 miles off, of course, we came home in the dark (with a moon, however). Now Lady Leigh is quite blind and utterly careless, and the daughters all blindly warned me that I should most likely be killed; however, I kept a bright lookout for obstacles ahead, and we managed to get home safely until we reached the turning into the court, where of course we both thought all was safe – not at all – up we go, bang! against the post and chains; there was a wrench, a struggle, and a thundering <u>crunch,</u> and we subsided quite gently into the attitude of people sitting in an armchair with the hind legs off. There was no question of being hurt or frightened. I tumbled out into the mud and then saw what had happened: the hind wheels had *fait divorce* from the rest, and were standing – axle and all – quite unhurt in the road, while the pony carriage had <u>sat down </u>on the ground. It was so utterly absurd that I went off into convulsions of laughter, which affected Lady Leigh so that she could hardly extricate herself, or I help her. It was such an achievement to have torn off one's own hind wheels at one's own door! I could not get over it, and while still under the influence of my fit of the giggles, I marched into the house where I suddenly found myself *nez à nez* with nobody but a very smart man I had never seen before (the newly arrived Mr Pember) and was utterly unable to give a rational answer to his questions – for the moment I attempted to speak, I burst into a fresh paroxysm of laughing, whence (as I afterwards learnt) the poor man not unnaturally concluded that I <u>must</u> be in hysterics.

As to our plays, I am ashamed to say we were remarkably in-expert in our parts, especially the 'genius' who had talked in the most offhand way of the facility of learning his – but he was the making of us nevertheless. He acted so well, improvised for himself and his neighbours, and sang well into the bargain; and he resorted to all kinds of mean shifts – newspapers, books etc., as a pretext for reading what we knew least of our parts – and as we had an un-discerning and partial audience of tenants and villagers, we received more applause than we at all deserved.

When I came home on the 2nd, I found Constance Hunter installed here for a week, while her husband was campaigning as a Militia man at Reading. She was very well, and as usual made no end of tender enquiries after you. They hear continually of or from Sir Charles Russell, who is a great friend of theirs . . . .

Mamma sent you a box of goods in HMS *Malacca*. I mention it again lest a letter she wrote to you to tell you so should not come to hand. If so, you'll be surprised to find a chuck full of ink bottles! The history of that is that they had been got for me to contribute to the Crimean Army Fund owing to the complaints I saw in the privates' letters in the newspapers of the difficulty of getting pens, ink and paper – so she got me some pens and ink in London, and finding that when she packed your box that she had extra room, she stowed them in there. And as there will be <u>a little</u> more ink and a <u>few</u> more pens than you can possibly want for yourself, please give them to such of your men who want them. There was hardly any paper to go with them, but that is added in another parcel which Papa has sent you by the son of our neighbour, Mr. Dugdale, who is going out (*en amateur*) in the *Caesar*. We hope said parcel is safe on board her – it contains some waterproof things that Papa sends you. The paper above-mentioned of mine with a packet of <u>foreign</u> paper for your own use, which I thought you might like, as I get it from Paris and like it better than the English paper – and a pair of warm slippers and a pair of night caps which I knitted. If you don't like such things (of course <u>nobody</u>

140

would here, but in that climate they may) you can always give them to somebody who is particular about keeping their ears warm. Mamma added a comforter which she knitted and which she says you can give away to a friend (as well as my slippers) if you don't want them; because before you get them you will probably have received a specimen of each (with one or two other things, I forget what) which were in a little parcel taken charge of for you by <u>Mr. Brackenbury</u>, whom I think you know, and who is gone out as a commissioner of the Crimean Army Fund, and will no doubt arrive before the *Caesar*. I am making this illegible with crossing, and it is getting pitch dark, so I'll leave off. If I have not commented on your letter, you must not suppose that we are not all <u>very much</u> interested in every detail you can send us – but it is useless writing all <u>our</u> ignorant reflections back to you. Papa thanks you very much for your long and interesting letter, and will soon answer it. The Zouave dinner sounds <u>wonderful</u> and must have seemed out there and amidst such privations like a scene in a fairy tale. I hope you will have such <u>good medicine</u> often.

Yours very affectionately,
    I. Percy

As he departed, Henry also got Josceline's account of his own journey home: quite an eventful one, judging by the number of times he had to visit 'the bogs' on the way – evidently not helped by his brother's advice that he should stay in the Hotel Byzance.

Torquay
Jan 18th 1855

My dear Henry,

I was so very bad in the stomach that I felt that it was more than probable that I should be a burden to you as well as to myself, so it was perhaps as well that I was ignorant of your having again been taken ill. Not till after 8 days at sea did I become anything like well, and sailing through France was a terror to me. I had a warning. A French officer in the *diligence* to Lyons was taken ill towards daybreak near Lyons, and being unable to stop the carriage, jumped out as it was going on, and I saw him instantly rush to a wall, and down with his breeches. I watched and saw him pull up his trews in haste, and run on to catch us, which I warned him he could not do. Again I saw him squat like a dog, and though I beckoned to the *Conducteur* in vain, we left the poor fellow behind.

At Paris I dined not, still at the time ill, and at Boulogne I passed the few hours before 6 in the morning at the bog. However, I reached London without further alarm on Sunday morning last. The doctor told me it must be stopped at once or dysentery would be the result, and I am still in a curious state. Therefore I suspect there would have been a pair of us if I had gone to Sebastopol . . . .

Do not go to the Byzance. It stinks abominably and poisoned me, I believe. I could not continue another night in the 2nd floor room over the bog. [You must] avoid all the rooms over the bogs on the side of the mid-landings of the staircases. The whole house stinks awfully. One night in a front room to which I changed, the stink was so loud as to awake me, and obliged me to open the door and window . . . .

If you are still ill, do not go to the Hospital. The Physician of the Embassy, Lady Guernsey said, had worked wonders with sick officers, but the Hospital is too crowded and confused to be wholesome. May the New Year restore your health and give us Peace. I never thought the miseries of war were so great as they are.

Yours affectionately,

J. Percy

Josceline was thoroughly depressed on his return to England. He had considered it his duty as an MP, and as one who had some experience of hospitals, to go out to the East on a mission that was officially sanctioned by the Secretary at War. He was paid nothing for his troubles and he had refused to accept any expense allowance; he'd managed to get Mary Stanley's party of nurses out to Constantinople without mishap, and in good time – just when they were most needed, as the crisis was approaching its climax. But instead of being welcomed with open arms, he had received a thick ear from Florence Nightingale, and the only thing he had to show for the whole expedition was a nasty dose of diarrhoea. He came home in the knowledge that all the newspaper reports about Scutari were only too true, and that he had been unable to do anything about it.

In fact, many of the nurses that Josceline accompanied to the Crimea did end up being extremely useful. After the row that followed their arrival, Lady Stratford did her best to take them under her wing and found some of them employment in hospitals other than the Barrack Hospital. A number of them, like Elizabeth

Davis, made it to Balaklava Hospital, where they did good works for the rest of the war. Davis later published *The Autobiography of a Balaclava Nurse,* pointing out that Nightingale's hospital presented 'the greatest amount of least alleviated misery of any war hospital belonging to the British Army of the East'.[14] Frances Taylor was another, who in 1857 published the book *Eastern Hospitals and English Nurses.* One should also recognize the contribution of Mary Seacole, the Creole from Jamaica, who, having been rejected by Liz Herbert for employment on Josceline's expedition, made her own way out to the Crimea in early 1855 and instituted the 'British Hotel' entirely under her own steam. For the rest of the campaign, she provided sustenance and medical relief to the troops, often exposing herself in the trenches to enemy fire. She was immensely popular and made many friends, including Lord Rokeby, who became a lifelong supporter.[15]

Josceline did his best when he got back to England to raise awareness of the needs of the sick and, early in 1855, he made a speech in the House of Commons, reported by Hansard:

> There prevailed a deplorable want of proper clothing for the sick and wounded, and very often the only clothing they had were those which the marines and sailors had given them while on their voyage from the Crimea, and very often men were sent thence as convalescents, who, on arriving at their destination, were found to be so ill that they were obliged to be sent back again. He therefore urged on the Government to provide proper clothing in the different hospitals for convalescents going out to the Crimea, and also for those returning to England. He must also allude to the stoppages made to the soldier's pay for hospital allowances. He knew an incident in which several hundred sick and wounded were landed from the *Acorn* at Scutari, who arrived at the hospital in such a state as to be incapable of taking care of themselves, much less of their kits. The authorities refused to supply them with knives and forks, because, by the regulations, a soldier was obliged to find these articles . . . . He had seen a letter from a sick officer in which he stated that his doctor had to attend to sixty-nine men and nine officers. Now, by the French regulations there was one doctor appointed to twenty-five wounded men, and one doctor to every fifty *malades ordinaires.* It was impossible for the medical men of our army to do all the business that was thrown upon them.[16]

The ultimate catalyst for decisive change was a motion tabled on 26 January by the Radical MP, Mr Roebuck, to establish a committee 'to inquire into the condition of the Army before Sebastopol and the conduct of those departments of the Government whose duty it had been to minister to the wants of the army'.* The passage of this motion by a large majority led to the fall of Lord Aberdeen's government.

The Duke of Newcastle and Sidney Herbert both left office, and their responsibilities were thenceforth combined in one post, Secretary of State for War, to which Lord Panmure succeeded. Panmure, whose own brother had died of disease in Varna, immediately ordered a Sanitary Commission to investigate the state of the buildings and hospitals being used by the army in Turkey and the Crimea, and this was the crucial event that at last facilitated an improvement in the mortality rate at Scutari. For all Florence Nightingale's reputation as the saviour of the British soldier, her undoubted organizational expertise and her single-minded determination to shake a moribund supply chain into action, she had singularly failed to slow the number of deaths occurring at Scutari. Hugh Small, in his book *Florence Nightingale: Avenging Angel* (1998), attributes the analysis of mortality figures that Miss Nightingale saw after the war as the cause of her nervous collapse after 1857. She realized that 'the epidemic which had killed 18,000 men out of an army intended to number 25,000 had *not* been caused by inadequate food, overwork or lack of shelter as everyone believed. It had been primarily caused by bad hygiene. The worst affected places had been those where overcrowding had aggravated the effect of poor sanitation. And by far the worst of these, where 5,000 men had been killed by bad hygiene in the winter of 1854/5, was Florence Nightingale's own base hospital at Scutari. In the five months before the Sanitary Commission arrived, between November 1854 and March 1855, Nightingale had not been running a hospital. She had been running a death camp.'[17]

To give Miss Nightingale her due, however, she thoroughly

* Josceline Percy was one of the MPs who from personal experience of the Scutari Hospitals were able to give valuable reports and suggestions to the Select Committee. As *The Times* put it in June 1855: 'By these means, much suffering was alleviated, the spirits of the men were raised, and many lives were saved.'

approved of and cooperated with the Commission's work, and indeed was largely instrumental in urging Lord Panmure to establish it in the first place.[18] In March 1855 the Commissioners set to work and soon discovered that the sewers running under the Barrack Hospital were in a 'murderous' condition, choked and overloaded to such an extent that the porous plaster walls of the hospital were soaking up liquid sewage. Poisonous gasses came up through open privies and permeated throughout the whole building. Worst of all, they found that the water supply was contaminated by the carcass of a horse, and the storage tanks were next to additional privies that had been hastily erected to cope with the flood of diarrhoea.[19]

As soon as these problems were tackled and the place was cleaned up, the death rate fell dramatically: in contrast to the five months of 1854–55 which cost the British Army nearly 10,000 deaths from sickness, the same period the following year saw only 500 deaths, when the army was twice the size it had been the previous winter.[20]

Chapter 7

1855: New Resolution

That winter, while the men were preoccupied with politics and the progress of the war, Louisa, Caroline and Isabel devoted their hearts and minds into collecting things for the 'Crimean Army Fund', the purpose of which was to provide whatever materials might ease the suffering of the troops in the Crimea. In charge of the fund was the Earl of Ellesmere, who detailed his son, the Hon Algernon Egerton, and Mr Thomas Tower to proceed to the Crimea in his own private yacht *Erminia*. Together with two screw steamers that they had also chartered, over a thousand tons of goods were conveyed to the Crimea, where they arrived in mid-February 1855. This first consignment represented some £60,000 worth of gifts,[1] most of them purchased using financial contributions to the Fund, others specific gifts in kind. There were all manner of things, including 37,000 flannel shirts and jerseys, assorted food hampers, wine and beer, even down to brushes and combs.[2] Lord Ellesmere's agents made a better job of distributing Crimean Army Fund's wares than had the Commissariat the previous year, when things had piled up on the quayside and rotted in Balaklava while troops froze to death on the heights above Sebastopol. They brought their own transport with them and, with the aid of some workers who were building the new railway out from Balaklava, they set up storehouses at the small settlement of Kadikoi, just outside the port. Most things were given out to the troops for free; a few luxuries were sold at heavily subsidized prices, such as sherry at 24s per case.[3]

For all the effort on the part of private individuals that had gone into the preparation and distribution of the Crimean Army Fund, the tangible benefits were not as great as their contributors would have hoped when they had collected everything together the previous November and December, in the aftermath of the hurricane. By Christmastime the breakdown in logistics that had led to the disasters of the winter was on the mend, and by the time the Crimean Army Fund really got going in March, the weather had improved markedly. One sentry, when asked by a staff officer whether he was comfortable, responded, 'I should be, sir, if I hadn't got so many bloody clothes on.'[4] All the extraordinary bits of new attire, woollen 'Balaklava' helmets, sheepskin coats, knitted waistcoats etc., were in fact now largely superfluous. A doctor described 'enormous quantities of useless clothing, fit only for a polar expedition' or a fancy-dress party.[5]

The real benefit, though, was intangible: it showed to the Army of the East that numberless private individuals at home were taking great pains to show solidarity with the troops and in doing so were implicitly concurring with *The Times*' verdict on the mismanagement that was the cause of so much of their suffering. As Kinglake put it, Lord Ellesmere's schooner 'brought nothing less than an Embassy – an Embassy of affection and gratitude from our people at home to the survivors of that valiant army which had borne the privations and hardships of November, December and January, and was still locked in strife with its foe.'[6] For this, Lord Raglan told Egerton and Tower, 'I cannot speak in terms of sufficient praise of the total disregard of personal convenience which you have exhibited in the prosecution of the laborious task to which you devoted your whole time and attention from the first to the last; of the benevolent way in which you distributed what the Crimean fund have provided for the comfort and use of the British army, or the earnest desire you have ever manifested to meet the wishes of all. Your success in this endeavour fully shows how much we all owe you; and in expressing my warmest acknowledgements, I speak the feelings of the many thousands who have so largely benefited by your exertions.'

The contributions made through the Crimean Army Fund, *The Times*'s Fund (which was for comforting the sick and wounded) and the Patriotic Fund (to provide for the widows and orphans of those who died, and the families of the wounded) were supplemented by many other unofficial private donations. In her confusion as to what the Yacht Committee would or would not accept, and 'distrusting all Associations', Louisa Percy preferred to send her contributions to the Crimean Fund by independent means. Unsurprisingly, this was perhaps not the best recipe for the most efficient distribution of her wares and her last package arrived in the Crimea when Henry was in Scutari, by which time he felt that by the need for yet more woollens had passed. Henry wrote to his father from his hospital bed:

> I hope poor Louisa has got notice of my departure in time to stop her generous but <u>torrential</u> flow of warm clothing. I have given away all to be divided if possible between the men, or if not the officers, and the good things I have given to my friends. The candles to my company, which will be an immense treat to them, for though Lord Raglan issued an order reciting the number of candles to each individual, the Commissariat could not supply them, as usual.

As well as trying to supply the men in Henry's company who were still serving, his father and sister were keen to do something for the families of Henry's soldiers who had died or were wounded. At Christmas Lord Beverley had sent £100 to provide 'a Xmas box for the men of your company who came out of the fight with you at Inkerman'. Later, he deposited a further £100 in Henry's account, which Henry got wind of while he was laid up in Scutari:

> I am very much obliged for your 2nd donation – most magnificent, but I cannot give money to men for fighting, and the way to dispose of it will be to distribute sums to the wounded of my company who come home to be invalided, and to whom a little assistance will be really useful. The men in camp have lots of money – more than they can spend, poor fellows. Their sufferings haunt me, and when I compare them with the French, and the way their Government manages, I am filled with bitterness . . . . *The Times* is right in all it says.

On his return to England, Henry entrusted £85 of this second donation to Captain Hatton, with instructions to distribute it to widows or to men requiring assistance on being discharged invalided. Hatton made sure that it was the needy from the 8th Company who received this charity; Henry himself distributed the other £15 when he reached England. Louisa did her best to look after the privates' wives – the widows of Stacey and Cook* especially.

* Sergeant Reuben Cook, a member of Henry's 8th Company, was killed at

Meanwhile, Lovaine busied himself in Parliament with the Militia Bill and the Enlistment of Foreigners Bill. He was Major of Militia No. 27, the Northumberland Light Infantry, of which Lord Beverley was Colonel and whose captains included representatives of the local gentry – familiar Northumbrian names like Potts, Craster, Riddell and Burrell. Lovaine told his brother in January how little he relished the prospect of going up to Alnwick to do duty with them, though at least he would be quartered with his cousin, the Duke, at the castle:

> I anticipate but a poor muster, and the poor wretches will have a disagreeable time of it, for the billets they are put into are wretchedly bad and cold – though doubtless to you they would be palaces. Lord Grey has persuaded my father into agreeing to suspend appointing officers just at the moment when they are most wanted. The latter was his error, but of course there will be no changing the pig-headedness of Father, so we shall have a lack of subalterns just as they are wanted most. However, this must appear to you sublimely ridiculous . . . .
>
> [By] Heaven, I cannot write something that was amusing to you, for I really am ashamed of my stupidity, but you need not answer it if you don't chance taking it as a simple expression of the affection which makes me cudgel my brains to produce four pages of nonsense simply to assure you that I am your affectionate
>
> Lovaine.

The Militia Bill, which was debated in Parliament in December 1855, was drafted to enable units of the Militia to serve abroad. Lovaine opposed the measure, and clashed repeatedly with Lord Palmerston, Secretary of State for War, on the floor of the House of Commons.[†] He reminded the House that the Militia was now voluntary, unlike during the Napoleonic wars, and that its role was solely for home defence; it was a condition of the existing legislation that volunteers were only withdrawn from their civilian employments for military drill and exercises for a maximum of twenty-eight days per annum.[7] He asked who would be left for

---

Inkerman. Private Thomas Stacey died of disease aboard the hospital ship *Kangaroo* on 23 November.

[†] Lord Palmerston, being an Irish peer, did not sit in the House of Lords; neither did Lord Lovaine, who held only a courtesy title until his father died.

home defence if the Militia regiments left their counties, and if Militia service brought with it the likelihood of serving abroad, how could they expect to recruit more men? Lovaine was conscious that there was widespread suspicion within the ranks of the Militia of any attempt effectively to push them into the regular army, with its poor reputation and derisory pay. The officers, who were usually from the landed gentry, as in Northumberland, were equally reluctant to allow their labourers to be removed from their employment on a permanent basis, particularly at a time when the price of grain was high owing to shortages caused by the blockade of Russia.

The Enlistment of Foreigners Bill, which attempted to recreate the successful British foreign legions of Napoleonic times, caused even more consternation among its opponents. By enlisting hastily convened and ill-trained foreigners, who as mercenaries were probably of dubious or even criminal character, to serve alongside the British army, the country's morale would be damaged and it would advertise to the world that Great Britain was in a poor state. Opponents of the Bill were also concerned that it would cause political problems in Germany and Italy (which along with Switzerland were the countries to be targeted), perhaps even widening the war.

In the event, both the Militia (Service Abroad) Act and the Foreign Enlistment Act received Royal Assent on 23 December 1854. The fact was that without conscription the British Army was in desperate need of more manpower: in 1854 the pool of potential recruits was diminished by an agricultural and industrial boom, and a rising rate of emigration. The only alternative was to increase the enlistment bounty and army pay, but this had to an extent already been tried, with little effect. Opponents of these measures, like Lovaine, may have been considered reactionary and have failed to come up with any other practical suggestions, but, as subsequent events would show, the misgivings they had about foreign legions were entirely justified.

As the year drew to a close, therefore, the feeling on the home front was ambivalent. On the one hand, all were profoundly depressed by *The Times'* reports and could see no end to the war in sight, let alone an improvement in the condition of the army; on the other hand, they were able to draw inspiration from the individual tales of devotion to duty that filtered through from the Crimea, and indeed from Britain's own provinces, and take comfort from the fact that everyone from the Queen and Prince Albert downwards was trying to do their bit, even if the Government seemed incapable of alleviating the plight of the army in the Crimea. Uncle Charles' new year message to Henry encapsulates the mood:

Guy's Cliffe 31st Dec 1854

My dear Henry,

First and foremost, this huge sheet shall convey to you Caroline's and my best wishes for the New Year . . . . As you scold us for our gloomy letters, I don't mean to touch on your situation before Sebastopol – all I say is that *The Times* has published such terribly gloomy articles, and in so bad a spirit, that we are all low and angry by turns. I hear that HM has prohibited that paper at Windsor, that she and the Prince are very unhappy at the hardships you have undergone and the unlucky or unskilful arrangements made for your comfort and for the arrival of necessaries, and that the Queen is hard at work knitting for the Army, saying 'I know it is of no use, but it is a comfort to be doing something for the brave army.' The Prince made some remonstrance as Colonel of the Grenadiers, <u>and was snubbed for it.</u>

I am glad to hear that Raglan writes cheerfully and hopefully. Everyone is knitting or sewing or crocheting for the soldiers, and I hear that warehouses are filled with piles of warm comforts for men and officers, waiting for ships to convey them. When my wife was in town she wished to send you some conveniences, and she was told there was an opportunity if she sent them <u>on that particular day.</u> Accordingly, she and her maid got what they could, not what they wanted, and forwarded them forthwith to go by the *Malacca*. Conceive her indignation when in yesterday's paper she sees that the *Malacca* had only just sailed, instead of her packet of goods being as she hoped by this time at Balaklava. She wrote to tell you what she had sent, but in case you did not get her letter, you will find a box about 2 feet long and nearly as wide, containing woollen shirts (she says for your men) and sundry stockings (ditto) – some finer Shetland sleeves, a comforter, caps and leggings, which she thought fit for yourself; a box of pickles, marmalade and soap, and a large supply of ink, which Isabel intended for the army, but which was stuffed into the box with a very small supply of paper, which was all they had at hand. She subsequently sent you through Lady Hunter and Mr Brackenbury a comforter of her own work, and mufflers, a pair of slippers made by Isabel for sleeping

151

in, 2 Camphor balls for chapped skin, and some 'old man's plaister' – good for Rheumatism, and to be put on the joint and remain there as long as it will – and 2 chest plates for warmth. I have a waterproof suit, galoshes, gutta-percha soles and a bottle of stuff to apply them with, some letter paper of Isabel's, some thin foreign paper, a rug and some oil cloth which I hope to send soon if I can. I shall put up Kohl's *Russia* with them. I am, I'm afraid, too late for the *St. Jean d'Arc*, but I believe it will go out by a neighbour's son, who goes out in the *Caesar*. Nobody's goods go by the ships they intend, and nobody can give one certain information.

I have heard from your father at Torquay, where they have Meyrick's house – The Cove, in a charming situation; but they do not seem satisfied with it, but say <u>we</u> shall be charmed with it when we visit them in February. Your sister in law, M. Percy, is with them now, and is always a great comfort to them, for she suits them exactly. I am afraid Louisa's eyes are no better for her doctors. We hear poor accounts of Lady Lovaine.

I am angry with the Foreign Enlistment Bill – not that I don't wish you had 10 or 15,000 good Foreign troops with you, but that if they are to be drilled first at home, I think they might as well have drilled our own people, who were all jealous, but whom this clumsy bill will disgust and dishearten. Your father does not approve of the Militia Bill and the sending of the Militia to the Mediterranean. However, as there is no reserve, I do not see what else could be done.

I wonder whether you see the papers? Once or twice I think Caroline sent you a paper, but we suppose that you see them tolerably regularly. People seem pleased with Louis Napoleon's speech, and we are all pleased that Austria leans to, instead of <u>from</u> us – I feel persuaded that she will be fighting with us in the spring, and I hope her doubtful position keeps the Russian troops from the Crimea now . . . .

Dunkellin was congratulated by the Russians on being taken prisoner, as the allies on the 5th, <u>no quarter given</u>, and they were to be driven into the sea. The other day a young officer who, on leave from India, found the expedition about to sail for the Crimea, joined it and was attached to the 20th Regiment and saw everything to Inkerman, came home after this last battle to see his family, whom he had quitted 9 years [previously]. Soon after his return, he went out hunting, and all the field took off their hats and cheered him as he came on the ground. I mention this to show you the feeling for the Army now in England . . . . Young Amherst is going on well, and is reported to be anxious to get back to his duty . . . .

I wonder whether you will see Josceline; I think he will take a passage from Scutari to Balaklava – if he is sure of one back. What a pity he did not marry Miss Nightingale! Some neighbours of ours, the Bracebridges, are with her at Scutari, and we sometimes see some of their interesting letters. She is a very clever woman, and they are both excellent people, but marvellously ugly. It is a bad job for Charles Bagot to spend his Xmas at Newcastle under Lyme, with the 3rd Staffordshire Regiment, instead of in his home with his wife and bairns. Admiral Josceline has had a severe fit of gout, but is mending. Of Admiral William, I have heard nothing, except that he was to pass his Xmas at Hatfield. Lord Dormer's son has changed from the Blues to the Foot Guards, that he may see active service.

God bless you.

C.B.P.

Henry arrived back in England on 26 February, almost exactly a year since he had embarked for the East. On his first night in London he dined at the Travellers' Club with Lovaine and a couple of friends. He was still feeling 'very seedy', however, with occasional diarrhoea and weakness in the limbs, and spent his first full day at home in the company of his father and Louisa; Josceline came round to visit and they no doubt swapped notes on their experiences of Scutari and its effect on their bowels.

Despite his health, he was keen to return to the front and persuaded the doctors not to refer him to a Medical Board, but to let him go straight back to the Crimea in April. 'A Doctor Scott, an Indian doctor highly considered, told me that my staying on here longer would not diminish my chance of fever, and that it was better to go now when the heat was not intense than in the middle of great heat. He gave me no end of advice and prophylactics, particularly quinidine – a remedy which has proved very effective – in order to get acclimatized before the oppressive heat of the summer.'

Henry therefore only spent six weeks back in England, and there is little of relevance to this narrative to report on this period, except that he had an interview with Prince Albert, Colonel of his Regiment, and dined one night at Buckingham Palace with the Queen, who thanked him for the 'exceptional gallantry' he showed at Inkerman. Lady Raglan was one of those he called in on during this time.

There didn't seem to be any sign of the coveted staff appointment, in spite of several opportunities. The Kingdom of Piedmont-Sardinia had joined the allies on 26 January and resolved to despatch a force to the Crimea under General De La Marmora.* Cadogan, who had by now recovered from his illness, did secure an attachment to the Sardinian Army, though Henry did not think that his friend had been treated very well by the War Office, observing that Cadogan was only 'Corresponding Officer', without any of the step up in rank, or additional pay or allowance which normally came with a staff appointment. Henry himself had recently had dinner with La Marmora, and came away from the meeting with the impression that their new ally was a very able man. The feeling was mutual, as another who was present on this occasion told Lord Beverley:

> I must tell you of the effect produced by your son Henry on 2 rather distinguished men. Lord Lansdowne,† to whom he talked a long time, told me afterwards he had never talked to any officer whose intelligence and manner had more favourably impressed him. De La Marmora had 2 hours with him, and said he got more information and instruction and useful advice from him than from all the French officers he had received. He added 'I see the Papers full of complaints that merit cannot make head[way] in this country against wealth and connexion in England. But how is it that such merit and service, with the aid of wealth and connexion, leaves such a man in command of a company? In Piedmont, I should give him a Battalion immediately, and keep my eye on him for a Brigade.'

If Henry had hoped to be appointed to La Marmora's staff on the back of this, he was disappointed: the day before he departed from England, 'I got a pompous document . . . saying I could not be approved Commissioner, or on the Staff of La Marmora, as the Government were not going to send <u>anybody.</u>' A month later, the authorities evidently relented on this, for Cadogan was in May elevated to the post of Military Commissioner to the Sardinian Army. For his part, Percy concluded that it was only by going in

---

* Alfonso Ferrero, Marchese De La Marmora (1804–78), Italian general and statesman. He was Prime Minister of Piedmont-Sardinia in 1859, and of the united Italy from 1864 to 1866.
† The 3rd Marquess of Lansdowne (1780–1863) was in Lord Aberdeen's cabinet.

person to see the new Secretary of State for War, Lord Panmure, that one could get any appointment, and if so, that was too bad. He embarked for Paris on 14 April.

After spending a few days in Paris, where he was surprised at the indifference to the war among the French upper classes, apparently because they had so few persons '*de notre société*' serving, he arrived on 5 May in Turkey, where he spent ten days, mostly shopping in the bazaar (for example to find some material to get a coat made for his father), and in the evenings dining at the embassy as guest of Lord and Lady Stratford, Lord Beverley having paved the way by thanking them profusely for looking after his son the previous winter. One day, Lady Stratford took Henry to see her hospital at Koulali, and he was much impressed with what he saw – particularly pleasing, given that it was staffed by some of the nurses that Josceline had brought out five months previously. Otherwise, he told his father, there wasn't much to report, apart from the fact that 'the Turkish Ministry is all changed, owing to some French intrigue, I am told. But I do not think it worthwhile to tell you the names of the new lot. A little beheading would do no harm, perhaps!'

On 18 May his ship arrived at Balaklava, and he was greeted with a scene which could not have presented a greater contrast to his last impressions the previous winter. Most obviously, the weather was exceptionally fine: 90 degrees in the shade. More importantly, however, the Guards were in fine fettle, with a new camp down beside Balaklava, huts instead of tents and plenty of food and fuel; at last also, a ship containing over a thousand Guardsmen had just arrived from England. Included in that draft was another veteran of the earlier campaign, Captain the Hon W.H. Wyndham-Quin, who had been with the Regiment in Varna and invalided home the previous summer.[8]

General La Marmora was among the first to offer Percy an invitation to dinner, though for the moment he was unable to accept, as Colonel Ridley (now in command of the Grenadiers) and Major General Lord Rokeby (commanding the Brigade) had already booked Henry as their guest for his first two evenings back in the Crimea. On the third night he dined with Lieutenant Colonel Strange Jocelyn* of the Scots Fusilier Guards, who described his

---

* The Hon Strange Jocelyn, later 5th Earl of Roden (1823–1897).

summer accommodation almost in terms of rapture: 'The view from my hut is beautiful. I put my Arm Chair (another luxury I have got) outside my hut and read, with a magnificent view of Mountains and Sea, and the town of Balaklava and its own Castle, before me.'[9] It must have seemed to Henry a world away from the snowbound tents which had been his only shelter on the heights overlooking Sebastopol five months previously. These could almost be described as halcyon days: there were regular race meetings, a Zouave theatre,[10] fishing in the Black Sea and picnics convened with a view to picking flowers and Crimean crocus bulbs to send home.[11] There were even one or two women around, Lord George Paget's wife having come over with the Stratfords, though Henry Percy was certainly not minded to consort with them, or the train of pompous dandies who followed them around:

> Lady George Paget is here with a great proportion of the Paget beauty and from what I hear, the whole of the Paget presumption and insolence. But as she and a Mrs Duberly* are the only ladies here except the *revêche* nurses, she is in full plenitude of power, and rides out with a cortege composed of officers from every regiment (though principally the Dragoons) who can only say 'ya-as'.

He was far more interested in catching up on military matters and the *on dits* that he had missed during his four-month absence. He found Lord Rokeby in fine form. The old boy was past his prime physically and rather deaf, but hugely respected (he had been at Waterloo)[12] and much liked by his fellow officers. Henry found the general 'in great spirits and as furious at Estcourt as I used to be', and thought his irreverent remarks were 'great fun', though he was very eccentric. Rokeby did have a reputation for being headstrong, to say the least. He was present on an expedition at the end of May organized by Lord Ward (who Henry described as displaying 'all the ostentation of a millionaire') to take his steam yacht down the coast to Aloushta. Far from this being a spying mission or some other clandestine operation, it was unashamedly an officers' jaunt, organized with a view to seeing some of the famous palaces up and down the coast belonging to the Russian nobility. The most spec-

---

* Fanny Duberly, wife of an officer of the 8th Hussars, and author of *Journal Kept During the Russian War* (1855).

tacular of them belonged to Prince Woronzoff, Sidney Herbert's uncle. Here, the English architect Edward Blore's masterly combination of Turkish and Scots baronial architecture stands on cliffs overlooking terraced gardens leading down to the Black Sea. Colonel Jocelyn was one of those on board the yacht as it anchored off the Woronzoff Palace:

> We sailed quite close in to the shore, not 100 yards off . . . close into the beautiful town of Yalta; all the inhabitants turned out to look at us and we took off our caps to them from the decks of the steamer. There was 'Mounting in hot haste' amongst the Cossacks! Rokeby and Ward wanted very much to land, but if we had we should to a certainty have all been made prisoners, and this letter most likely been dated from some Russian Fortress. Rokeby is like a boy, and Ward, as you know, mad; but luckily General Rose was on board, who represented the folly of the thing, and it was abandoned, though we had our boats lowered. So Rokeby was obliged to postpone his visit to the beautiful damsels he fancied he saw walking along the shore. I think 'Old Rag', as we call him, would have been rather astonished if he had learned that two of his Generals, and a host of Field Officers, had landed at Yalta and been taken prisoners; for it so happened we none of us even had leave! We dined on Board, and after dinner the Steamer lay to, and some of our party bathed, taking headers off the paddle boxes. The Sea is very deep all round this Coast, and quite black in colour. We reached home about 9 o'clock.[13]

It had taken some weeks for Rokeby to attain this carefree state of mind, for his mood when he first reached the Crimea on 1 February could not have been more different. He had arrived as successor to Brigadier General Bentinck, nominally in command of a Brigade of 3,000 men; Rokeby had of course known only too well that he would not find it at full strength, but there had been recruits sent out from England, so he expected to find 2,000 or so. He was therefore deeply shocked when he encountered barely 500 effectives, and none of the briefings from Horse Guards or private sources nor any newspaper accounts had remotely prepared him for the miserable sight he saw before him on parade early that first winter's morning. Strange Jocelyn was one of those present when Rokeby first addressed the Brigade's officers:

[He read] them most flattering letters from the Queen. But as he read, the sight was too much for him. He burst into tears and could not go on. When he came to speak of the wretched remnant of the Brigade of Guards he saw before him on parade that morning, he said he could not believe any such pitiable misery existed. He saw before him 140 of our Battalion, all that were left, and about the same number of each of the other Battalions, about 450 in all, instead of 3,000 – men, he said, who looked haggard and worn out, half naked, and was this what Her Majesty's Guards had arrived at? . . . He said, 'I thought I was coming out to command a magnificent Brigade, and I find a miserable half-starved set of old soldiers and raw recruits, and my only duty now is how to save these few left.'[14]

The Brigade had reached its nadir later that month, by which time its strength had ebbed away to between three and four hundred men, of which the Grenadiers made up barely 150,[15] only sixty of which were from the original draft of a thousand which had left England a year before. It was this state of affairs that had resulted in the high command ordering the Guards to quit their camp before Sebastopol and proceed to the neighbourhood of Balaklava, where they might be relieved from the duties of the siege and recuperate their health in the new wooden huts which had been sent out from England.

While they were so under-strength at Balaklava that spring, the Guards were engaged in mundane duties around the town, either at the wharves or manning precautionary defences. It is fair to say that they had a comparatively easy time, particularly the officers, who amused themselves by making excursions to Kamiesch in search of delicacies, riding off into the valleys of the Tchernaya or Baidar, or making excursions to view progress in the trenches for a few hours. The French trenches were better for observing the siege, and from Percy's point of view also attractive because one didn't have to talk to cavalry officers there, 'whose ignorance and affectation and swagger is really unbearable. They ask military questions a child would be ashamed to ask, at the top of their voice and in their peculiar detestable accent.'

Early on the morning of 25 May the ground leading up to the Tchernaya River was occupied by French, Turkish and Sardinian forces whom Percy accompanied *en amateur*. The Russians, however, did not resist, other than by lobbing a few cannon shots from across the river. Later that same day he rode up to investigate the abandoned Russian camp near Tchorgoun, 'a very pretty village, with very fine trees, but evidently a most malarious spot, from the appearance of the vegetation and the marshes caused by the overflowing of the river . . . . The country here is enamelled, to use a poetical phrase, with beautiful flowers – sweet smelling and of every colour.' He admitted to a sense of excitement, cantering alone beyond the line of outposts over *terra incognita*, and half-hoped he might chance upon some stray Cossacks. The Russian camp was well laid-out with wooden huts, and there seemed to be plenty of food and luxuries about, though the smell indicated a degree of filth and misery. The playing cards that he found scattered around the ground indicated a hasty withdrawal.

Exchanging notes at dinner with General La Marmora a few days after this excursion, he was told that the valley of Baidar was even more beautiful than the valley of the Tchernaya; La Marmora had just returned from reconnoitring the area, and related how the peasants of Baidar had besought him to leave some men to guard them against the Cossacks, whose return filled them with dread. A good many of them loaded themselves and their property up and followed the Sardinian troops; others apparently had begged La Marmora to shoot them at once, rather than be left to the Cossacks' cruelty. As dinner progressed, they ruminated about the progress of the war, and Henry left with the impression that the General had a very low opinion of Lord Raglan's Staff.

The siege was heating up again. April had seen the Second Bombardment (the First being the previous October), which was the fiercest display of artillery fire ever seen until that time: some 500 guns firing more or less continuously for ten days. The logistics had been made easier by the development of the Balaklava Railway, which ferried vast quantities of heavy ammunition and men up to the heights above Sebastopol. Despite there being over 6,000 Russian casualties (as against 1,585 French and 265 British),[16] the Russians still managed to keep their defences intact. The only advantage the allies gained was in pushing their trench parallels a few hundred yards further forward into some advance Russian rifle pits. During one of the brief armistices that were held in order to bury the dead, one Russian officer was alleged to have said to a British counterpart, 'Why *don't* you go? You bore us so.'[17]

But the war of attrition continued, the Guards all the while remaining in reserve as they gradually recovered their strength. In an attempt to break the stalemate and open up the Sea of Azof to allied shipping, thereby cutting off the Russian supply lines, two expeditions were despatched to the Straits of Kertch in May. The first ended in fiasco owing to a shambolic chain of command, which caused the flotilla, already well under way, to abort the expedition at the last minute. The second sailed on 23 May and was successful, the allied landing being unopposed. The Russian batteries there were blown up, and within a few days four hundred Russian supply ships were either destroyed by allied shipping or scuttled by the Russians themselves.[18] It was an important victory, but entirely marred by the orgy of murder, rape, looting and pillage that took place afterwards. None save the Russian inhabitants were innocent in this shameful episode and, in descending order, it seems the blame lay with the rebellious Tartars first and foremost; they in turn encouraged the Turks to join in, who were aided and abetted by a few drunken French sailors – none of whom were stopped by the British, who stood idly by and watched. Henry Percy, of course, reckoned that the Turks were being made scapegoats:

> It appears that French sailors behaved very ill at Kertch, destroying the museum which was full of curious antiquities. The bestial sailors went in with sticks breaking everything. This I know from good authority. General Brown seems to have behaved like a vandal – we ought at once to have put a sentry over the museum. The inhabitants were glad to see the allied troops and came out with the best intentions, but the Tartars came down and began to pillage. The inhabitants then sent to Brown for protection, to which he replied they must form their own police. All this is very bad and will not raise the Allies' name. The evacuation and destruction of Anapa by the Russians is true, so that they now have not a *pied à terre* south of Sebastopol. I do not believe that the French committed many horrors at Kertch – they say the Turks did, but that is very easy to say. I believe Brown shot some Turks, who I dare say did not deserve half as much as the French. They say Kertch was a very nice town with every comfort, but they have only destroyed the Government buildings. I understood that it was all burnt, but that is denied. It is

stated that Liprandi has been obliged to detach some of his force to keep the Tartars under, who are in insurrection.

Whilst the campaign at Kertch was an important move towards increasing the stranglehold on the Crimea and it boosted the morale of the allied armies, it had no immediate impact on Sebastopol. So long as the city remained open to the interior of the Crimea, it could only be captured by being utterly destroyed and then stormed. So, on 6 June came the Third Bombardment, in which still more guns were brought into play. Unlike the ten-day barrage of April, this bombardment was concentrated into twenty-four hours, after which the French stormed the Mamelon, a Russian-held knoll lying between the French trench lines and the walls of Sebastopol. This they captured, thereby enabling covering fire to assist the British in taking the Quarries ahead of their own front line. These features were immediately turned from being Russian defences into salients ready for the next offensive. Henry, while not directly involved in this action, could not resist going up to witness the attack. Its success put him in a fever pitch of excitement, for it represented the first step change in the siege and he felt that it would only be a matter of time before they would deal the decisive blow by taking the two most formidable Russian defences on the edge of the town: the Malakoff, a 350-yard-wide fortress encompassing 62 guns, whose centrepiece was a prominent stone-built tower which menaced the French sector; and the Great Redan, a massive network of gun emplacements, several hundred yards across, which commanded the British sector. He wrote a few days after the attack:

> The attack on the Mamelon was most brilliantly executed by the French, who in their ardour made a rush at the Malakoff Tower, and not succeeding there were pursued by the Russians to their own trenches, when the French supports came up and settled the business. Had these supports been nearer at hand the French would I think have taken the Malakoff. The French took 2 other batteries and 400 prisoners, and another battery was evacuated by the Russians and destroyed. A miserably small body of English at the same time took possession of the Quarries near the Redan, but they were attacked three times during the night and lost 650 men and 43 officers *hors de combat*, retaining however possession, and they are now well entrenched. The use of this is that they are so close to the

Redan that they keep up such a fire on the embrasures the [Russians] cannot work their guns. I think it was a pity when the French were in such good spirits not to have attacked the Malakoff, but Pélissier* would not hear of it. The firing has been tremendous and the Russians are evidently a little staggered. It slackened yesterday, so they will repair damages, but as the French have got such a hold of the Mamelon, the Malakoff cannot last . . . .

In the armistice, I went into the Mamelon. I never saw such chaos and so many horrors. I wanted to converse with some of the Russian officers, but I came late and a sentry who had been blown up for letting too many through got sulky and turned me back.

These frontal assaults were very costly, even in the aftermath of intense artillery bombardment, but the fact that, within the space of two weeks, the stalemate which had endured for seven long months had been broken on two different fronts indicated to the whole army that one final push might settle the business. Therefore Lord Raglan and General Pélissier decided that the denouement should take place on 18 June, symbolically chosen for being the anniversary of the Battle of Waterloo. The day before, at 4 am, the Fourth Bombardment commenced: six hundred siege guns in action this time, of which the British mustered 166, including 30 thirteen-inch mortars and 8 sixty-eight pounders.[19] The original agreement was that the firing should stop for a time during the night, before opening up again for two hours before 5.30 on the 18th, when, at the signal of three rockets, the French infantry would launch their attack on the Malakoff. The British would attack the Redan shortly afterwards.

Late that night, however, Pélissier changed his mind and decided to move at three in the morning, and for some reason without the preliminary artillery barrage. Lord Raglan was informed of this, but had no opportunity of persuading the French to stick to the original plan: the losses that had been sustained by the British at Inkerman and the devastation to which they had been subjected the previous winter (from which the French had barely suffered in comparison), coupled with the large number of French reinforcements that had been sent out by Napoleon III, meant that the British were now very

* General Pélissier had become Commander-in-Chief of the French forces on 19th May 1855, following Canrobert's resignation.

much the junior partners on this campaign. However unfair, Lord Raglan could do nothing except send out a revised set of orders to his commanders, for any refusal to commit his troops to this new arrangement would not only meet with derision in the French camp, but imperil the whole operation, with only a combined assault on the two fortresses, which covered each other's approaches with crossfire, having any likelihood of succeeding.

From that moment on, there was chaos. A few minutes before the appointed hour, just as first light was beginning to appear in the eastern sky, a stray shell trailing a burning fuse was mistaken by General Mayran, commanding the French right, for the expected rocket signal. Over-anxious and expectant, he did not heed the advice of officers who had not shared his mistake and gave the order for his division to advance. When Pélissier saw what was happening, he realized that he had to order his other two divisions to attack as well, but facilitating this took time, as the French sector in front of the Malakoff spanned about a mile of very broken ground, including the great Careenage Ravine. Mayran's troops were already being decimated by the time their comrades were able to join in. Not only was the French advance in disarray, but the Russians, despite sustaining enormous casualties in the previous day's bombardment, had on that cloudless night (illuminated still further by the fires burning all around) seen the allies preparing their assault and taken advantage of the end of the bombardment to fill up their defences with infantry at the ready. This was no mean achievement, given that they had sustained the loss of several thousand men in the artillery barrage.[20]

As the French advanced they were subjected to every conceivable projectile, exploding or otherwise, as well as rudimentary land mines planted in no-man's-land before the Malakoff, some of which were fired using electricity. Lord Raglan quickly saw that this was developing into a gut-wrenching massacre, but he felt that his only option was to get his own troops into the fray as soon as possible. He explained to Lord Panmure afterwards that he was 'quite certain that, if the troops had remained in our trenches, the French would have attributed their non-success to our refusal to participate in the operation.'[21]

So, two British columns of infantry, one drawn from the 4th Division under General Sir John Campbell and one drawn from the Light Division under Colonel Yea, were ordered over the top of the trench parapets. They had nearly 500 yards of ground to traverse in broad daylight, encumbered with wool bags for filling the ditch in front of the Redan and ladders for scaling the walls. Like the French, they were met by a hail of grapeshot and rifle fire, coming not only from the work that they attacked, but also the Russian batteries on either side. Those few who reached the Abattis, an outwork of sharpened branches 80 yards in front of the Redan, were disappointed to find it still intact in spite of the previous day's shelling and, given the hail of fire coming from the front, there was little possibility of engineers opening up the way with grapnels, never mind the fact that nearly all the scaling-ladder bearers were killed or wounded long before they reached the Redan. There were, however, one or two gaps or weak places here and there in the Abbatis through which men might push their way, so Colonel Yea's leading Engineer, A'Court Fisher, consulted with his chief, who had arrived at the head of his storming party, sword in hand. 'I am the Engineer officer, sir; shall I advance?' he asked. At that moment, Yea fell backwards, shot dead. Fisher then accosted a fellow Engineer, Captain Jesse: 'Well Jesse, what's to be done?' Before he could answer, Jesse too staggered back, with a bullet in the head. A'Court Fisher then spoke to several others successively, but, in Kinglake's words, 'as though his charmed life had been given him on some fell condition importing that all he accosted must die – it so happened that those he addressed were stricken, one after another, before they could answer his words.' It turned out that only 150 effectives were still available, a hope-lessly small number to complete the final assault, so they resolved to lie down, seeking as much shelter as they could in shell holes etc., until the reserve was sent forward.

Lord Raglan personally experienced the intensity of the Russian fire, observing the action from the parapet of his trench lines; indeed a man standing next to him was killed by grapeshot.[22] He saw only too clearly the folly of committing any more men into this hopeless situation, so sent no second wave, leaving the survivors to make their own way back across no-man's-land. As soon as it was safe to do so, artillery support was brought to bear on the Russian fortress, at last affording some relief to the allied infantry. If an artillery barrage had preceded the infantry by a few minutes, rather than vice versa, the whole outcome of the attacks on the Redan might have been different. Instead, it was a black day indeed: nearly 800 men were killed or wounded, including 62 officers, as well as General Campbell and Colonel Yea, leading the two columns involved.

The Guards were in reserve and had moved up onto the heights in readiness for being in the second wave of the attack. The idea had been that, once the Redan was occupied, the Brigade would come up in support and defend the work against the inevitable Russian counter-attack. Strange Jocelyn wrote:

We did not parade till 3 o'clock, and as we marched up the top of the hill at a little after that hour we saw the whole thing open in the grey of the morning before our eyes, where we were posted till it was all over . . . . Without the French being able to get into the Malakoff, for some reason or other our storming party was ordered to attack the Redan. The fire had not been in the least bit subdued by our guns, and was perfectly terrific. Nothing could stand against it; whole sections [of the line] being carried away before they got near the place. They found the ditch of the Redan 18 feet deep full of men with fixed bayonets, and the parapets lined, too. The Abattis was so strong that the hatchets could not cut through it. A very few men managed to creep through, and were instantly put to death. Colonel Yea of the 7th Fusiliers led the storming party, as he was the general of the day in the trenches. He was shot first of all in the leg, but he kept on in front with his cap on his sword, cheering on the men, until a Russian got behind him and shot him in the back. He then still crawled on along the ground, and they finished him by knocking his brains out with a stone.

Thus perished one of the finest Officers in Her Majesty's army, who had gone through everything from the time the army left England. He had just received a pension for distinguished service, and was about to retire in three months from the Service. I consider, and we all consider, he and the whole of the storming party, out of whom scarcely 2 or 300 got back, were all massacred by the Authorities. The idea of storming such a place when their guns had not been in the least silenced was a piece of downright madness. Fortunately they did not send up their supports as they saw the uselessness of the whole thing. Therefore the sufferers were only the stormers, out of whom there were 700 men killed and wounded, and 44 Officers [actually 64], including two Generals; and all this sacrifice for nothing – for worse than nothing.

165

The only aspect of 18 June that was successful was an attack on some ground to the west, between the Great Redan and the Flagstaff Bastion, but control of this area on its own was of little strategic benefit and it too was achieved at great cost: 562 casualties from a Brigade of 2,000. Total casualties for the day therefore amounted to 3,500 French, 1,500 English and 1,500 Russians (the latter having also lost 4,000 in the bombardment the previous day), and of the six French and English commanders who had led the attacks, four were killed (including Mayran, who had precipitated the attack prematurely) and one was severely wounded.[23] It had been hoped that another glorious and decisive victory would be celebrated thenceforth on Waterloo day; instead, the events of 18 June 1855 are immortalized by the phrase 'lions led by asses', first uttered by Russians trying to explain their attackers' folly on that day.

Percy, now writing to his father from the heights above Sebastopol, where the Guards were needed on trench duty to fill the gaps created by the failed offensive, was furious:

> There is some foul mismanagement . . . . Fancy men being ordered to storm an earthwork with a ditch 18 feet in depth and defended by successive swarms of Russians. There is but one way to take the place – *viz.* placing sixty 13 inch mortars and a hundred 68 pounders in position (and 1,000 rounds per gun). Lord R. has sent for another siege train of pop guns, and I suppose about October we shall have another *brutum fulmen*. It looks almost as if madness pervaded every authority. If the people who place these attacks had to lead them they would look out better . . . . I hope *The Times* is satisfied at the destruction of officers: 93 to 600 men is a fair proportion . . . .
>
> Unless we have a stronger armament than we have now, I doubt much our making more than a 5th abortive bombardment. I hear that a proposition was made to employ the Electric Light, which thrown on the enemy's batteries from an inaccessible point would keep them in a glare of light, and that our batteries and trenches would be proportionately obscured. From what is known of the success of this Light in London I cannot see why it should not be tried at least. I hear that Brunel said that he would undertake for £100 a night to keep the enemy's batteries in a glare of light nearly equal to day, also that the plea is under the 'consideration' of the Government. If the proposal was made to the HQ Staff here it of

course would meet with derision, as did the railway at first – at which the fine ass General Airey* laughed outright. And if the Government don't make haste, the Russians will have it and use it with effect . . . . The Russians showed considerable jealousy at the last armistice for fear we should see any of their works – poor geese – they don't know that our Staff have neither eyes for observation nor brains to comprehend! I hope you are as well as the annoyance you will feel at the news of our blunders and those of the French will permit. I have had a slight liverish attack, very slight, but am cured.

The mood was becoming increasingly bitter. The Guards were now back where they had come from before their rest cure down on the plains by Balaklava, and yet, despite four months of fighting, there was still no end in sight. The renewed frustration expressed itself once more in agonies of bitterness about the lack of promotions, and Percy's views on this subject were widespread at the time.

They say the Sultan offered us all the Medjidie, his Order, and Lord Raglan refused it for the army, taking it for himself and Generals Brown and Burgoyne.† I wish Lovaine would ask in Parliament whether it is true, for I think it hard that Lord Raglan is in every way to deprive us of any small distinction. He was asked to recommend more officers for promotion etc. and refused, saying it was yielding to a cry: if he had been just in the first instance, there would have been no cry on that score, but the Government have I believe not insisted on him doing so. They have, I am credibly told, found out that many have not been mentioned that ought, and also that many have been promoted who ought not – and an instance exists of one who was promoted for Balaklava, when at the time he was actually on board ship sick . . . . Since I have been out here, I have heard so much about Lord Raglan's injustice and officialdom that though I might not attack, I would not give myself the trouble of defending him. Whether he is right or wrong in the military conduct of the war, I cannot of course decide or pronounce, but I am sure that as far as the interior economy and management of the army, he is not fit for it.

* Airey crossed out many years later.
† In 1858 the Sultan did bestow the Order of the Medjidie on a number of Grenadier Officers, including Percy. In addition, the Turkish War Medal was granted generally to all officers and men who served in the Crimean campaign.

167

Henry had been avoiding contact with Lord Raglan since he had arrived for the second time in the Crimea, as he considered the Commander-in-Chief must have something against him personally. He couldn't understand how, after going on wounded at Alma and showing widely recognized leadership at Inkerman, and then volunteering to return to the Crimea after being invalided home, there was still no sign of any promotion, nor any appointment whatsoever. This was particularly disappointing given that Lord Raglan's nephew had tipped Henry off that his uncle was looking for something to give him, and that was nearly a year ago, before any of the aforementioned reasons might have provided Lord Raglan with an excuse to act on his apparent intention. Despite getting on so well with La Marmora, nothing had come of that either; instead, Cadogan had been appointed Military Commissioner to the Sardinian army. Back in Constantinople he had been sounded out about taking a Brigade in the Turkish Contingent; there can't have been many senior British officers who spoke fluent Turkish, so he had felt that this was a likely prospect, and the pay was excellent too. Again, nothing came of it and his hopes were dashed again. Little could he imagine that, within a few months, he would be corresponding with the Secretary of State for War, the latter addressing Percy with the words, 'My dear General'.

After the débâcle at the Great Redan, Lord Raglan was a broken man, and there was no way he could disguise his sorrow. On Sunday 24 June the Adjutant-General and Lord Raglan's right-hand man, James Estcourt, died of cholera, which was now sweeping through the army again and had recently claimed the life of La Marmora's brother. Lord Raglan was so upset by this new blow that he dared not attend Estcourt's funeral, so afraid was he of breaking down. He had defended Estcourt to the hilt at great cost to his own reputation, when the Government had demanded he be dismissed the previous winter; now all he could do was pray silently for him by his grave.[24] The following day he himself was taken ill, and on the night of the 28th his life quietly ebbed away as the sun sunk below the horizon.[25] The doctors said he died 'without sufficient physical reason. It was *not* cholera. The diarrhoea was slight, but he was so *depressed* . . . the more by reason of his apparent equanimity which never failed. Peace be with him and his hecatomb of twenty thousand men.'[26] All the allies, even the brutish General Pélissier, were greatly affected by this unexpected blow, and throughout the French camp, they mourned '*Le pauvre vieux Père Crees Mass*', who the previous winter had spent a considerable sum of his own money on little comforts for their sick and wounded.[27] As Florence Nightingale put it, he was not a *very great* general, but he was a *very good* man: 'It was impossible not to love him.'[28]

Henry immediately penned a note to his father, so different in tone from his recent references to the old man: 'poor Lord Raglan died last night of exhaustion, caused by a fit of cholera. He was quite well in the morning. Poor man, the worst defect they can impute to him is being too confident in the capacity of his inferiors. I am very sorry for him. Another gentleman less in the world . . . . I wish it was [just rumour] that he was dead, but it is too true; his death was painless.'

By an extraordinary irony, within a few hours of Lord Raglan's death, Percy received news from London that he was promoted to Brevet Colonel. Four days later, there was more:

To my great surprise, the Telegraph announced here my appointment as ADC to Her Majesty – which announcement has put me in some good humour . . . .

I always told you that I knew that Lord R's powers were not like those of the Duke of Wellington, and I feel convinced that it will turn out that Lord R. was cribbed and confused and worried by the government and the Duke of Newcastle. Gordon told me he hoped [Raglan's correspondence with the Duke of Newcastle] would be published. I hope it will, and that the consequence of its publication will be that no civilian will be permitted in future to be Minister of War.

I believe there is no doubt that we shall be here for the winter. Lord R's remains are to be sent on board ship in state tomorrow. I believe the French are going to make a very strong demonstration of respect. Pélissier is said to have said '*en perdant Lord Raglan, j'ai perdu un vrai ami,*' which from him, who is universally stated by the French to be *un homme dur et brute,* is pretty. My General Cler said that he would not truck upon Lord Raglan's merit as a [general] but that he was convinced that Lord R. had been of the greatest use as a diplomat in this business – '*il a adouci bien des choses*' – and that he would be very much regretted by the French army . . . .

Is it not curious that Pélissier, who as I say is a brute, and burnt women and children etc. etc. is a slave to the purpose of flowers and gardening? He was quite annoyed at the sight of Lord Raglan's orchard, and nothing would serve him but sending ever so many soldiers to put it into order, though Lord Raglan begged him not to, saying he did not care about gardens.

A few days later, the Grenadiers provided a guard of honour of a hundred men for the funeral of Lord Raglan. A procession from British headquarters to the *Caradoc* in Kamiesch Bay stretched six miles, all the way lined on either side by British, French and Sardinian soldiers. It was the end of an era: Alexander Kinglake's exhaustive eight volume history of the war finishes purposely at this point, as does William Howard Russell's first volume of his history of the war. This time also coincided with a new chapter for Henry Percy, though he did not yet know it. His penultimate letter from the Crimea that summer encapsulates his attitude: a touch impatient, but ever keen for a more efficient prosecution of the war effort and open to any new ideas that might facilitate this; personally ambitious and above all, strictly unsentimental.

July 13th Camp Sebastopol

My dear Father,

Nothing has occurred worth mentioning. I was in command of the Trenches the other night with about 2,600 men, and we were well peppered by the Russians, who threw every description of projectile in profusion, as the place where my post was was only 200 yards from the Redan. I had a very pleasant night of it, and what with anxiety, heat during the day etc., I was not sorry when the relief came. 24 hours under fire is enough. I of course got hit by a stone from a shell which fell near me – in the arm, in the inner part of the elbow joint, but only bruising my arm. But with a very little more power, I should have had the artery cut through, the surgeon said, so I am very lucky. I saw a dreadful wound – *viz* a poor fellow had his right hand taken off horizontally as clean as possible, and the other cut off except just a fragment. We are so near our enemies that the shells we send burst amongst them, and the pieces come amongst us. Alas, a great many of our shells are bad, and explode at the mouth of the gun, and of course the pieces come amongst us. I received 2 of your letters at once, the post having made one of its usual blunders.

The dislike and contempt I have for our engineers does not decrease. Our parapets are bad, and our scientific arrangements

170

careless. They are going to try and blow up the bridge across the Putrid Sea beyond Genitchi. They have examined it without being found out; they are only waiting for a peculiar wind which gives additional depth to the channels. There is also a project of blowing up a ship in Sebastopol harbour: a man has invented an almost invisible boat by which he means to get under the bows of one of their largest ships and blow it up. It appears that he has been round all the ships in our squadron and bored a hole in the bows of each ship without detection, so clever is his contrivance. The French are getting on well with their battery near the harbour. Health is fair, and the weather not insufferably hot, though very hot.

In consequence of a new commander-in-chief being appointed, I have made a formal application for a Staff Appointment. If I do not get it, I think it will be worth thinking of changing into a Line Regiment, for _entre nous_, the service of the Guards with Sir C. Campbell and Rokeby is getting disagreeable, and Rokeby is I think a little insane. I have had no collision with either, but R. takes such a strong line about everything, that even an innocent person may not escape. He uses mallets to kill fleas. Sir Colin Campbell is a Scotchman – _c'est tout dire_. We are having some promotion, at which Rokeby denounces, but really it is hard upon married men – and others who have no immediate prospect of coming to the Battalion – to force them to stay.*

I hope you are quite well. Give my love to Louisa. Many thanks for the cigars which will doubtless arrive safe. Though I have been seedy at times, I have no doubt that the course of quinidine does good. I suffer here principally from restiveness. We have had some very severe wounds here, but our surgeon, who is very clever, says that he thinks the climate is favourable to wounds, which is odd. Some think that there will be another assault in six weeks time. I know not and have made up my mind to pass the winter, though I feel convinced our situation will be little better than last year. The railway is badly constructed for wet, and sundry other things lead me to suppose so. There is a Colonel Munro here, a great geologist, who says that if Murchison had been here, he would have made the roads hard for the winter.

Your most affectionate

H. Percy

* If middle-ranking officers were not granted the option of retiring on half-pay, or were pressurized not to sell out, there was little opportunity for junior officers to rise up the ranks.

Chapter 8

Pyrrhic Victory

It was a quirk of fate that no sooner had the perceived bar to all of Lieutenant Colonel Percy's frustrated ambitions passed away a hat-trick of promotions appeared as if from nowhere. First, the Colonelcy, followed shortly afterwards by the appointment to be Queen's ADC, in Lord Hardinge's words, 'as representing an officer from the Brigade of Guards whose bravery and devotion to his duty was second to none'.* Finally, two weeks later, came an offer from the Secretary of State for War to command the British Italian Legion in Piedmont, with the local (i.e. temporary) rank of Brigadier General.

He agonized over whether or not to take the appointment up. It was without doubt beyond his wildest dreams: 'I should have been contented with a humble situation here', he wrote. If he refused it, people might take a dim view of a Queen's ADC being 'luke-warm'; on the other hand, there might be a certain shame in leaving the theatre of operations for an altogether more comfortable situation. Whatever the pros and cons, he had to make up his mind without really knowing the nature of the appointment, as the telegraph contained no particulars whatever. The advice he was given, however, was almost universal: General Sir James Simpson, who had replaced Lord Raglan as Commander-in-Chief, urged him to accept, as did La Marmora (obviously), Rokeby and two other generals that he consulted.

* Later that year Prince Edward of Saxe-Weimar (1823–1902) was also made Queen's ADC. He ultimately reached the rank of Field Marshal.

He wrote home to say that it was a pity he had to accept without waiting for his father's advice or approval, but that 'by all accounts I should have committed a folly in not taking it, and as the answer required immediate attention, I had to settle and sign.' Higginson wrote to his own father on the subject:

> Percy has got the command of the Italian Legion; he goes to-morrow to Genoa. As yet he knows nothing whatever beyond the fact that he has the appointment; but what the strength or duties of the corps are, he knows no more than I do. The reason I mention this is that, immediately upon getting the appointment, he came to me and offered me to be adjutant-general, should there be such an office or any post similar to it. Of course, I did not say yes, as it will take a great deal of promotion to induce me to quit the Brigade, even though it took me away from this place; the more so as I have the Brigade majorship in prospect; but if the acceptance of such a post were to carry with it a lieutenant-colonelcy and other advantages, the question is whether I am justified in saying no.[1]

In the event, Higginson decided to remain in the Crimea. In actual fact he did eventually receive a message from his father to the effect that he should accept the appointment; for some reason, though, this advice didn't arrive until mid-September, even though it came by telegraph directly from Lord Panmure. So Percy alone was hauled off to the sea in the greatest hurry on 21 July. Robert Lindsay considered it 'a very fine appointment'. It was, however, by Percy's subsequent admission, 'a fatal moment'.

The passage of the Foreign Enlistment Act in December 1854 was greeted almost immediately by a change of Government, and with it a new Secretary of State for War, replacing the Duke of Newcastle. Right from the start Lord Panmure was far from convinced that the foreign legions which were supposed to come out of the Act would materialize, partly because the amount of money being granted to them was very limited and partly because he could see that the internal politics of the host nations were unlikely always to coincide exactly with British interests. For example, some states in the German Confederation, notably Prussia, violently objected to a perceived attack on German neutrality.[2] Notwithstanding these concerns, in early 1855 measures were put in place to raise mercenaries in Germany, Switzerland and Piedmont-Sardinia.

The Kingdom of Sardinia at this time incorporated not only the island of Sardinia, but also Piedmont, Savoy and Nice. The country's capital city was Turin, and its king was Victor Emmanuel II of the House of Savoy. The Prime Minister was Count Cavour,* whose dream was to see a united Italy, beginning with the liberation of Lombardy from Habsburg rule. It was in pursuit of this goal that Cavour had taken Sardinia into the Crimean War on the side of France and Britain, for he knew that he would need Napoleon III's support in any future war with Austria and that Great Britain would play a pivotal role in the redrawing of southern European boundaries that would surely take place as the absolute monarchies of Austria, Turkey and Russia gradually relinquished their hold on southern Europe in the face of nineteenth century progress.

Compared with Germany and Switzerland, therefore, Sardinia's entry into the war was likely to be more conducive to the success of a foreign legion. Both Cavour and Sir James Hudson, the British Minister in Turin, believed that there was a vast pool of potential recruits for a such a force: there were thousands of officers still nominally on the strength of the Sardinian army following the recent war with Austria who had failed to obtain their correct discharge papers by virtue of mess debts; there were 50,000 Lombard exiles who had been granted political asylum in Sardinia following the uprisings of 1848–49; there was the impending disbandment of 3,000 men from the army of Parma; and a further pool was created by rising unemployment.[3] Every communication from Hudson to Lord Panmure indicated the utmost confidence that the British Italian Legion would be up and running in no time. For his part Percy, comforted by the knowledge that La Marmora's 'Sardines' in the Crimea were competent and well turned-out, had every reason to look forward to his new challenge as he sailed up the Mediterranean that August, particularly as he was on intimate terms with Sir James Hudson, whom he had known since their schooldays. Reassuringly also, Sir James' brother, Colonel Joseph Hudson, was the individual at the War Office in London who had responsibility for the Italian Legion.

* Count Cavour (1810–1861). Prime Minister of Piedmont-Sardinia 1852–59 and 1860–61. First Prime Minister of Italy 1861.

When he first arrived in Turin on 8 August the Brigadier General was put up by Hudson at the Embassy and was promptly introduced to the King and dining with Cavour. The first day, he set about trying to establish exactly what he was supposed to be doing, and was staggered to discover that the British Italian Legion thus far consisted of just one man – himself. It soon became apparent that he was expected to start the whole enterprise from scratch, from appointing the first officers in charge of recruiting (though it wasn't even clear at this stage whether these should or could be Italian or English officers) to finding somewhere to house the new force. Far from having replaced trench duty with a spell of drill, training and exercise, he found his new role to be confined to a desk, pushing papers in three different languages.

Percy has been accused of impeding the recruitment process by being too rigid about adhering to all the legal formalities, e.g. by insisting on seeing the correct discharge papers from anyone entering from the Sardinian army. It is true that his high standards were not conducive to cutting corners, but it was for entirely practical reasons that recruiting did not get under way quickly: nothing could sensibly be done until the Legion had secured some suitable accommodation. Cavour had originally promised Hudson the use of some barracks at Novara, but when Brigadier General Percy investigated, he was 'thunderstruck' to find the building roofless. Other buildings offered by the Sardinians included a roofless monastery (empty for fifty years) and a dilapidated cow house.[4]

Within two weeks of his arrival in Turin, he was totally despondent:

Aug. 22nd. Turin

My dear Father,

I write you nothing pleasant. I am utterly disgusted with this work, utterly. Hudson is a very quick clever man, who sees the end of his journey, but not knowing anything of the road does not take nuts for the rats one has to encounter [on the way]. I am sure some civil spirit must have proposed that poor Lovaine go and mention my name for an appointment which at any other time he would have sneered at. Foul fell the moment in which, instead of consulting my own thoughts, which were always opposed to this, I went and asked those stupid generals their opinion.

I get inadequate instructions from my own Government, not an answer to vital queries – nothing but what Lord Panmure <u>said</u> to Hudson etc. The War Office could not find me a paymaster who had served in the army, and have sent me a young man, a gentleman luckily, but who is inexperienced. My ADC is sick, and I am not very well. I work all day from 6 am to 6 pm-ish, but don't advance a bit. In short, I never have been so utterly miserable as I have been in the last 2 days.

A lot of people came over the frontier [from Lombardy] to enlist without being asked. The Piedmontese authorities wanted to know whether I would take them: I said not, as I had not asked for them and was not ready, but Hudson and my Recruiting Committee said I would have to take them on, or it would stop the whole business altogether. Luckily the good nature of the Piedmontese Govt. have given me a respite . . . . Of course, do not say to anybody, particularly Lovaine, what I have told you, but try to think how I can slip my head out of this noose. I have been to see Madame La Marmora, a vulgar noisy woman, but aristocratic. Hudson is very quick and clever, luckily . . . . You must pardon my not writing oftener – I have so much to do and I have a stupid secretary, who of course as usual here was recommended as something wonderful. I hope you are quite well; give my love to Louisa, and believe me

Your most affectionate son,
H. Percy

Henry's spirits did pick up when the redoubtable Captain Burnaby appeared as his Aide-de-Camp, and de Fonblanque arrived as Assistant Commissary General; but in the main, good English officers were not allowed to come, despite Sir James Hudson urging his brother at the War Office to get some sent out, the problem being, he said, that Italian officers are profligate and assume that England can afford anything. But these appeals fell on deaf ears and even one of Percy's favourite sergeants was prevented from joining him, though he wished to come. He admitted that he could hardly fault the Secretary of State for this, as 'I believe in him, and he has behaved like a gentleman to me; the fault was commencing without having everything ready – a month's delay would have cost nothing.'

After a month of getting nowhere, he decided to write to Lord Panmure personally, in a desperate attempt to acquaint him with the true situation in Piedmont – namely that the Government there was all talk and no action, but glad enough to have England's money, for England was financing the Sardinian expedition to the Crimea, as well as the Italian Legion. Although the tone of his letter to Panmure was entirely measured, his true feelings came out in his correspondence with his father: 'I am, I feel, going insane. You need never be surprised at seeing me returned on your hands a raving madman, whom the word Italy will throw into convulsions, or a cretin.'

For reasons which will soon become apparent, pressure of work meant that Panmure was unable to give the matter immediate attention.

28th Sept.
War Dept. London

Dear General,

I have to acknowledge the receipt of your private letter of the 11th which would have been answered sooner if a continued succession of pressing business had not occupied my mind.

So far from thinking that you take a liberty in making your opinions known to me confidentially, I have to thank you for it, and wish you to continue to give me every information which you think will enable me to judge correctly of the real progress you are making and the amount of reliance which I ought to place in the promises of the Sardinian Government.

I confess to being disappointed in the quick formation of this Legion, because Sir James Hudson certainly led the Government to suppose that little more was required than the unfurling of the English Flag to attract all Italy to it.

I remain my dear General,
Yours faithfully,
Panmure

This letter crossed in the post with another, for Henry could take it no more.

28th Sept.
Turin

My Lord,

I have the honour to state to your lordship that I feel that I am unequal to the post respecting which, without having been able to make any enquiries to ascertain the circumstances, I have so rashly and unfortunately accepted.

177

I have done all I possibly could to forward the views of HM Government but from the circumstances I am in, I feel that I am not likely to succeed in giving satisfaction. I have been more than once on the point of taking this step I now propose, *viz* that of tendering my resignation to your Lordship, but have refrained in the hope of smoothing all difficulties.

The perpetual references that are made to me and the absolute necessity of doing everything myself leave me no time to attend to the organisation and discipline of the Legion.

Should your Lordship have the goodness to relieve me from this duty, I ask for nothing but permission to return without delay to the Crimea, from which I ought never to have departed.

I have the honour to be, my Lord, your humble and obedient servant,

Henry Percy

Compounding this misery was news of Uncle William's death. When he had last seen him shortly before he had returned to the Crimea the previous spring, he had looked strong and hearty, though Henry remembered that the old man had muttered something about not seeing him again, which he had assumed was a reference to the possibility of his own death from battle or disease.

Oct 14th

My dear Father,

Poor William's death has caught me in such a state of my own miseries that I can hardly think of anything. I rejoice to hear that his latter days were not passed in actual suffering.

For myself, I am quite at the end of my tether with this infernal Italian Government, who throw impediments in my way, don't fulfil their promises, and at the same time are fair spoken. How anyone can have devised such a mad scheme I cannot imagine. If they don't accept my resignation, my only alternative will be to leave the Army, as it is impossible to succeed or prosper here. The difficulties of adopting a system like ours to the formation of a foreign legion out of England are perfectly staggering. Our code is too mild and our clerks are too rooted in the spirit of the country to enable a man to cut through difficulties which are unfettered by regulation . . . .

I have but one consolation to offer – that everyone in London said, 'You don't expect to keep Percy in Italy when there are active operations: he won't stop.' It is very fine, but I should have considered myself bound to stop if I had had a chance of success. Give my love to Louisa and to Charles.

Your most affectionate son,

H. Percy

It was becoming widely known that his health, both mental and physical (for his nervous breakdown had brought on a renewed onset of Crimean fever) was in a very precarious state, and his resignation was accepted without further ado. Perhaps sealing his fate was a communication between Cavour and the Sardinian ambassador in London, who he instructed should convey his misgivings to Palmerston and Clarendon: 'Percy is a good fellow, but narrow minded; the least difficulty stops him, and he loses courage. He is a good soldier, but a detestable organizer. Another man in his place would have recruited two regiments by now. But he hasn't got two companies together. If he goes on, there will be no foreign legion for ten years.'[5]

The command was given to a Lieutenant Colonel Constantine Read. Burnaby, whom Percy had repeatedly put forward for promotion, was at his suggestion made Assistant Quartermaster General. Annoyingly, Read arrived just as the Sardinian Government at last consented to the use of the barracks at Novara. Although there would be many recriminations during the course of the next two years, in the main Percy departed on good terms with those he left behind and the Hudson brothers were amazingly conciliatory, given that they had both experienced the rough end of his tongue towards the end of his three months in Turin, although, in his defence, he was careful not to blame either of them publicly, or speak ill of them to Lord Panmure. Joseph Hudson penned a kind note to Lovaine, telling him he believed that Henry had done the best that could have possibly been expected in 'one of the most wearisome jobs under the sun', and that he had 'done the most difficult part, and laid the foundations from which others will benefit . . . and that he mustn't regret having taken up the appointment in the first place'. One of his parting letters to Henry said, 'You were right to blow me up [about a muddle over supplies sent from England] . . . . All your old friends lament that you are going away just as the fruits of your labours are beginning to show themselves. You have, however, every credit for your exertions, but with a threatened return of Crimean fever and rheumatism, you are just as well out of it.' Again, he wrote:

Nov 8th
War Dept.

My dear Percy,

Many thanks for your letter of November 3rd, and the hints you give me and which I assure you will not be thrown away. You are quite right in your estimate of me that I am easily led and have not resolution enough in my composition to avoid being humbugged by the refugees and adventurers who set upon me here. I often deplore it myself for it gives me endless trouble and some loss, seeing that I lost 30 shillings by a vagabond last week for whom I got a place in the Army Work Corps who borrowed 30 shillings from me to buy his outfit and then deserted. Serve me right? Oh I know it. But with regard to Read, you don't seem to be aware that every man with brains and resolution is now engaged in the Crimea or elsewhere. Those who remain at home are mere idlers and without interest for the job of President of the Committee of Appointment. I thought Read certainly the best man I could find. Remember in my letter to you about him I said I preferred sending him out as a recruiting officer in order that you might after conversing with him decide where to place him. I certainly thought he would be useful in recruit hunting, but I never contemplated more; however, when the Medical Officer said you were threatened with a return of fever and other Crimean ills and were likely to be laid up, I could find no one to go on with the work.

As to the other staff officers, I did my best but was always reliant on others' testimonials. It is very difficult to find good people. I tried to get officers transferred from the Crimea, but General Simpson immediately put his veto on any officer of decent ability leaving. The Turkish Legion pay so well that all clever unemployed men went to them, and the market was swept out before we came into the field . . . .

You are well out of it. There are much better things at your command in our own Service . . . .

Everything is very dull and dreary here. I wanted to get a month's leave to run out to Turin and go with my brother to shoot deer and moufflon* in Sardinia, but Lord Panmure would not hear of it . . .

Adieu my dear Percy,

Yours always sincerely,

Jos. Hudson.

* A type of wild sheep.

The poor Hudson brothers showed astonishing patience; perhaps in the eyes of a man of action not used to politicking and the niceties of diplomacy, their patience was in some ways their greatest failing, as it aggravated his sense of impotency by giving a semblance of apathy. Henry found a degree of solace in the company of Mr and Mrs de Fonblanque, with whom he spent his final days in Italy. It was about this time that the Fonblanques made their friend godfather to their baby boy, whom they christened 'Percy'. For several weeks, though, Henry's letters home displayed a great deal of anguish, which resulted in him lashing out in all directions, Lovaine included:

Genoa Nov 10th

My dear Father,

I have arrived here and of course have found no means of getting on to Marseilles till tomorrow. I am by no means in a state of happiness, though delighted to have retired from the company of dissembling ministers, English diplomatists and cheating Italians. If Lord Panmure would have seen the business in the right light – *viz.* the necessity of collecting a good English Staff, I could have done very well, but as I could get no one (all being employed) that were good for anything, and those that I applied for were refused to me on one plea or another, and the others were not desirous of changing permanent employment for temporary ones without extra advantage being attached. In fact my brain and health sunk under the constant supervision I had to exercise – not at all mitigated by the knowledge that I was from the want of assistance only half doing my work. When anyone considers that to join to the detail of organising a Corps, officers and all, was added a correspondence in 3 languages, they will not be surprised at one man finding himself incapable of directing the whole to his satisfaction. I at last sunk into a state of nervous irritation that I never slept an hour without awaking, and could not sleep again, and tormented by every vague apprehension, and to such a degree that I would have handled with pleasure a fever or accident only to relieve me for a space from care or worry. The Medical Officer of the Legion wrote to me and spoke to me often advising me to go away for a time, but I could not do so – how could I? There was no one to take my place, and Burnaby, who was the greatest use to me, was more than fully occupied in his share of the business.

Whilst promotion and honour are lavished, in addition to fabulous pay, to officers serving in the Turkish Contingents, I was told that my energy and decision must find officers.

I wrote privately to Lord Panmure to tell him in what a state I was, imploring him to allow good officers to the Legion, but with that extraordinary blindness to his own interests, [the War Department] seemed to prefer my getting a chance, and not (for a little money) to encouraging experienced men to offer their services. Militia men, swindlers, half-decayed Cheltenham half-pay officers were all I could get. I should have had the additional work of teaching them their business, and if they failed, of course, the responsibility of their appointments would rest on me.

I must have gone mad or shot myself if I continued. *Entre nous* the two Hudsons have been obstacles to my success. The Minister [Sir James] obviously wants to spare the London Government, and the Government in reality hates the Legion . . . . The men I appointed to the committee, recommended and introduced by Sir James Hudson, for I could of course know nothing about them, were unfit both morally and socially for the place – and I do not despair of them being yet found out. Hudson is in the hands of a clique, and I of course from my ignorance of the people, fell into the jaws of the clique. I extracted myself when I found what they were, but too late.

When I think of what I have lost by not being in the Crimea, and the lapse of time before what I have done and why I resigned will be appreciated, I could dash my brains out against the wall with vexation. I have but one consolation – *viz* that all the Italian Officers nearly wept when I went and declared openly my [resignation] – and indeed they have found the difference between a gentleman and a snob, for my successor is detested by them. I sanctioned his being appointed and did all I could to get him another step of rank. The moment I resigned, he treated me as much like a dog as a man can do. I would give anything that you would consent to my leaving the army. I am thoroughly disgusted having been so trapped by Lovaine's unpardonable folly; he had no business to mention me for a duty he must have known was alike contemptible and precarious.

Pray give my love to Louisa, and don't send out warm clothing till you hear from me. My stomach is so deranged, I never have a sound sleep, and am more furious than I can express.

Your most affectionate,
        H. Percy

182

He left Genoa on 11th November, still fuming about the Legion, but happy to have received orders to return to the Crimea once again.*

While Percy and Burnaby were bogged down in their own private stalemate in Italy, the real army in the Crimea was nearing victory. The first engagement in open territory since Inkerman had taken place on 16 August, when the Russian Army launched an attack across the Tchernaya River, with a view to capturing the Fedioukine Heights which they could then use as a strongpoint for pushing on towards Balaklava. The French under General Cler and the Sardinians under General La Marmora held the south side of the river, and they soundly repulsed the Russians, who saw their final chance of breaking the siege of Sebastopol fail. The allies celebrated their success with a Fifth Bombardment.

With the exception of one artillery battery, the British army was not involved in the Battle of the Tchernaya, and the Guards continued to do their trench duty. By early September it really did look as though the campaign was finally coming to a head, with the Russians visibly making preparations for the evacuation of Sebastopol via a thousand-yard pontoon bridge that they had constructed across the harbour to the north side. On 5 September, the Sixth Bombardment, which comprised 592 French guns and 183 British (the latter firing off 28,476 rounds in three days)[6] began: this was a still more awesome concentration of fire than that which had preceded it and it destroyed whole swathes of the city. Not that the lulls in between these organized bombardments were necessarily all that quiet: Higginson recorded an incident which took place on 3 September:

> We had a gallant thing done by one of our men last night. He saw a shell fall between two barrels of rifle ammunition from which the men in the fifth parallel were filling their pouches. He jumped forward, and seized it with both hands, the fuse still burning, and threw it clear of the powder, where it burst and did no harm. Had it remained and burst where it fell, many lives must have been

* For the subsequent history of the British Italian Legion and Burnaby's part in it see Appendix I.

sacrificed. Had he been in the French army, by this time he would have been *décoré*.*

The final assault – a phrase that had been used prematurely three months earlier – was set for 8 September. Early in the morning on the appointed day, three French mines were exploded in front of the Malakoff; but the infantry did not immediately follow this up with an attack, so the Russians withdrew most of the redoubt's occupants (who had been placed there in the expectation of an imminent assault) so that they could shelter from the continued shelling. To surprise the Russians, the French attack was scheduled for midday, and the tactic worked, for the closest French parallels had come to within twenty or thirty yards of the Malakoff, so when the infantry did come, they were on the skeleton Russian force too quickly for them to react. Once they were in, a savage Russian counter-attack did its best to dislodge them, but in the end the French held their ground.

At ten past twelve the French tricolour could be seen flying above the Malakoff tower. This was the signal for the British sector to attack the Great Redan, which, being an open earthwork and on a lower elevation than the Malakoff, was covered by the higher bastion. In actual fact this probably rendered the British assault on the Redan superfluous, for once the Malakoff was in allied hands the fate of Sebastopol was effectively already sealed. But the British wanted their part in the fall of the city they had besieged for so long, and in conducting what should really have been no more than a diversion to enable the key French objective to be secured, they believed they had the opportunity of exorcizing the memory of 18 June.

Owing to the lie of the land, it had been impossible for the British to bring their trenches within 250 yards of the Great Redan, because, if they had done so, they would have been permanently exposed to Russian fire from above; nor, given the distance between the two lines and the solid rock foundations of the Redan, had British sappers been able to undermine the Russian position to the same extent that the French had. Accordingly, as on 18 June, British infantry had to cross a large expanse of open ground in full

* Private Alfred Ablett was later awarded the Victoria Cross.

daylight before they could begin the task of dislodging the enemy from the earthwork. The bulk of those in the front line were not seasoned troops, but fresh-faced young recruits, a large number of whom fell before they had traversed half the ground before them; the rest seemed only capable of lying down and firing wildly and ineffectually at the face of the Redan. Despite the valiant efforts of a few officers, nothing could be done to move them forward and get them to use their bayonets. A number of officers did reach the Redan; a few, like Colonel Charles Ashe Windham (afterwards known as 'Redan' Windham), managed to clamber over the ramparts and in through the embrasures, the recent bombardment having completely destroyed the Abattis which had proved so problematic three months before. But after an hour or so, in which they were at least able to spike the Russian guns, these gallant few were ejected by the Russian counter-attack, for, despite repeated requests, no reserves were sent. General Codrington, commanding the assault, fully admitted: 'They won't go.'[7]

The Russian counter-attack caused undisguised panic among those who had got within striking distance of the Redan, and nothing could induce them to stand and fight. The disproportionate casualty rate among the officers that day is partly attributable to so many being shot by Russian marksmen as they stood up on the parapets and implored their men cowering below to fight. William Howard Russell's despatch to *The Times* reported:

Bleeding, panting, and exhausted, our men lay in heaps in the ditch beneath the parapet, sheltered themselves behind stones and in bomb craters in the external slope of the work, or tried to pass back to our advanced parallel and sap, having to run the gauntlet of a tremendous fire. Many of them lost their lives, or were seriously wounded in this attempt. The scene in the ditch was appalling. Although some of the officers have assured me that they and the men were laughing at the precipitation with which many brave and gallant fellows did not hesitate to plunge headlong upon the mass of bayonets, muskets, and sprawling soldiers – the ladders were all knocked down or broken so that it was difficult for them to scale the other side, and the dead, the dying, the wounded, and the un-injured, were all lying in piles together. The Russians came out of the embrasures, plied them with stones, grapeshot, and the bayonet, but were soon forced to retire by the fire of our batteries and riflemen, and under cover of this fire a good many of our men escaped to the approaches. In some instances the Russians persisted in remaining outside, in order to plunder the bodies of those who were lying on the slope of the parapet, and paid the penalty of their rashness in being stretched beside their foes; but others came forth on a holier errand, and actually brought water to our wounded.[8]

In an hour and a half at the Redan the British army lost nigh on as many men as they had done in nine hours at Inkerman. Over 500 were killed and some 2,000 wounded. It turned out to be the costliest day of the entire war, for French casualties were over four times what they had been on 5 November, at 7,500 killed, wounded and missing; and the Russians lost well over 10,000 between the two sectors of the line, of which 3,000 were killed (again, almost on a par with Inkerman). Although the action was successful in that the Russians had been driven once and for all out of the Malakoff, many would remember it as a day on which the British army was disgraced – a sense of shame reinforced by the knowledge that victory had been achieved by the French. Apart from the fact that the British had fewer troops at their disposal and a more difficult objective, the cause of this disaster was as much a failure in leadership as it was mass cowardice among the troops: the generals did not commit enough men into the action and those they did send forward were among their least experienced; they did not send reserves when it might have made a difference; and, given the lessons of 18 June, they probably shouldn't have entered into such a hazardous engagement across open ground again in the first place – especially as complete neutralization of the Great Redan was militarily unnecessary.

The proof of this last statement is that, on the night of 8 September, the key bastion in Sebastopol's defences having been captured, the Russians abandoned their lines. That they still nominally held the Redan on the evening of the 8th did not matter: Sebastopol was doomed once the Malakoff fell into enemy hands.

Before this was known, the Guards and the Highlanders had been told that they would be leading a renewed assault on the Redan the following day. But during the night loud explosions came from all parts of the town, and around ten o'clock the Highlanders manning the forward trenches discovered that the morrow's objective was now devoid of any living thing, save one wounded Russian officer. By morning it was clear that the Russians were abandoning the whole of the south side of Sebastopol, blowing up all the magazines and stores they left behind, setting fire to the houses and sinking the remaining battleships in the harbour. Such was the conflagration engulfing the whole town that the allied high command, wary of booby traps and mines, allowed only a few advance parties into the town before they officially took possession on Wednesday the 12th. William Russell was there at the first opportunity:

Of all the pictures of the horrors of war which have ever been presented to the world, the hospital of Sebastopol presents the most horrible, heart-rending, and revolting . . . . Entering one of the doors, I beheld such a sight as few men, thank God, have ever witnessed! In a long low room, supported by square pillars, arched at the top, and dimly lighted through unglazed window-frames, lay the wounded Russians, who had been abandoned to our mercies by their General. The wounded, did I say? No, but the dead – the rotten and festering corpses of the soldiers, who were left to die in their extreme agony, untended, uncared for, packed as close as they could be stowed, some on the floor, some on wretched trestles and bedsteads, or pallets of straw, sopped and saturated with blood, which oozed and trickled through upon the floor, mingling with the droppings of corruption. With the roar of exploding fortresses in their ears, with shells and shot pouring through the roof and sides of the rooms in which they lay, with the crackling and hissing of fire around them, these poor fellows who had served their loving friend and master the Czar but too well, were consigned to their terrible fate. Many might have been saved by ordinary care. Many lay, yet alive, with maggots crawling about in their wounds. Many, nearly mad by the scene around them, or seeking escape from it in their extremest agony, had rolled away under the beds, and glared out on the heart-stricken spectator . . . . The bodies of numbers of men were bloated and swollen to an incredible degree, and the features distended to a gigantic size, with eyes protruding from the sockets, and the blackened tongue lolling out of the mouth, compressed tightly by the teeth, which had set upon it in the death-rattle, made one shudder and wheel round. In the midst of these 'chambers of horrors' – for there were many of them – were found some dead and some living English soldiers, and among them poor Captain Vaughan of the 90th, who has since died of his wounds. I confess it was impossible for me to

187

stand the sight, which horrified our most experienced surgeons; the deadly, clammy stench, the smell of gangrened wounds, of corrupted blood, of rotting flesh, were intolerable and odious beyond endurance. But what must the wounded have felt, who were obliged to endure all this, and who passed away without a hand to give them a cup of water, or a voice to say one kindly word to them? Most of these men were wounded on Saturday – many, perhaps, on the Friday before – indeed it was impossible to say how long they might have been there. In the hurry of their retreat, the Muscovites seem to have carried in dead men to get them out of the way, and to have put them on pallets in horrid mockery. So that their retreat was secured, the enemy cared but little for their wounded. On Monday only did they receive those whom we sent out to them during a brief armistice for the purpose, which was, I believe, sought by ourselves, as our over-crowded hospitals could not contain, and our over-worked surgeons could not attend to any more.[9]

The fall of Sebastopol was therefore far from the joyous occasion that might have been expected. Captain Henry Clifford of the Rifle Brigade, who had so distinguished himself at Inkerman, summed up the feeling of the whole army:

If a few days before, I had been told, 'on the morning of the 9th September at five o'clock Sebastopol will be in the hands of the Allies, and you will stand in the Redan held by the English', I should have said, 'Oh! That will be a proud and happy moment, that will repay us for all we have gone through, even the loss of so many lives, so much suffering and hardship will not have been thrown away in vain!' But no, I stood in the Redan more humble, more dejected and with a heavier heart than I have yet felt since I left home.

I looked towards the Malakoff, and there was the French Flag, the 'Tricolor' planted on its Parapet. Yes, the French had taken the Malakoff, but the English had not taken the Redan. No flag floated on the Parapet on which I stood, and if it had, I could have seized it, and dashed it into the ditch we could not pass, or hid it in the bosom of the young officer, dead at my feet inside the Redan. I could not stand it long.[10]

As Higginson wryly noted in his first letter home since these momentous events had taken place, 'So ended Russian power in the Black Sea for many a long day to come.'[11]

Sebastopol may have fallen, but the war was not over, for, as Lord Palmerston said, 'After what had occurred at Sebastopol, it was impossible that the war could be brought to any other conclusion than that which would secure for Europe safety against the future aggression of Russia.'[12] The Baltic naval campaign continued as before, blockading and harassing shipping and coastal defences. Nor were the Russians yet defeated in Asia Minor – in fact, quite to the contrary: the town of Kars, in Turkish Armenia, was threatened by an army under General Muravieff. The beleaguered British officer in charge of the Turkish Army there, acting Brigadier General William Fenwick Williams, had been holding out for several months, but by November his supplies were running out and he was completely surrounded by the Russian force.

Because Sebastopol had been the main objective of the war and because the French, being the senior ally, insisted that the main Turkish army remain in the Crimea until Sebastopol fell, Williams' pleas for reinforcement repeatedly fell on deaf ears. Omar Pasha was in no position to disagree, as he depended on his allies for transport, and it was only on 29 September that Pélissier released the Pasha's army from the Crimea. On the same day Muravieff and his 30,000 troops made a determined effort to capture Kars; he failed at considerable cost, but the defenders also lost over 1,000 men.[13] On 19 November, Williams sent a final message to the outside world:

> Tell Lords Clarendon and [Stratford de] Redcliffe that the Russian Army is hutted, and takes no notice of either Omar or Selim Pashas. They cannot have acted as they ought to have done. We divide our bread with the starving townspeople. No animal food for seven weeks. I kill horses in my stable secretly and send the meat to the hospital, which is now very crowded.[14]

Selim Pasha headed another Turkish army, which had landed at Trebizond on 22 October, and was nominally on its way to Kars. However, it had stalled at Erzerum, perhaps because there was very little love lost between these Pashas and Williams, who had spent the whole of the last year exposing their poor leadership, corruption and downright cowardice to his superiors (and indirectly therefore to the Sultan) in Constantinople.

While all this was going on Percy proceeded to Constantinople, in some trepidation that his resignation of the Italian Legion command would have damaged his reputation and precluded him from being asked to take on any further position of responsibility. He was therefore pleasantly surprised to find that Lord Stratford de Redcliffe considered his arrival on 27 November to be most opportune, believing that Percy was just the man to be a Pasha (General) in the Turkish army, and who could sort out the situation at Kars.

Pera Dec 14th

My dear Father,

Lord Stratford de Redcliffe proposed me to go to Erzerum to try to liberate General Williams by bullying the Pashas and forcing them to march, and at least menace Muravieff. I accepted at once. Whilst the necessary preparations were being made with the Government, the news came that Kars was to capitulate on the 25th November, 2 days before my arrival here. Lord S. deemed it therefore useless to send me – a grand opportunity *manqué*, and which if I had succeeded would probably have made me a Major General – a step I earnestly desire for my own reasons.

Lord S. some days after offered me General Williams' post – *viz.* British Commissioner [in Armenia]. After some deliberation, I refused. You must discriminate in these matters: the first was a purely military business, the second involved diplomacy *dont je me sens peu capable et pour laquelle je n'ai point de goût* – rather *dégoût* after my late taste and insight into the profession. I don't think I am fit to be tryster of vacillating, timid and <u>perhaps</u> bribed Pashas to inspire them with activity and courage. I have no doubt that the non-relief of Kars is owing to the French not having allowed any of the Turkish army to leave Eupatoria, where they are doing nothing. 10,000 men sent 6 weeks or two months ago must have forced Muravieff after the action of the 29th September at Kars to move off. The French don't wish to destroy the Russian influence in Georgia – *c'est notre affair*, not theirs, and Pélissier having got his baton of course won't risk anything, and probably is dying to return. All this had better not be repeated, but I am pretty certain of my premises. Lord S. seems to have done what he could, but you have no conception of the ridiculous state everything is in. The Generals of the army in the Crimea jealous of the Turkish Contingent, the Admirals jealous of the Army, each man abusing his neighbour, injustices at home, and nonsense everywhere.

Every military man says that I was quite right to resign the B.I.L.

under the circumstances, and I am quite satisfied with their opinion. I hope you are quite well. Give my love to Louisa and Lovaine. A merry Xmas to you all – I shall be in the Crimea by that time.

Your most affectionate son,
H. Percy

Lord Stratford privately admitted to Percy that the whole enterprise had probably been something of a forlorn hope, so it may have been a blessing in disguise that the expedition was called off before it got under way. When Williams surrendered, Muravieff treated him as a hero and allowed his men to bear arms as they marched out of Kars. He remained a prisoner of war for a brief period, and was repatriated the following spring.[15]

On 30 December 1855 Colonel Percy rejoined his regiment in the Crimea. Once again, he did not have to wait long before another interesting task was given to him. In January 1856 he was sent on a special mission by the Commander-in-Chief, now General Sir William Codrington, with directions for making himself acquainted with the proper places for landing an army in Asia Minor and to report on them and the several roads leading to the interior, as, in the event of the war continuing, it might be necessary to land allied troops in these parts to check any further progress of the Russian army from Georgia.[16] Ultimately, this involved visiting a series of places with unpronounceable names, which were scarcely marked on any map, but apart from meeting Omar Pasha (who 'talked indecorously of women and played with dogs. A well bred Turk never mentions the first, nor touches the second'), the job was entirely uneventful, and completed so quickly that he was back in the Crimea by the 31st of the same month. Codrington was pleased with the maps and sketches he produced, but in the event none of it was of any use, for the campaign never recommenced.

In the weeks and months after the fall of Sebastopol the occupying force busied itself with razing to the ground any edifice of military significance, including the enormous naval dry dock and the forts commanding the harbour's entrance, which were blown to smithereens. Apart from the odd shell lobbed by Russian artillery over the expanse of water from the north side of the bay and occasional skirmishes in open country, hostilities in the Crimea effectively ended, and the year of 1855 ended quietly.

191

Peace talks dragged on throughout the winter. London wanted to take a tough line in the negotiations and was prepared to prolong the war – to which end Britain continued to pour troops into the Crimea, making maximum use of the efficiencies they had learned from the disaster of the previous winter (including the Balaklava railway, new roads, huts, hospitals with improved sanitation, etc.). Paris, however, was keen to settle, not least because the French army was now itself experiencing a similar crisis to that which had afflicted its ally the previous year – and on a greater scale. In the winter of 1855–56 between thirty and forty thousand French troops died of disease in the Crimea and the Bosphorus, a figure which compares with British deaths in the same theatre, for the entire duration of the war, from battle or disease, of 21,000.*

The first five months of 1856, before the troops returned home, saw a more permanent return to that brief interlude of relaxation which had pervaded the camp at Balaklava in May 1855. There were drag-hunts and 'no end of Brigade theatres. I think the officers of the British Army have mistaken their profession, and are better as mimes than warriors.'[17] Amateur dramatics being the antithesis of Henry's idea of amusement, he preferred to fill his time riding about the fertile valleys of the Crimean countryside which had for so long been off-limits; among the places he visited were Alma and the Tartar capital of the Crimea, Bakshi Seräi. Unusually for a British officer, he spent the greater part of his spare time pursuing his linguistic studies in the Tartar villages and identifying the differences between their language and Turkish. These charming people seemed to reinforce his conviction that Moslem culture was much more refined than anything Orthodox, be it Russian or Greek. One day he and a companion had to stop at a Russian camp in order to change one of their horses' shoes. The soldiers there were very civil, and one officer ushered the two men into his den, where they found four others 'lolling on a bed with a *lady*, and the host said, "*permettez moi de vous présenter ma fille de joie.*" I was forced in and made half sick by the filth, fleas, stink and general beastliness of the place – not to mention the toying of

* The Grenadier Guards lost 150 killed by enemy action and 750 from disease – the vast majority of these from the 1,678 who arrived in the Crimea before 31st December 1854. A total of 2,458 Grenadiers landed in the East from first to last.

these gentlemen with the aforesaid lady.' He recorded another time, too, when General Lord Rokeby and two of his staff were completely served up as they visited a Russian general at an outpost. They were physically torn from their horses and carried aloft on a chair, to cheers of 'Queen Victoria!'

Fraternization between the two sides became more common from the official armistice on 1 March, though relations were necessarily guarded while peace talks were still going on. The British camp was divided on its view of the negotiations and Percy, along with most of the new arrivals who had yet to see action, was firmly in Lord Stratford's camp: the war should be brought to a decisive conclusion. Every time he thought about the proposed Peace, his mind flashed back to Inkerman and the Russian treatment of his wounded comrades.

It is understandable that the scars of Inkerman, the extended suffering of that first winter and the awful finale at the Great Redan might have instilled a desire in some people for Russia's unconditional surrender. However, while the British army, refreshed and re-equipped, was well prepared to continue the war, the other participants had reached the limits of their endurance. Since hostilities had first broken out between the Ottoman Empire and Russia back in October 1853 in excess of half a million men had lost their lives, four out of five from disease, and the vast majority Russian; 95,000 Frenchmen had died, along with over 40,000 Turks, making British and Sardinian losses, at 22,000 and 2,000 respectively, a small proportion of the total.[18] The diplomats at the Paris peace conference were therefore determined to reach a settlement, even if it did not resolve the fundamental issues of the Eastern Question – namely the continued decline of the 'sick man of Europe' and the future of the Balkan nationalities.

Russia's acquiescence was hastened by Austria's threat to join the allies: if she would agree to the freedom of the Danubian principalities, free passage for international shipping on the River Danube, and to the Black Sea becoming a neutral zone, the Russians could keep Sebastopol, and the Tsar his dignity. The wider conflict, that at times during 1855 had seemed destined to bring central Europe and America into the war, was averted for two generations, and the Treaty of Paris was ratified on 27 April 1856.

Epilogue

On 24 February 1857 the names of 85 soldiers, sailors and Royal Marines appeared in *The London Gazette* as having been awarded the Victoria Cross. Among these names were the following citations:

Brevet-Major Sir Charles Russell, Bart., Grenadier Guards
>Offered to dislodge a party of Russians from the Sand-bag battery, if any one would follow him. Sergeant Norman, Privates Anthony Palmer, and Bailey (who was killed) volunteered the first. The attack proceeded.

Private Anthony Palmer, Grenadier Guards
>Present when the charge was made in defence of the Colours, – and also charged singly upon the enemy, as witnessed by Sir Charles Russell – said to have saved Sir C. Russell's life.

Sergeant Alfred Ablett, Grenadier Guards
>On the 2nd September 1855, seeing a shell fall in the centre of a number of ammunition cases and Powder, he instantly seized it and threw it outside the trench; it burst as it touched the ground.[1]

Others on the list included Brevet Major Robert Lindsay, Scots Fusilier Guards, who had defended the colours at Alma, and Brevet Major Gerald Goodlake, Coldstream Guards, whose sharp-shooters had so distinguished themselves at Inkerman. There was, however, according to one correspondent 'a universal expression of surprise' at there being no mention of Colonel Henry Percy on

194

the list of recipients. Names were in fact still being put forward under a selection process that was being coordinated by HRH the Duke of Cambridge, who had succeeded Lord Hardinge at Horse Guards: applicants for the new Order were invited to submit their claims directly, and regiments were also instructed to conduct their own selection process, submitting any suitable candidates to a committee composed of the Duke himself, General Sir James Simpson, Major General Lord Rokeby and Colonel the Hon W.L. Pakenham. In his letter of 2 February to Lord Panmure, Secretary of State for War, the Duke spoke of 'very numerous applications', warned him that the first list was by no means comprehensive and that he should expect further names to be recommended for the Victoria Cross in due course. This could, he said, take some months, as a number of regiments were serving abroad, and had therefore been unable to submit names to the committee.[2] Ultimately, it would take more than a year for the process to be finished, and the February list was only the first of several batches which eventually made up a total complement of 111 Crimean VCs.

It had been Queen Victoria's own idea to institute a new order with which ordinary soldiers in the field could be rewarded. There was a widespread belief that the campaign medal for the Crimean War had been awarded far too liberally. William Russell reported in *The Times* in December 1855 that 16,000 clasps for Inkerman had been issued, when only 8,000 men were on the field. He claimed that people were rushing up to the Crimea from Constantinople solely in order to get the campaign medal. In his discussion of the 'Order of Merit of Victoria' that he understood the Queen was trying to institute, Russell suggested that each one should have engraved on it the number of bombardments the recipient had suffered. He knew a man who had endured over a hundred![3]

At that time there was no satisfactory way of honouring an officer's bravery and devotion to duty other than promotion in the field, being mentioned in the Commander-in-Chief's field despatch or receiving the Order of the Bath. The chances of a regimental officer being mentioned in an official despatch were very slim – as shown after Inkerman. Equally, as Prince Albert, who was closely involved with both the design of the Victoria Cross and the terms of its bestowal, observed in a memorandum dated 22 January 1855, the Order of the Bath was not available to anyone below the rank of Major. The position regarding non-commissioned officers and ordinary soldiers was also unsatisfactory: although they were eligible for a variety of good conduct medals and annuities, these were awarded on a limited basis, and not necessarily for gallantry in the field. Prince Albert pointed out that, in a disaster like the Charge of the Light Brigade, the troops, in receiving no adulation for their immense bravery on that occasion, had effectively been punished for the mistakes of their commanders. He went on to say:

It is now proposed to establish a 3rd mode of reward, neither reserved for the few nor bestowed upon all, which is to *distinguish on a liberal scale individual merit in the Officers of the Lower Ranks, in Sergeants and in Privates.*

I admit fully the want of such a reward, but it must practically have great difficulties as renouncing either of the above principles. How is a distinction to be made, for instance, between the individual services of the 200 survivors of Lord Cardigan's Charge? If you reward them all it becomes merely a Medal for Balaklava, to which the Heavy Brigade and the 93rd have equal claims.

The only mode I see, in which the difficulty could be overcome seems to me to be something like the following:-

1. That a small cross of Merit for *personal deeds of valour* be established.
2. That it be open to all ranks.
3. That it be unlimited in number.
4. That an annuity (say £5) be attached to each cross.
5. That it be *claimable* by an individual on establishing before a jury of his peers, subject to confirmation at home, his right to the distinction.
6. That in cases of general actions it be given in certain quantities to particular Regiments, so many to the Officers, so many to the sergeants, so many to the men (of the last say 1 per company) and that their distribution be left to a jury of the same rank as the person to be rewarded. By this means alone you could ensure the perfect fairness of distribution and save the Officers in command from the invidious task of making a selection from those under their orders, which they now shrink from in the case of the Bath. – The limitation of the Numbers

to be given to a Regmt at one time enforces the *necessity* of a selection and diminishes the pain of those that cannot be included.[4]

After a year's deliberation on the subject, the Warrant Instituting the Victoria Cross was signed by Queen Victoria on 29 January 1856. The terms broadly reflected Prince Albert's original outline, although the annuity was set at £10 a year, and would only be paid to non-commissioned officers, privates etc.

It seems that some time after the first list was published in *The London Gazette*, Henry Percy was persuaded to write to Colonel Wood at Horse Guards, enquiring of his eligibility for the new order, for Wood explained in a letter to him dated 17 April that he had been accidentally left out of the original list of those gazetted on 24 February owing to a bureaucratic muddle, and that he had long since remedied this omission. He closed with the words: 'You are undoubtedly due a Victoria Cross.'

The process of adding Percy's name was already well under way and, as it happened, the day after Wood wrote to Percy, the Duke of Cambridge sent the details of the next four recipients, including Percy, to Lord Panmure: 'I now transmit a further list of officers named in the margin, together with a statement of their services, whose claims to the Victoria Cross have in my opinion been established in each case agreeably to the requirements of the Royal Warrant, and I am therefore desirous, in the event of your Lordship's concurrence, that the names of these officers should be submitted for Her Majesty's approval with the view to their being granted the high distinction for which they are recommended.' Interestingly, Panmure didn't just rubber stamp it all before sending it on to the Queen for her final approval. He made comments on three of the recommendations, and removed the first paragraph of Percy's proposed citation[5] – a mention of the fact that he had continued fighting after being wounded at Alma and insisted on remaining with his Regiment for some days afterwards. Lord Panmure correctly considered this to have no bearing on Percy's claim to the VC, given the terms of the Warrant governing its issue.

Within a few days, the Queen approved the supplementary list and the four names were gazetted on 7 May 1857. Colonel the Hon H. Percy's citation read as follows:

> At a moment when the Guards were some distance from the Sandbag Battery at the battle of Inkerman Colonel Percy charged singly into the Battery, followed immediately by the Guards; the embrasures of the battery, as also the parapet, were held by the Russians who kept up a most severe fire of musketry.
>
> At the battle of Inkerman Colonel Percy found himself with many men of various regiments who had charged too far, nearly surrounded by the Russians, and without ammunition. Colonel Percy, by his knowledge of the ground, though wounded, extricated these men, and, passing under a heavy fire from the Russians then in the Sandbag Battery, brought them safe to where ammunition was to be obtained, thereby saving some 50 men and enabling them to renew the combat. He received the approval of His Royal Highness the Duke of Cambridge for this action on the spot. Colonel Percy was engaged with, and put *hors de combat,* a Russian soldier.[6]

As the Victoria Cross has evolved over the years, it has on average become less 'easy' to win, though it would be both fruitless and unfair to compare individual cases with hindsight, particularly given the changed nature of combat operations since those days. However, one should remember that there are now numerous ways of rewarding men for distinguished service or valour in the field, whereas in 1857 there was no such thing as the Distinguished Service Order (DSO) or the Military Cross (MC) etc. Some who were awarded the VC for their services in the Crimean War would today have only merited one of these lesser orders. One must spare a thought, however, for all those who were killed in their act of gallantry, for the Victoria Cross was not awarded posthumously until 1906* – although interestingly, Colonel Hood, who was killed in the trenches in 1854, had his name appear in *The London Gazette* the following year as one of the officers who would have received the Order of the Bath for his conduct at the Alma had he lived.[7]

While it may now be more 'difficult' to win the Victoria Cross

---

* It was retrospectively awarded to Lieutenants Melville and Coghill, who had saved the colours at Isandhlwana during the Zulu War of 1879, as well as several who had fallen in the Indian Mutiny and the Boer War.

than it was in the time of the Crimean War, this has not been a smooth progression. The selection process in 1856–7 was probably a great deal more rigorous and comprehensive than it was for a number of later campaigns, and as such its outcome represents the nature of what the VC was originally intended to be all about – something that, in theory, could realistically be earned by any serviceman, and which would thereby encourage acts of valour in pursuit of an award. As Queen Victoria put it in the terms of the Warrant: 'We are desirous [that it] should be highly prized and eagerly sought after by the Officers and Men of our Naval and Military Services.'[8] Later in the nineteenth century, however, there were occasions when VCs seem to have been awarded rather more liberally than was originally intended. The Indian Mutiny of 1857 gave rise to 182 VCs – one more than in the whole of the Second World War; some of these were apparently handed out on a discretionary basis by local commanders.[9] As the century progressed, minor colonial conflicts would see a surprising number of VCs being awarded. In contrast, the vast majority today are awarded posthumously, other medals and decorations being available to those who live.

Methodical though the selection process was in 1856–57, there are inevitably some inconsistencies, despite the Duke of Cambridge's committee and Panmure between them doing their very best to be fair. One name that it is perhaps surprising did not make the grade is that of Captain Edwyn Burnaby. He was a modest and unassuming man, who appeared to be somewhat unambitious, though like all his contemporaries he was not afraid to apply for promotions and staff appointments.[10] Without seeing the complete minutes of all the meetings which considered who should be awarded the Victoria Cross, it is impossible to know why he was rejected, if indeed he was considered (which he surely must have been) by his peers. His most notable act of bravery, when he and just 18 men delayed a large Russian column and prevented them from overrunning the Grenadiers' colours, was probably not, by its very nature (because he was surrounded by the enemy), actually witnessed by another officer; Burnaby may also have been disadvantaged by the fact that, at the time names were being put forward for recommendation to the VC, he was still serving on a Staff employment abroad (though he was by no means 'out of the

199

loop' in this respect, for, like the other officers present at Inkerman, he was asked by Colonel Wood for his views on which officers should be put forward for a VC Recommendation).* His pamphlet, *An Account of the Right Flank Company of the 3rd Battalion of the Grenadier Guards defending the Right of the British Position and subsequently the Colours of the Battalion, when Surrounded by the Enemy at the Battle of Inkerman, 5th November 1854,* which contained statements from eight surviving privates and one sergeant, was not drawn up and privately printed until late 1857. Notwithstanding the fact that, for whatever reason, he may have been overlooked for his lone rearguard action, Burnaby had still performed another more public deed in the same place, at practically the same time, and in an almost identical manner as the one which earned Sir Charles Russell his VC.

Early on the morning of Friday 26 June 1857, a huge parade of nearly 9,000 men from all branches of the services gathered in Hyde Park. Thousands of spectators also assembled and on the side nearest to Grosvenor gate, 'galleries were erected for the accommodation of 7,000 persons, who by a pleasing fiction were denominated the public, though, of course, the distribution of the tickets which admitted to the enclosure was as exclusive as a presentation at Court.'[11] The ground outside the enclosed space was left open to anybody who wished to come and look – and look they did, a great crowd, in places thirty or forty deep. The occasion was the first investiture of the Victoria Cross, at which the Sovereign in person would bestow the medal on each of the sixty-two recipients present.†

---

* Wood wrote to all of those officers who were present at the saving of the colours at Inkerman, saying that, in his opinion, the thirteenth rule in the Queen's Warrant governing the award of VCs (namely that, in a situation such as this, members of a company could select from among their number one officer and/or three other ranks to receive the VC) would enable him to recommend up to three of those officers for the award. In the end, perhaps because the answers he received were so diverse (e.g. Burnaby recommended Higginson and Fergusson said that, with one exception, they all behaved brilliantly), none of them were decorated. Russell and Percy, neither of whom were present when the colours were surrounded, were singled out for individual acts of gallantry.
† Although eighty-nine men had thus far been gazetted VCs, a number were unable to attend the first investiture, for example because they were serving abroad.

The privileged visitors, including Lord and Lady Palmerston, arrived in their carriages from around 7.30 am, while for some hours the West End was in a state of high bustle, with officers on their chargers galloping in haste to their appointed places.[12] The sky was completely cloudless, and *The Times* reported that:

> The heat throughout the entire proceedings was intense; the ladies seemed to suffer much from it, and even strong hearty gentlemen were not too fastidious to extemporise rude fans from coat-tails, handkerchiefs and morning journals, or any suitable material at hand. Not a breath of air seemed stirring, and the standard which marked the Queen's position drooped heavily down, as if it too suffered from the sun and was incapable of fluttering or active motion. Everybody simmered into a state of aggravation, and everybody gasped and said how hot it was, in a tone of private communication, as if the temperature was a State secret which must not be bruited abroad. In less tropical nooks, beneath the trees, costermongers drove a brave trade in the retail of liquids from portly-looking barrels, which we fancy must have contained something better than water, as policemen formed the staple of their customers.[13]

A few minutes before 10 o'clock the recipients arrived, marching in single file towards the Queen's allotted position in front of the handsome dais beneath which the medals were arranged. This small band of heroes created a sensation in the crowd who had come to witness their moment of glory. The enormity of the occasion dwarfed them, and their mixed attire contrasted with the splendid display of regiments before them. Among them were Guardsmen, infantrymen from the Line, members of the Light and Heavy Cavalry Brigades and the Rifle Brigade, as well as Artillerymen and Engineers, together with representatives from the Royal Navy and the Royal Marines. One man was now a policeman, another a park-keeper – the latter formerly a corporal of the 23rd, who had volunteered on 8 September 1855 to go out, under a murderous fire, to the front after the attack on the Redan, and carry in a Lieutenant, mortally wounded; both now civilians, and dressed accordingly. Three or four others were in private clothes, having quitted the ranks. As they waited for the Sovereign to appear before them, officers stood beside privates and able seamen, without regard for rank – Sir Charles Russell next to Private Ablett and one away from

201

Private Palmer, who had saved his life. They were commanded by the senior officer among them – Colonel the Hon Henry Hugh Manvers Percy. Acting as his adjutant for this occasion was one of the bravest of them all, one John Knox, commissioned from the ranks, who in the failed attack of 18 June had continued to advance on the Redan until his left arm was first broken by a bullet and then all but torn off by grapeshot.[14]

The Queen's cortège, including Prince Albert and the Duke of Cambridge, arrived a few moments after the recipients had found their station by the dais in front of the grandstand, overlooked by the troops on parade. As the Royal party approached this enormous line of continuous columns – a serried mass of bayonets, rows of glittering helmets and gleaming cuirasses flashing and sparkling in the rays of the sun – there was a dull heavy rattle as the whole force presented arms, the bands simultaneously striking up the National Anthem. The Queen wore a dark blue skirt and scarlet riding coat, with a gold sash, and Prince Albert was dressed in the uniform of Field Marshal. They rode slowly all along the front ranks of the whole long line, and then returned to the centre of the gallery, to where the recipients were patiently awaiting their own pivotal moment in the proceedings.

It was intended that the Queen should dismount from her charger and stand beside the small table beneath the dais on which the bronze crosses were arranged, but in the event, she preferred to remain mounted, stooping down each time as Lord Panmure handed her the medals in turn. Robert Lindsay's mother had secured a spot right behind the Queen:

> There were thousands and tens of thousands of spectators, but except a lucky few, among whom we were, everyone had to stand on the most uncomfortable sloping platforms, their toes lower than their heels, under a burning sun. The excitement to get tickets was furious. The sight was as beautiful as a sight could be. The Queen looked pretty and rode well, and smiled as she attached the Cross to the little loop made to receive it. She said a few words to Bob but he could not make out what they were.[15]

The actual ceremony scarcely lasted ten minutes. It was so short, in fact, that the crowd hardly realized it had begun. The recipients, on whose breasts were just visible that new mark of such honourable distinction, filed back sufficiently far in front of the Queen to allow the whole assembled force to march past twice between them and their Sovereign. The drill was impeccable, the Guards setting the standard for all. Nearly all regiments had a mascot. The Grenadiers had a noble-looking Newfoundland; another regiment also had one, who sat waiting patiently for his masters to complete their operation, before falling precisely in line with his allotted position in the march past. The Rifles were attended by their Crimean ram, who had apparently been bleached for the occasion, and who caused considerable amusement in his attempt to keep pace with the quick march of his regiment.[16]

When all was over, the course taken by the recipients as they dispersed across the park could be traced by scattered throngs of spectators following each one; everyone was anxious to get a glimpse of the Cross, which was made by Hancock's from metal taken from guns captured at Sebastopol, and hung beneath a crimson riband for the Army, or a blue one for the Navy, with the reverse being engraved with the name of the recipient, the relevant action and its date. *The Times* was surprised that such a high honour could look so drab: 'all found more or less fault at the very first . . . . [It was] poor looking and mean in the extreme.'

Such is the picture of that glorious occasion as it was presented by reports in *The Times* and *The Illustrated London News*. Henry Percy, however, left some notes suggesting a fair degree of chaos beneath the veneer of careful choreography. On his arrival in Hyde Park, in the knowledge that he was responsible for the party of men receiving the Cross, he reported to General Sir Colin Campbell, commanding the parade. Campbell, in his thick Scots accent said, 'Paircy [*sic*], you are the senior. Take charge of the recipients. I leave all to you. I don't know anything about parades, and you do.' As he turned away, the Colonel couldn't help muttering under his breath, 'Old Humbug has been at plenty at Dublin'. Unfortunately, it wasn't that easy for him to marshal the recipients to their allotted place in front of the stand, as the 'fussiness of Horse Guards' had prevented him being mounted, and he really needed a horse on such an enormous parade ground, with so many people getting in the way. He was particularly irritated, as he had a right to be mounted, being Queen's ADC. The net result was that he had to run about all over the place, in full dress, including sword and bearskin; it would have been hot work, even on a cold day. Sir Colin Campbell 'was evidently not of temper' at all, and kept well out of the way all this time.

The newspaper reporters may have thought the dress of the recipients was somewhat disorganized, but what they didn't know was that the festivity of the occasion, combined with the unusual heat, had fuelled a number of the men's drinking habits – even at that early hour. Just before they filed past the Queen, a Quartermaster from the ranks enquired of Percy: 'Colonel, for the love of Heaven, where could I get a drop of gin? For I am dying with thirst.' He wasn't the only one in need of refreshment. One private of the Royal Engineers was so drunk, he recalled, that ordinarily he would have sent him off in disgrace; this time, however, he simply 'blew him up and gave him in charge to a stout dragoon and infantry soldier – with orders not to leave sight of him, and suppress by quiet strength any undue effervescence.' Just as he was beginning to get this motley crew into some sort of order, the Chief Policeman started to interfere, as did the Royal Grooms and, worst of all, the Press reporters stuck their noses in. He made short work of them all, quelling the reporters by threatening to have the police at them!

The drunken Royal Engineer, meanwhile, was becoming decidedly fractious and declared he would rather be damned than have the VC, and kept out in the sun. Somehow, however, the two stout soldiers that had been entrusted to look after him managed to keep him on the straight and narrow and, in the event, they all survived the ceremony without mischief.

When the march past was finished, there was a mad rush on the part of the eminent personages to a reception at Buckingham Palace – among them Sir Colin Campbell, who simply disappeared from the parade he was commanding, without giving any orders at all to Percy. Nothing by way of refreshment or invitation was offered to the VCs and Henry had no idea what to do with them. So, while the rest of the recipients were receiving congratulations from their friends and lovers, he borrowed a horse from a senior officer and galloped off after the Staff to get an idea of what he was supposed to do with his charges; by this stage it was very difficult to get past the crowd, though he noted they were 'very gracious, and cheering'. When eventually he did catch up with someone who was supposed to know what the orders were, he was simply told to send the VCs back to their barracks.

In short, there was a regular stampede, led by 'the jealous, prejudiced, indignant old Scotchman Sir Colin Campbell, who did not want to leave a chance of <u>his</u> luncheon with royalty', and the 62 officers and men for whose benefit the whole day had been organized were completely ignored. It seems extraordinary that they weren't given something at Buckingham Palace, or even a lunch at Horse Guards.

Interestingly, none of the newspapers, in their exhaustive accounts containing every detail, mentioned Henry Percy's role on that day. He concluded that he had been spited because of his heavy-handed treatment of the reporters.

Henry's subsequent career must have seemed to him rather frustrating. He spent the next four years with his Regiment on various duties at home and in Ireland, commanding a Battalion from 1860. As the author of a book on drill and tactics, which General Hamilton wrote in his *History of the Grenadier Guards* 'was so favourably thought of that every officer of the Regiment was ordered to be supplied with a copy', he was placed in charge of the Prince of Wales when he joined the Regiment at the Curragh. Ever the wanderer, though, his heart hankered after further adventure abroad, and on successive occasions he applied to the War Office for postings in various parts of the world, from Western Europe to the East Indies. Unfortunately, these were in most cases situations of his own invention and the standard response usually was that the Government had no current intention of sending an observer to the Spanish Army fighting in Morocco, or of despatching any force to Persia, etc., etc.

His opportunity came in December 1861, as civil war broke out in the United States of America, when he was sent out to Canada in command of the 1st Battalion Grenadier Guards as part of an expeditionary force needed to support the existing garrison there in the event that the conflict would escalate beyond the borders of the United States. On their embarkation, the veterans of the Crimea among them had an uncomfortable feeling of *déjà vu*. The ship in which they crossed the Atlantic was totally unsuited for the conveyance of troops; Higginson, who had been asked by the Colonel to inspect the transport arrangements at Southampton, wrote:

> Little seemed to have been learnt since our Crimean days, except a desire to show activity and zeal on the part of each department. The representatives of the Admiralty, Woolwich Arsenal and the Commissariat vied with each other in activity and punctuality, but each worked independently of the others. When a consignment from one department arrived, the hour of its receipt was recorded in a departmental book, and then off went the official, his responsibility being at an end. Consequently, furs and blankets required during the voyage had to be extracted from under shot and shell; fresh provisions were carefully deposited, only to be covered up by stores which would not be required till long after the troops had disembarked. I could only look on, having no authority to remonstrate. Up to the very last moment before the arrival of the troops, the carpenters had not completed the arm-racks, and heaps of shavings, which it was nobody's business to collect, lay around the ''tween decks', inviting the most dreaded enemy on board ship – fire. I explained the state of affairs as best I could to Colonel Percy when the battalion arrived to embark; when I rejoined him later at Montreal, he told me that the ship had twice been on fire, and that the fresh meat was in such a condition that the men only had it twice during a voyage of nearly three weeks' duration.[17]

On arrival in New Brunswick, any realistic prospect that there might have been of seeing action soon faded, but they nonetheless all endured a harsh winter with equanimity. However, six months of snow and temperatures down to 40 degrees below zero[18] rapidly took their toll on Henry's health. The arm that had been shot through at the Alma was permanently rheumatic and on some days he could barely move at all, his joints were so seized up. In fact, though he was only forty-four, his constitution had never fully recovered after the Crimean fever from which he had nearly died seven years before.

He had a further, equally pressing, problem. The rank of full colonel represented a crisis point in an army officer's career. The vagaries of the Purchase System meant that it was the last rank from which an officer could sell his commission. In other words a colonel still had the option of retiring with the all capital he had invested still intact, investing the sale proceeds and living off the income; if, on the other hand, if he decided to stay in the army and become a Major General, he would wave goodbye to a lifetime's accumulated capital and therefore effectively be financially bound to the army for the rest of his working life. Ironically, one of the worst things that could happen to a colonel who was contemplating retirement was to be 'caught in a brevet' and unexpectedly receive early promotion to Major General.[19]

Either way, Colonel Percy faced a huge decision: retire at the age of forty-five from the career he had always lived for, or soldier on in the face of increased competition, plagued by ill-health and with no possibility of selling out again. There was, however, one possible and much sought after compromise, namely to retire on half-pay. This was the mechanism by which an officer who had purchased his commission could retire from active service, but receive a basic annuity from the government if he consented to be still available for service in the future. He would 'receive the difference' through a partial sale of his commission, most probably to officers below him in his own regiment, some of whom would be prepared to pay varying sums to the colonel on the basis that his retirement would free up their own promotion prospects. The beauty of it also was that a part time officer on half pay would continue to receive promotions by seniority, while at the same time being able to invest that portion of his capital which was released in an annuity to supplement his income.

In March 1862, after something of a mid-life crisis, Percy finally applied from Canada to the War Office for permission to retire on half-pay. 'If I defer it too long, I shall find myself caught in some trap from which there will be no release . . . and I shall die if I remain a soldier . . . . It is better to be free and poor than poor and fettered.' As he agonized all summer as to whether his application would be accepted, the surgeon-major told him that, whatever the outcome, he must return to England before the next winter for the sake of his health. In the event, his wish was granted later that year.

In spite of the rather anticlimactic end to his regimental duties, Henry's time in Canada was a success. His letters home during this period reflect none of the 'croaking' that had been such a feature of the Crimea and, in contrast to that earlier campaign, he got on extremely well with his superior, Sir Fenwick Williams (who had been the hero of the siege of Kars, and whose relief, ironically, Percy had been co-opted to organize back in 1855). Sir Fenwick was 'wonderfully good' and very understanding about his application to go on half-pay. Some of Percy's views, though, would never change: 'I will not be pooh-poohed by staff officers, however brilliant they may be.'

The Colonel left the Regiment with an enormous sense of pride at the way the men had conducted themselves, in spite of so many hardships, interspersed as they were by long periods of boredom and every conceivable temptation. That autumn he issued the following address in his last battalion orders:

> Colonel Percy cannot resign the command of the First Battalion Grenadier Guards without expressing his sense of the efficient and hearty support he has received from the Officers and Non-Commissioned Officers of the Battalion, and of the excellent and soldier-like conduct of the men, which is well known and thoroughly appreciated by the authorities at home in Canada. He feels that had it been the destiny of the Battalion to be employed against an enemy, that its conduct would have been as distinguished in war as it has been in peace. It is with deep regret, though modified by the knowledge that promotion would at no distant period have caused his retirement, that Colonel Percy leaves the Battalion, in whose welfare and honour he will always feel the deepest interest, and to have commanded which will always be a source of pride to him.[20]

In 1865, his eighty-seventh year, Lord Beverley became 5th Duke of Northumberland on the death of his cousin. In the same year, Major General Lord Henry Percy (as he now was) stood for Parliament and was duly elected as Conservative MP for North Northumberland, the seat vacated by Lovaine. But though he spoke occasionally on army matters, Henry was no political animal and soon came to detest the in-fighting of the House of Commons; he also felt that Parliament was incompatible with staff duties and was disappointed that, because of this, he had reluctantly to give up the command of a Brigade at Aldershot, the place to which, back in 1853, he had first brought the army. He did not stand again in the general election of 1868 and the seat went to his nephew,

Earl Percy, for Lovaine had gone to the House of Lords when he became 6th Duke of Northumberland in 1867.

Although the Purchase System was abolished in 1871 under the Cardwell reforms, Percy remained on half-pay, becoming Colonel of the 89th (The Princess Victoria's) Regiment of Foot* in 1874. His continued involvement with the army included being sent out by the Duke of Cambridge as an observer with the Prussian army at Sedan during the Franco-Prussian war, and he eventually attained the rank of full General in 1877 under the new Army Scheme.

But just two months after he had reached this pinnacle of his ambition, the following announcement appeared in the newspapers:

> We have to announce the death of General Lord Henry Hugh Manvers Percy, brother of the Duke of Northumberland, who was found dead in his bed at four o'clock on Monday afternoon at his residence in Eaton Square. His lordship had been out for his usual carriage drive in the morning, and after luncheon retired to his bedroom, as was his custom. Not making his appearance in the drawing-room, his personal servant, on knocking and entering the room, found his lordship on the bed apparently asleep, and on attempting to disturb him found him dead. Medical aid was immediately obtained, when it was supposed he had been dead about an hour. Lord Henry had long been a great sufferer from neuralgia. Death resulted, we are informed, from angina pectoris.[21]

At first it was thought probable that he would have a full military funeral, but owing to the Duke's aversion to pomp and ceremony, it was decided that the service should be as unostentatious and private as possible. It was, however, held in the grand surroundings of Westminster Abbey, where the Percy family have a vault. Among the mourners were companions in arms from the Crimea, including Colonel Burnaby, now commanding the Grenadiers, and Major General Brownrigg. But Lord Henry's friends were by no means all officers: also present, long since discharged from the army, but once again conspicuous by the medals on his breast, was

---

* This regiment was subsumed into the Royal Irish Fusiliers in 1881 and is now part of the Royal Irish Regiment.

James Bancroft, the private soldier whose long record of imprisonment and docked pay has to be seen to be believed, but who during the Battle of Inkerman had single-handedly accounted for nine Russians (in between spitting out his teeth); another very old soldier had served under the deceased as far back as 1838, when they were in Canada together. The coffin was covered with a silk Union Jack and was preceded down the aisle by old soldiers of the Grenadier Guards in double file. On the pall were the General's cocked hat, his sword and sash, together with the decorations of the Order of the Bath and the Victoria Cross.[22]

Appendix I:

Postscript on the British Italian Legion

Percy's exasperation with the Italian Legion had a number of causes, some of which are touched upon in the chapter dealing with that period. His biggest bugbear, and the main cause of his breakdown in relations with the British Minister in Turin, Sir James Hudson, was that every communication with the Sardinian Government, either way, had to go through the Foreign Office's man as intermediary, despite the fact that Percy, fluent in Italian, was Brigadier General in command, and directly answerable to the War Office. For example, when supplies were needed, Hudson presented a list, as specified by Percy, to the Sardinian Ministry of War, which in turn asked its suppliers to furnish the necessary equipment. Any small error or mistake in the specification entailed a lengthy paper chain backwards and forwards.[1] Percy detailed some examples in a memo he wrote in 1856: 'In one instance some material for making Staff Sergeants' coats was not itemized in the statements, and so everything was kept back for a week. Another time, the Quartermaster General of the Legion was kept for 12 hours a day for 7 days at the Custom House by the vexatious conduct of the employees, who doubtless had received orders to be as strict as possible.' The whole system was a recipe for inefficiency and profligacy, but on every occasion, 'the Italian money-mongers were backed up by Sir James Hudson, from his slavery to Cavour.'

Percy's departure from the Italian Legion coincided with the resolution of one important problem, namely the release of the barracks at Novara, without which obviously recruiting could not properly get under way. The timeliness of Lieutenant Colonel Read's arrival had the unfortunate effect of making it look as though Percy himself had been a hindrance to the Legion's success. Ironically, it was his vociferous complaints to the War Office which prompted Lord Panmure, who was acutely aware of the need for more troops for the Crimea, to insist on a number of changes to the administration of the Italian Legion. The Sardinian Government was pressured into removing much of the red tape that had restrained the recruiting process, and progress was made on a number of other measures that had first been advocated by Percy, such as dispensing with unnecessarily severe punishments (e.g. flogging) in order to stem the rate of desertion, and employing British officers on the recruiting committee (there being very few good Italian officers who wanted to serve as mercenaries on their own country's soil).

According to one London newspaper, 'the soul of the whole recruitment is Major Burnaby, of the Guards, a young officer of great ability, and particularly remarkable for his administrative powers. He occupies the post of Assistant-Quartermaster-General, and by his perfect knowledge of the language and conciliatory manner has been of the greatest possible utility in forming the Legion.'[2] Unlike Percy, who was a lot more cool-headed when under fire in the field than he was sitting behind a desk, Burnaby initially seemed to be relatively relaxed about the continuing challenges, although he did have the added motivation of at last seeing some of their labours bear fruit. By early December 900 men had been signed up:

12th Dec 1855
Turin

My dear Percy,

I am most anxious to hear from you, and to know you are safely arrived in the Crimea. I think of you very often indeed, and so do your old friends. I sometimes call on Mrs Fonblanque, who always talks much about you, and we wonder what you are about. The cold frosty weather has fairly set in, but the days are sunny and warm . . . .

I have not much to tell you about the Legion since I last wrote to you. Lindsay* arrived and was appointed Major Commandant, much to his disgust, as on leaving England he had been led to expect

---

* Sir Coutts Lindsay, Bart, was Robert Lindsay's brother. He had retired as a Captain of the Grenadier Guards in 1850.

he would be Lt. Col. [Burnaby then bemoans the fact that Panmure wouldn't promote him to the local rank of Lieutenant Colonel, on the grounds that he could only go up one step at a time.] The daily routine is carried out with a certain degree of regularity (from you having laid it down), but there is much more required, and irregularities are constantly arising which frequently are allowed to continue, and nothing can be so detrimental to a system or organisation. Pinelli too soon felt he had lost you, and minds Lindsay's appointment. He is at Novara with 750 men – the remaining 250 go tomorrow, so the first regiment is complete as regards men. [We are all finding it very difficult to work under Lindsay]. The recruiting is going on at the rate of 20–30 men a day . . . .

Can I send you anything from here? Only tell me what you would like – I could put anything in a box and send it by a steamer with the troops. My family leave for Rome in a few days.

Believe me my dear Percy yours most sincerely,

E. Burnaby

Read exercised a firm hand, and successfully enrolled a good number of men, such that the Legion's strength amounted to nearly 2,000 by 19 January 1856. However, because a blind eye was being turned to the origin of these men, many of them were deserting conscripts from the Austrian imperial army in Lombardy, the very undesirables whom both the British and Sardinian Governments had sought to avoid. As a strict disciplinarian, Read was unpopular with men and officers alike; desertion from the Legion naturally increased and Read had a number of offenders shot.[3] There was a near-mutiny at Novara, with the malcontents openly declaring that they would desert if the Legion was posted to the Crimea.[4] In time the Sardinian Government became more uncomfortable about the implications of having British-paid troops on their soil, many of them agitators at that, and in the new year Cavour insisted that the entire force be moved to Malta.

In spite of all these problems, and the effective end of the Crimean War, there was no let up in the recruiting process. On 12 March Burnaby again wrote to Percy:

Old Read is a greater fool than ever and perfectly ignorant of the simplest military principles. Coutts Lindsay is worse and wants to have his own way. Sir James Hudson is worse than ever. I shall perhaps meet you soon when I shall give you an account of the shameful way we have been treated. The Novara barracks have I

213

fear cost more than I anticipated . . . . I have worked very hard, getting up at 6 and not finishing until dark. My great annoyance is I have no one to look up to. Can you do anything towards getting us a Brigadier? . . . We have orders to get 6,000 men in all, and are now sending estimates for raising cavalry. After Read, I am the senior officer, as Lord Panmure gave me my step of local rank to date from my Brevet Majority. Can I get you anything you wish for?

Burnaby unexpectedly got command of the whole Brigade (now amounting to three regiments of 1,000 men each) in Malta. He was not sorry to leave Read, who 'sat in his chair consuming 3 times his share of wood, and succeeded in writing one letter a day after having made many rough copies'. But the Legion's time in Malta was not a success, with ill discipline being such a problem that it verged on anarchy. Petty thievery, revolutionary songs and not a few fights seemed to be the order of the day. There was an attempt by a hundred recruits to release one of their number from the Palais de Justice, where he was being held under arrest. During the commotion, a police inspector, Vincenzo Caruana, was killed and there was a conspiracy of silence as to who was the culprit. Burnaby confined them to barracks and drew the whole regiment up on parade, demanding to know who was responsible, but he got nowhere. Then, on 8 May a number of legionaries clashed with the civilian population and, in order to prevent wholesale mutiny, the men were deprived of their ammunition and a British battle-ship was called in to train her guns on their quarters. The murderer of Caruana was never revealed, and the luckless Burnaby was relieved of his command.[5]

Colonel Read came out from Turin to replace Burnaby and tried to placate the islanders, but he too was fighting a losing battle. The Italian Legion had in a few months made the transition from a mere concept to an unruly mob, with nothing much tangible in between. The fact is that, even if they had been up to scratch, there was now no role for them. Cavour, disappointed that Sardinia had achieved virtually nothing by the Peace of Paris, sought to persuade Lord Palmerston that the Legion should be used to further the unification of Italy and deployed against the Kingdom of the Two Sicilies. Unsurprisingly, Palmerston was not keen on this idea and Cavour would have to wait until Garibaldi and the Thousand did their work in 1860.

On 16 May Lord Clarendon, Foreign Secretary, proposed to Hudson that the Legion should be disbanded and that it should leave Malta as soon as possible. Undoing this creation would prove to be almost as difficult as starting it. The Sardinian Government was in no mood to accept nearly 3,000 men of dubious character as its own responsibility, but reluctantly agreed that 1,700 who proved their citizenship could be shipped to Genoa at England's expense, so long as they were disbanded in small groups to minimize the risk of civil disturbance; the balance were Great Britain's problem, and the colonies, as well as Egypt, Algeria and Argentina were suggested as potential homes for them.[6]

In August, those who were prevented from going back to Sardinia were shipped over to England; on the way there was a mutiny and *Tudor,* one of the transport vessels, briefly passed into the hands of a few hotheads until their commanding officer, Major de Horsey (Grenadier Guards), persuaded them to give themselves up.[7] After a brief but somewhat riotous stay in England, Clarendon eventually persuaded the Sardinian Government to take back those stateless legionaries who wished to return to Italy. It was just one year since the first member of the Italian Legion, Henry Percy, had accepted his post.

The ensuing twelve months were filled with recriminations all round. Sir James Hudson, Henry Percy, Edwyn Burnaby and Edward Barrington de Fonblanque all wrote their own post-mortems. Fonblanque saw a private copy of Hudson's paper and told Percy that 'you and I got some harsh hits [in it]'. After a point-by-point rebuttal by Fonblanque, Hudson withdrew his paper. Percy's also, apart from the odd fragment, is lost. Burnaby's was printed in August 1857, under the title *Is it beneath the dignity of a Nation to Employ Foreign Soldiers?* (answer: not necessarily!) Fonblanque, ever the able commissary, produced the most comprehensive paper of all, which, as well as dispassionately going through all the reasons why the enterprise had failed, incorporated a full statement of the expenditure incurred in Turin by the Legion during its year of existence, from recruiting costs right down to the last postage stamp: £89,534,14s,6d.*

* The total expenditure was later put at £195,855 – about £14m in today's money.

215

Panmure was impressed, and ordered that it be printed by the War Department as the official account of what went on that year in Sardinia. When Fonblanque initially set out to write *Observations on the Administration of the British Italian Legion in Sardinia*, he tried his best to be magnanimous to all parties concerned. He felt that Sir James Hudson was 'a right good fellow, but as usual not in "the right place"'; but he soon became exasperated by Hudson's ceaseless attempts to absolve himself of any blame – preferably at Percy's expense. Fonblanque warned his friend to be on his guard, and told him:

> When there was everything to try your temper, you treated all us English Officers with courtesy at all times, and you never addressed to me one word that I should wish to forget. The Italians who knew you regretted your loss to a man, with two exceptions, and those were men who hoped to, and did profit by your absence. Sir James Hudson is, I am told, considered at the FO an expert but not a safe man. He handled the Legion clumsily enough, and considering all we have done for Sardinia, our influence in that country is not what it should be. I have no respect whatever for his character, either public or private.

Percy, however, over-sensitive as always, reckoned that Fonblanque's report did *him* injustice (which it didn't). The author felt that the whole affair was now so buried in oblivion that stirring it up again would do no good:

> I am sorry anything in my paper should have vexed you. It was entirely far from my intention to fail to do you justice, for I was a witness to your exertions and to your difficulties. Read is savage with me for giving you all the credit. Sir J. H. charges me with 'bolstering up a defence' for your 'failure'. Colonel Hudson thinks I hit him harder than he deserves. In short, I please no one which perhaps justifies me in thinking that I have written impartially.

Never again did the British Army attempt to raise significant numbers of recruits from Continental Europe.

Appendix II

The Gallant Grenadier,
by Harry Turner*

The Hon Henry Hugh Manvers Percy
The Heights of Inkerman, 5th November 1854

A grey mist cloaks those rugged heights
With a cloying, damp embrace,
It masks ravines and gullies
And obscures each soldier's face.

The broken ground is treacherous,
Sewn coarse with tufted grass,
And thickets ribbed with dragon's teeth
Over which each man must pass.

On that bleak November morning,
The Russian hordes advance
Towards the Sandbag Battery,
For 'tis here they see their chance.

They've poured forth from Sebastopol,
And seek to drive a wedge
Between the French and British troops,
Then occupy the ledge.

* Reproduced by kind permission of Harry Turner from his book, *Wrapped in Whirlwinds: Poems of the Crimean War* (Spellmount 2005).

A pincer movement is the plan,
And the Russian generals' boast,
To isolate the British on the hill,
Cut all routes to the coast.

The British front line takes the shock
Of the surge of Russian troops,
As they stream in thousands up the slopes
Now emitting fearsome whoops.

Still early in the morning,
For dawn has scarcely broken,
And reinforcements to these British troops
Is now a need unspoken.

Down on the plain below the Heights,
The Brigade of Guards is waking,
Each man responding to the bugle call,
All heroes in the making.

Still groggy from sleep's warm embrace,
That nocturnal paradise,
They snap alert at their sergeant's cry,
Battle-ready in a trice.

No breakfast now, no warming cup,
No time to wash or shave,
No lingering over what lays ahead,
Be it glory or the grave.

The Russians swarm like insects
Onto that fateful hill,
Past sandbags and embrasures,
Each man intent to kill.

Grenadiers are there to face them,
With bayonets and swords,
A steady line of Englishmen
'Gainst howling Russian hordes.

The fighting is ferocious,
Men stab and cut and hack,
The enemy is repulsed, and yet -
Those Tartars have come back!

Six times or more – no man keeps score,
The Sandbag Battery's taken,
Then lost again midst murderous toil,
Each charge faced down and shaken.

The Russians mass and charge again
As they scramble up the slopes,
And for a moment – scarcely more,
They raise up Russian hopes.

The Grenadiers are fading fast,
Their casualties horrific,
They need to rally desperately,
With energy prolific.

Each weary soldier racked with pain,
Lungs burning fit to burst,
And sweat or blood on every brow,
On every lip a curse.

And just ahead, upon the hill,
A heaving, human tide,
A living, breathing testament
To vaulting Russian pride.

The British troops observe this scene,
The hill is thick with Russians
Can they be driven off again
Without fatal repercussions?

But then among those weary men,
The wounded and the dead,
Henry Percy holds his sword aloft
And moves up to their head.

'Now come on boys,' is his trenchant call,
      'Our duty is quite plain,
We must attack, we must go back
      And take that hill again.'

Then into that press of human flesh,
      Now swarming on the hill,
Young Percy plunges, as Russian lunges,
      Surround him for the kill.

He sees the Russian musketeers,
      Fire downhill at his men,
But he finds this 'quite impertinent'
      As he scales the slope again.

Breathless he climbs the parapet,
      Exchanging cuts and blows,
When a chunk of stone is hurled at him,
      Smashing hard into his nose.

The fight around him rages on,
      With the British in full cry,
As Percy regains consciousness,
      Though he's half blind in one eye.

A subaltern revives him
      With brandy from his flask,
And Percy's on his feet again,
      Keen to complete his task.

But now the tide is turning,
      How strange the twists of fate,
For the enemy's retreating fast,
      At a tumbling, stumbling gait.

Although his sight is clouded,
      Henry Percy too has seen
The Russians fanning down the hill
      To St. Clement's great ravine.

He charges now in hot pursuit,
With ninety of his men,
And other troops upon the hill,
Are keen to go again.

Yet just beyond the deep ravine,
Lies a mass of Russian steel,
Packed ranks of gleaming bayonets,
British flesh is soon to feel.

But Percy sees the danger there,
At the gaping mouth of hell,
His gallant lads face certain death
If they tumble down pell-mell.

Half-blinded and face blackened,
Dead soldiers at his feet,
His orders are to 'stand fast',
No advance and no retreat.

'Keep firing lads,' is Percy's cry,
''Till every round is spent,'
But all about the Russians swarm,
Each man on victory bent.

Ammunition is in short supply,
Each moment it grows shorter,
They have to disengage at once,
Or they'll face bloody slaughter.

Here skill and field craft and quick wits
Are now deployed by Percy.
He's seen a bank, close by a spur
That might offer, briefly, mercy.

They find a sheep track on their right,
By Inkerman's great knoll,
But fire, alas, from their own troops,
Adds more death to the toll.

221

And thus, exhausted, wounded,
Henry Percy and his men,
Reach camp at last, depleted,
Having lost a score and ten.

Relief and pride that they've survived,
Is soon replaced by pain
As those unharmed are soon re-armed,
And sent back to fight again.

The battle flares till four o'clock,
But at last is dearly won,
And many thousand men will die
Before the setting of the sun.

The Grenadiers' own losses
Are prodigious on the day,
Forty-six percent are hurt or killed
In that awesome, bloody fray.

But those who live to tell the tale,
Those spared by God's great mercy,
Remember one fine gallant man,
His name, why Henry Percy.

References

References to Henry Percy's papers have not been made in every case, as it is usually obvious from the text. The title of the source is only given when the author has more than one entry in the bibliography.

Introduction (pp xiv–xxix)

1	Bagot
2	Holmes
3	Wheeler
4	Airlie
5	Fonblanque: *Money or Merit*
6	*Vanity Fair*, 14 June 1884
7	*Hansard*, March 1855
8	*Hansard*, March 1855
9	Fonblanque: *Treatise on the Organisation and Administration of the British Army*
10	Cameron
11	Martin
12	Lord Henry Percy: *Election Manifesto* 1865
13	Royle

Chapter 1 Alma (pp 1 – 23)

1	Higginson
2	Tipping
3	Higginson
4	Burgoyne
5	Fergusson
6	Tipping, Hamilton

7	Fergusson
8	Fergusson
9	Brown
10	Tipping
11	Tower, Higginson
12	Higginson
13	Burgoyne
14	Neville papers, Balgonie
15	Fergusson
16	Tipping
17	Fergusson
18	Burgoyne
19	Hibbert
20	Hamilton
21	Wantage
22	Kinglake
23	Hibbert
24	Tipping
25	Hamilton, Hibbert
26	Hamilton, Burnaby: *The Right Flank Company of the 3rd Battalion of the Grenadier Guards at Inkerman*
27	Airlie
28	Royle
29	Neville
30	Higginson
31	W. H. Russell: *The War*

Chapter 2 Balaklava (pp 24–47)

1	A Regimental Officer (Lieutenant Colonel C.T. Wilson)
2	Hibbert
3	Higginson
4	Higginson
5	*The Times*, Friday 13 October 1854
6	Hibbert
7	Higginson papers
8	Hood
9	Hood
10	Higginson
11	Hamilton

12   Cooke
13   A Regimental Officer (Lieutenant Colonel C.T. Wilson)

Chapter 3 Inkerman (pp 48–69)

1   Higginson
2   Balgonie
3   Hibbert
4   Moore
5   Mercer: *'Give them a Volley and Charge!' Inkerman 1854*
6   Hibbert
7   Ross-of-Bladensburg
8   Todleben. Hamilton says 'over 76,000 men'.
9   Massie: *The Crimean War: The Untold Stories*
10   Kinglake
11   Clifford
12   Sir Charles Russell, published in *The Guards Magazine*
13   Hibbert
14   Hamilton
15   Higginson papers
16   Tipping
17   Sir Charles Russell: *ibid.*
18   Kinglake
19   Burnaby: *The Right Flank Company of the 3rd Battalion of the Grenadier Guards at Inkerman*
20   Carmichael
21   Percy: *Rough Notes on Inkerman*
22   Kinglake
23   Hamilton
24   Hamilton
25   Higginson papers
26   Barthorp: *Heroes of the Crimea*
27   Higginson papers
28   Higginson papers
29   Hamley

Chapter 4 Aftermath (pp 70–96)

1   Kinglake
2   Mercer: *'Give them a Volley and Charge!' Inkerman 1854*
3   Mercer: *ibid.*

4   Mercer: *ibid.*
5   Fergusson
6   Hamley
7   Reynardson
8   Percy: *Rough Notes on Inkerman*
9   Hamilton
10   Neville
11   Higginson
12   Neville
13   St. Aubyn
14   Tipping
15   Benson, Esher and Buckle
16   St. Aubyn
17   Kinglake
18   Clifford
19   Maxwell: *Evening Memories*
20   Maxwell: *ibid.*
21   Maxwell: *The Life and Letters of the Fourth Earl of Clarendon*
22   Neville
23   Neville
24   Neville
25   Percy

Chapter 5 Winter Siege (pp 97–121)

1   Higginson
2   Hibbert
3   W. H. Russell: *The War*
4   W. H. Russell: *ibid.*
5   Royle
6   Skene
7   St. Aubyn
8   St. Aubyn
9   Eyre-Todd
10   *The Times,* 23 Feb 1857
11   Percy
12   Percy
13   A Regimental Officer (Lieutenant-Colonel C.T. Wilson)
14   W. H. Russell: *The War*
15   Percy
16   *Hansard* Vol. 137, 1206

Chapter 6 Nurses and Hospitals (pp 122–145)

1   Burgoyne papers
2   Small
3   Hamilton
4   Balgonie
5   Woodham-Smith: *Florence Nightingale*
6   W. H. Russell: *The War*
7   Davis
8   Stanmore
9   Small
10 Woodham-Smith: *ibid.*
11 Stanmore
12 Woodham-Smith: *ibid.*
13 Woodham-Smith: *ibid.*
14 Davis
15 Robinson
16 *Hansard* Vol 136, 19 Feb 1855
17 Small
18 Woodham-Smith: *ibid.*
19 Woodham-Smith: *ibid.*
20 Small

Chapter 7 1855: New Resolution (pp 146–171)

1   Kinglake
2   Kinglake
3   Hibbert
4   Calthorpe
5   Hibbert
6   Kinglake
7   Bayley
8   Hamilton
9   Airlie
10 Hibbert
11 Balgonie
12 Higginson
13 Airlie
14 Airlie
15 Hamilton
16 Kinglake

17   Percy
18   Hibbert
19   Cooke
20   Kinglake
21   Kinglake
22   Kinglake
23   Kinglake
24   Hibbert
25   Kinglake
26   Hibbert
27   Skene
28   Hibbert

Chapter 8 Pyrrhic Victory (pp 172–193)

1   Higginson
2   Bayley
3   Bayley
4   Fonblanque: *Observations on the Administration of the British Italian Legion in Sardinia*
5   Bayley
6   ffrench Blake and Cooke
7   Fletcher and Ishchenko
8   W. H. Russell: *The War*
9   W. H. Russell: *ibid.*
10   Clifford
11   Higginson
12   Higginson
13   ffrench Blake
14   Royle
15   Royle
16   Hamilton
17   Percy
18   Baumgart

Epilogue (pp 194–210)

1   *The London Gazette*, 24 Feb 1857
2   Public Record Office: WO 32/703
3   W. H. Russell: *The War*
4   Crook

5   Public Record Office: WO 32/703
6   *The London Gazette*, 7 May 1857
7   Hamilton
8   Crook
9   Crook
10   Burnaby (Grenadier Archives)
11   *The Times*, 27 June 1857
12   *The Illustrated London News*, 4 July 1857
13   *The Times*, 27 June 1857
14   Lambert and Badsey
15   Wantage
16   *The Illustrated London News*, 4 July 1857
17   Higginson
18   Higginson
19   Bruce
20   Hamilton
21   *The Morning Post*, Wed 5 Dec 1877
22   *The Morning Post, The Newcastle Daily Journal* etc. 8 Dec
        1877

Appendix I (pp 211–216)

1   Bayley
2   *The Globe*, 10 December 1855
3   Bayley
4   Bayley
5   Bayley
6   Bayley
7   Hamilton

Bibliography

Adkin, Mark: *The Charge* (1996)

Airlie, Mabel, Countess of: *With the Guards we shall Go* (1933)

Aloysius, Sister Mary: *Memories of the Crimea* (1897)

Bagot, Mrs. Charles: *Links with the Past* (1902)

Baring Pemberton, W.: *Battles of the Crimean War* (1962)

Barthorp, Michael: *Heroes of the Crimea* (1991)

Barthorp, Michael: *Crimean Uniforms: British Infantry* (1974)

Bayley, C.C.: *Mercenaries for the Crimea* (1977)

Baumgart, Winfried: *The Crimean War* (1999)

Benson, Esher and Buckle: *Letters of Queen Victoria* (1906–1930)

Bentley, Nicholas: *Russell's Despatches from the Crimea 1854–56* (1966)

Blackwood, Lady A.: *A Narrative of Personal Experiences and Expressions during a Residence on the Bosphorus during the Crimean War* (1881)

Bostock, J.A.: *Letters from India and the Crimea* (1896)

Brenan, Gerald: *History of the House of Percy (1902)*

Brown, D.K.: *Before the Ironclad: Development of Ship Design, Propulsion and Armament in the Royal Navy, 1815–60* (1990)

Bruce, Anthony: *The Purchase System in the British Army* (1980)

Burgoyne, Sir John M.: *Some Bedfordshire Diaries* (1960)

Burnaby, Major E.S.: *The Right Flank Company of the 3rd Battalion of the Grenadier Guards at Inkerman* (Privately printed 1857)

Burnaby, Major E.S.: *Is it beneath the Dignity of a Nation to employ Foreign Soldiers?* (1857)

Calthorpe, Lt. Col. S.J. Gough: *Letters from Headquarters* (1856)

Clark, Major Frank A.O.: *Through Hell to Immortality: The First Suffolk Soldier to win the Victoria Cross* (Privately printed)

Clarke, Sir George Sydenham: *Atlas to Illustrate Kinglake's Invasion of the Crimea* (1899)

Cler, General: *Reminiscences of an Officer of Zouaves* (1860)

Clifford, Henry, VC: *Letters and Sketches from the Crimea* (1956)

Cooke, Brian: *The Grand Crimean Central Railway* (1990)

Compton, P.: *Colonel's Lady and Camp Follower: the Story of Women in the Crimean War* (1970)

Crook, M.J.: *The Evolution of the Victoria Cross* (1975)

Davis, Elizabeth: *The Autobiography of a Balaclava Nurse* (1857)

Eyre-Todd, G.: *Autobiography of William Simpson RI* (1908)

ffrench Blake, R.L.V.: *The Crimean War* (1971)

Fletcher, Ian; and Ishchenko, Natalia: *The Crimean War: A Clash of Empires* (2004)

Fonblanque, E.B. de: *Observations on the Administration of the British Italian Legion in Sardinia* (1856)

Fonblanque, E.B. de: *Money or Merit. The Army Purchase Question Considered* (1857)

Fonblanque, E.B. de: *Treatise on the Administration and Organisation of the British Army, with especial reference to Finance and Supply* (1858)

Fonblanque, E.B. de: *Annals of the House of Percy* (1888)

Gernsheim, H. & A.: *Fenton, Photographer of the Crimean War* (1954)

Hamilton, Lt. Gen. Sir F.W.: *History of the Grenadier Guards* (1874)

Hamley, Lt. Col. E. Bruce: *The Story of the Campaigns of Sebastopol* (1855)

Hibbert, Christopher: *The Destruction of Lord Raglan* (1961)

Higginson, General Sir George: *Seventy-One Years of a Guardsman's Life* (1916)

Holmes, Richard: *Redcoat* (2001)

Jagow, K. von: *Letters of the Prince Consort* (1938)

James, Lawrence: *Crimea 1854–56, from contemporary photographs* (1981)

Kinglake, A.W.: *The Invasion of the Crimea, Vols I-VIII* (1866–1887)

Knollys, Major: *The Victoria Cross in the Crimea* (1870)

Lambert, A. and Badsey, S.: *The War Correspondents: The Crimean War* (1994)

Lane-Poole, S.: *Life of Stratford Canning* (1888)

Lawson, George (ed. V. Bonham-Carter): *Surgeon in the Crimea* (1968)

Maxwell, Sir Herbert: *The Life and Letters of the Fourth Earl of Clarendon* (1913)

Maxwell, Sir Herbert: *Evening Memories* (1932)

Malcolm Smith, E.F.: *The Life of Stratford Canning* (1933)

Martin, Sir Theodore: *The Life of HRH the Prince Consort* (1875–80)

231

Massie, Dr. Alastair: *A Most Desperate Undertaking* (2003)

Massie, Dr. Alastair: *The Crimean War: The Untold Stories* (2004)

Mercer, Patrick: *'Give them a Volley and Charge!' Inkerman 1854* (1998)

Mercer, Patrick: *Inkerman 1854: The Soldiers' Battle* (1998)

Moore, Geoffrey: *Vincent of the 41st* (Privately printed 1979)

Neville, the Hon Henry and the Hon Grey: *Letters written from Turkey and the Crimea, 1854* (Privately printed 1870)

Nolan, E.H.: *History of the War against Russia* (1857)

Percy, Lt. Col. the Hon H.H.M.: *Brigade Movements* (1853)

Ramsay, Sir G. Douglas & Sir G.: *The Panmure Papers* (1908)

Regimental Officer, A (Lt. Col. C.T. Wilson): *Our Veterans of 1854* (1859)

Robinson, Assistant Surgeon General F.: *Diary of the Crimean War* (1856)

Robinson, Jane: *Mary Seacole: The Charismatic Black Nurse Who Became a Heroine of the Crimea* (2005)

Ross-of-Bladensburg, Lt. Col.: *The Coldstream Guards in the Crimea* (1897)

Russell, W.H.: *The War, Vols I & II* (1855–56)

Russell, W.H.: *General Todleben's History of the Defence of Sebastopol 1854–55: A Review* (1864)

Russell, W.H.: *The British Expedition to the Crimea* (1877)

Royle, Trevor: *Crimea: The Great Crimean War 1854–56* (1999)

St. Aubyn, Giles: *The Royal George: The life of HRH Prince George Duke of Cambridge 1819–1904* (1963)

Simpson, W.: *The Seat of the War in the East* (1855)

Skene, J.H.: *With Lord Stratford in the Crimean War* (1883)

Small, Hugh: *Florence Nightingale: Avenging Angel* (1998)

Stanmore, Lord: *Memoirs of Sidney Herbert* (1906)

Taylor, Francis M.: *Eastern Hospitals and English Nurses* (1851)

Tolstoy, Leo: *The Sebastopol Sketches* (1855–56)

Thayer, W.R.: *The Life and Times of Cavour* (1911)

Trevelyan, Sir Charles: *The Army Purchase Question, and Report and Minutes of the Royal Commission Considered* (1858)

Trevelyan, Sir Charles: *The Purchase System in the British Army* (1867)

Wantage, Lady: *Lord Wantage, VC, KCB: A Memoir* (1907)

Wheeler, Captain Owen: *The War Office Past and Present* (1914)

Wilkins, P.A.: *The History of the Victoria Cross* (1904)

Windham, Lt. Gen. Sir Charles Ashe: *Crimean Diaries and Letters* (1897)

Woodham-Smith, Cecil: *Florence Nightingale* (1950)

Woodham-Smith, Cecil: *The Reason Why* (1953)

Newspapers etc.

Hansard
The Berwick Journal
The Globe
The Guards Magazine
The Household Brigade Magazine
The Illustrated London News
The London Gazette
The Morning Herald
The Morning Post
The Newcastle Daily Journal
The Times

Manuscripts

Amherst, Lieutenant the Hon William Archer: *Letters* (National Army Museum)

Balgonie, Lord: *Correspondence and Papers* (The Earl of Leven and Melville)

Burgoyne, Lieutenant J.M.: *Letters* (Bedfordshire County Council)

Cameron, Captain W.: *Correspondence and Papers* (National Army Museum)

Carmichael, Lt. Col. G. L.: *Notes on the Battle of Inkerman* (National Army Museum)

Fergusson, Sir James: *Correspondence and Papers* (Sir Charles Fergusson, Bt.)

Hood, Col. the Hon Grosvenor: *Correspondence and Papers* (National Army Museum)

Officers of the Grenadier Guards: *Assorted Papers (Burnaby, Higginson, Henry Neville, Reynardson and Sir Charles Russell)* (Grenadier Guards Archives)

Percy, Col. the Hon Henry: *Correspondence, Notes and Papers* (Duke of Northumberland)

Percy, Col. the Hon Henry: *Diaries* (Staffordshire County Council)

Public Record Office: *War Office files*

Ridley, Colonel C.W.: *Letters* (The Viscount Ridley and the National Army Museum)

Tipping, Captain Alfred: *Diaries* (E. Skipwith Esq.)

Tower, Captain H.: *Diaries* (National Army Museum)

Index

Note, serving officers of the 3rd Battalion Grenadier Guards, with both their regimental and army ranks, are set in bold.

Abbott, Tpr., 49
Aberdeen, 4th Earl of, xxvii–iii, 114, 119, 144
Ablett, Pte. Alfred, VC, 183, 184, 194, 201
Acorn, 143
Adams, Brig. Gen., 82
Airey, Quartermaster General R., 25, 106, 167
Albert of Saxe-Coburg-Gotha, Prince, xxiii, xxv, 1, 90, 96, 151, 153, 195–197, 202
Aldershot, xxiii, 208
Algar, Sgt. Maj., 61, 73
Alma, 12–23, 40, 192
Aloushta, 156
Amherst, Lt. the Hon W. Archer, 54, 81, 116–117, 152
Anstruther Lt. H., 22
Armenia, 189, 190
Austria, 152, 174, 193
Azof, Sea of, 160

Bagot, Charles, 42, 153
Baidar, 159
Bakshi Seräi, 192
Balaklava, capture, 27;

description, 32; Battle of, 44–49; in hurricane, 98–101
Balgonie, Lt. & Capt. Lord, 3, 5, 50, 128, 129
Baltic Sea, 6
Bancroft, Pte. James, 61, 67, 210
Barents Sea, 6
Barrack Hospital, Scutari, 138, 142
Barrier, the, 54–55, 64
Bathhurst, Lt. & Capt. Frederick., 128
Belbec, River, 24
Bentinck, Brig. Gen., 14, 55, 82, 96, 112, 113, 157
Bessarabia, xxviii, 43
Beverley, 1st Earl of, xx
Beverley, 2nd Earl of, xx, 41, 90, 103, 108, 112–113, 124, 127, 129, 148, 155, 208
Bomarsund, 6
Bourliouk, 13
Bracebridge, Mr & Mrs Charles, 92, 137, 153
Brackenbury, Mr, 141, 151
Bradford, Capt. & Lt. Col. Ralph., 11, 121
Braybrooke, 3rd Baron, 82, 91, 94
Brigade of Guards (Grenadier Gds., Coldstream Gds., Scots

Fusilier Gds.), casualties, 19, 70–71, 192; strength, 74, 155, 157, 158
Britannia, 6
Britannic, 114
British Army, see under Cavalry, Infantry etc.
British Italian Legion, 173–183, 190, 211–216
Brown, Maj. Gen. Sir George, 82, 160, 167
Brownrigg, Lt. Col. Studholme, 106, 209
Brunel, I. K., 166
Bulganak, River, 12
Burghersh, Lord, 111
Burgoyne, Ensign & Lt. J. Montague., 16, 21, 41, 123
Burgoyne, Lt. Gen. Sir John, 31, 105, 106, 167
Burnaby, Lt. & Capt. Edwyn S., 60, 61, 66–67, 77, 128, 176, 179, 199, 200, 209, 211–215

Cadogan, Capt. & Lt. Col. the Hon George, 2, 22, 59, 61, 64–65, 67, 68, 120, 129, 136, 154, 168
Caesar, 140, 141, 152
Calamita Bay, 10, 50
Cambridge, Lt. Gen. HRH

Prince George, Duke of, 16, 17, 27, 44, 64, 65, 68, 77–80, 82, 99–100, 102, 105, 111–112, 133–134, 195, 197, 202, 209

Cameron Lt. & Capt. William G., xxiv–v, 3, 37, 38

Campbell, Brig. Gen. Sir Colin, 171, 203–205

Campbell, Brig. Gen. Sir John, 163

Canada, xxiii, 104, 205, 206

Canrobert, Gen., 51, 64, 68

Caradoc, 27, 170

Cardigan, 7th Earl of, xxi, 44, 120, 121

Cardwell Reforms, xx, 209

Careenage Ravine, 51–53, 68

Carmichael, Lt. Col., 62

Caruana, Vincenzo, 214

Cathcart, Lt. Gen, 2nd Earl (1783–1859), 91

Cathcart, Lt. Gen. Sir George (1794–1854), 45, 65, 66, 82

Cavalry, British, 12, 26, 44–47, 49, 50, 70, 71, 196

Cavour, Count, 174, 175, 213, 214

Chenery, Thomas, 28

Cholera, 3, 6, 8, 9, 12, 25, 27, 28, 30, 38, 168

Christmas 1854, 127–129, 148

Clarendon, 4th Earl of, 89, 179, 189, 215

Cler, Gen. Gustave, 108, 169, 183

Clifford, Lt. the Hon Henry, VC, 55, 80, 188

Codrington, Gen., 185, 191

Col Road, 101

Colombo, 29, 30, 130

Commissariat Dept., xxii–xxiii, 6, 11, 101, 103, 104

Constantine, Archduke, 81

Cook, Sgt. Reuben, 148

Cornwallis, Capt. the Hon C. C., 118

Corunna, xix

Cox, Capt. & Lt. Col. Augustus, 5, 27, 28, 38

Crimean Army Fund, 141, 146–148

Crimean War, causes, xxvii–xxix; conclusion, 191–193

Cumming, Dr., 134

Cust, Capt. Horace, 14

Dannenberg, Gen, 53

Danubian Principalities, see Moldavia & Wallachia

Davies, Ensign & Lt. F. Byam, 37

Davis, Elizabeth, 142, 143

Dawson, Lt. Col. the Hon T. Vesey, 79, 91

De Horsey, Major W. H. B., 215

Drummond, Capt. the Hon James, RN, 30, 31, 79, 99, 100, 102, 103, 128

Duberly, Fanny, 156

Dundas, Admiral, 114

Dunkellin, Lord, 114, 115, 152

Egerton, Hon Algernon, 146, 147

Ellesmere, Earl of, 146

Erminia, 146

Erzerum, 189

Estcourt, Maj. Gen., 82, 97, 103, 106, 107, 156, 168

Eupatoria, 9

Evans, Lt. Gen. Sir G. de Lacy, 66, 82

Fedioukine Heights, 101, 183

Fergusson, Ensign & Lt. Sir James, Bt., 4, 5, 11, 15, 17, 27, 73, 102, 3, 128, 200

Fisher, Lt. A'Court, 164

Flagstaff Bastion, 34, 166

Fonblanque, E. B. de, xx, xxi, 111, 176, 181, 215, 216

Foreign Enlistment Act, 150, 173

Forth, Lord, 87

Fortnum & Mason, 85, 86

General Hospital, Scutari, 136, 138

Genitchi, 171

Georgia, 190, 191

Golden Fleece, 2

Goldie, Brig. Gen., 82

Goodlake, Captain Gerald, VC, 51, 52, 194

Gordon's Battery, 34

Gortschakoff, Prince, 18, 46, 53, 68

Gregory, Arthur, 38, 9, 42, 43, 86, 91

Gregory, Mrs, 38, 86, 91

Greville, Lt., 75

Grey, 3rd Earl, 149

Guards' Camp, today, xv; in 1854, 34, 55, 74, 97, 103; in 1855, 155–158

Guernsey, Lady, 136, 142

Hamilton, Col. Frederick W., xxiii, 4, 16, 66, 128, 205

Hamilton, Ensign & Lt. Robert W., 16, 102, 128

Harcourt, Col., 120

Hardinge, Viscount, 90, 113, 172, 195

Hatton, Capt. V. Latouche., 35, 43, 58, 65, 90, 113, 114, 118, 148

Haygarth, Lt. Col. F., 22

Hayter & Howell, 117, 119

Heavy Brigade, 4, 26, 44–46, 49, 196

Herbert, Elizabeth, 122, 124, 143

Herbert, Sidney, 116, 122, 124, 125, 131, 132, 142–144

Higginson, Capt. George W., 2, 5, 9, 11, 21, 22, 27, 35, 37, 58, 65, 66, 68, 70, 74, 77, 89, 90, 102, 104, 109, 112, 128–30, 173, 183, 188, 200, 206

Hill, Quartermaster
Sergeant, 65
Holmesdale, Lord & Lady,
54, 91, 116
Home Ridge, 54, 55, 72
**Hood, Col. the Hon F.
Grosvenor**, 5, 15, 17,
21, 27, 36, 37, 38, 39,
42, 58, 113, 198
Hotspur, Harry, 64, 90
Hudson, Sir James,
174–176, 179, 181,
182, 211–216
Hudson, Col. Joseph, 174,
179–182, 216
Hunter Blair, Lt. Col.
James, 102
Hurricane of 14 Nov.
1855, 97–101
Hydaspes, 4, 28, 30

Inkerman, today, ix, xvi;
Battle of, 51–76;
despatch, 109, 110,
195
Infantry, British, 1st
Division, 16–18, 71;
2nd Division, 55, 56,
61, 66, 68, 71; 4th
Division, 45, 163; Light
Division, 16, 20–21,
163; 23rd Royal Welch
Fusiliers, xix, 17, 18,
51; 41st Regiment, 51;
93rd Regiment, 6, 44;
95th Regiment, 18, 62
Italian Legion, see British
Italian Legion

Jackett, Pte. George, 82,
129
Jesse, Capt., 164
Jocelyn, Lt. Col. the Hon
Strange, 155–158, 165

Kadikoi, 146
Kamiesch, 32, 53, 107,
158, 170
Kars, 189–191, 208
Katcha, River, 20, 24
Kertch, 160, 161
Kinglake, A. W., 17, 54,
147, 164, 170
Kitspur, 54, 63, 65, 66
Knollys, W. W., 59
Knox, Lt. J. S. VC, 202

Kola, 6
Korniloff, Vice Admiral,
26, 34
Koulali, 137, 155
Kourgané Hill, 12
Kronstadt, 39

Lansdowne, 3rd Marquess
of, 154
Leipzig, Battle of, xxviii
Light Brigade, 26, 44–47,
70, 71, 196
**Lindsay, Capt. & Lt. Col.
the Hon Charles**,
59–61, 128
Lindsay, Sir Coutts, Bt.,
212
Lindsay, Ensign & Lt.
Robert, VC, 17, 38, 61,
173, 194, 202
Liprandi, General, 43, 161
'Little Inkerman', 45–47,
49, 105
Lobanoff-Rostoff, Princess,
xxvi
London Gazette, The, 86,
94, 194, 197, 198
Lovaine, Lord, xx, xxii,
xxiv, xxv, 42, 85–89,
108, 119, 149, 150,
153, 182, 208, 209
Lucan, 3rd Earl of, 26, 44
Lyons, Rear Admiral Sir
Edward, 114

Mackenzie's Farm, 25
Malacca, 140, 151
Malakoff Redoubt, 34, 35,
161–166, 184, 186,
188
Malta, 2, 4, 134
Mamelon, 161, 162
Manilla, 1
Marmora, Gen. Alfonso
De La, 154, 155, 159,
168, 172, 174, 183
Maxwell, Sir Herbert, 89
Mayran, Gen., 163, 166
Meade, Lady S., 91, 92
Medical Dept., xxii–xxiii,
42, 123, 134
Mentschikoff, Prince, 26,
28, 53, 80
Menzies, Dr, 134
Meyer, Dr, 124, 132, 134

Militia Regiments, 85, 149,
150
Militia (Service Abroad)
Act, 149, 150, 152
Minié rifles, 2, 19, 20, 26,
57, 72
Mitchell, Lt. & Capt. A.,
126, 134
Moldavia, xxviii, 3, 6
Moore, Gen. Sir John, xix
Morning Herald, The, 58,
88–90
**Munro, Lt. & Capt.
Campbell**, 5
Muravieff, Gen., 189–191

Napier, Sir William,
119–121
Napoleon III, Emperor, xii,
xxviii, 151, 162, 174
Neville, Capt. Edward, 76,
77
Neville, Capt. the Hon
Grey, 4, 10, 44, 48, 49,
92–96
**Neville, Lt. & Capt. the
Hon Henry**, 2, 4, 5, 15,
17, 28, 32, 48, 49, 58,
75–78, 82, 92–96
Neville, Hon Richard, 75,
95, 6
Newcastle, 5th Duke of,
122, 132, 144, 169,
173
**Newman, Lt. & Capt. Sir
Robert**, 74
Nicholas I, Tsar, xxviii, 54
Nightingale, Miss Florence,
92, 122–124, 131–137,
142–145, 153, 169
Nikolayeff, 105
Nolan, Capt. L., 44
Northumberland, 4th
Duke of, xx
Northumberland, 5th
Duke of, see Beverley,
2nd Earl of
Northumberland, 6th
Duke of, see Lovaine
Northumberland, 9th
Duke of, x
Northumberland Light
Infantry, 149

Odessa, 6
Okhotsk Regiment, 65, 67

236

Omar Pasha, 189, 191
Orr, James, 5th DG, 95

Paget, Lord George, 120, 121, 156
Pakenham, Capt. & Lt. Col. Edward, 19, 40, 75, 112, 116
Palmer, Pte. Anthony, VC, 60, 194, 202
Palmerston, 3rd Viscount, xxvii, 132, 149, 179, 189, 201
Panmure, Lord, 132, 144, 145, 155, 163, 173–182, 197, 199, 216
Patriotic Fund, 115, 116, 127, 147
Paulet, Lord William, 137, 138
Pauloff, Gen., 72
Pélissier, Gen., 162, 163, 169, 170
Pennefather, Brig. Gen., 55
Percy, Algernon, see Lovaine, Lord
Percy, Caroline Greatheed-Bertie-, 38, 39, 81, 90–92, 146, 151–153
Percy, Hon Charles Greatheed-Bertie-, 38, 39, 81, 90–92, 151–153
Percy, Capt. the Hon. Francis, xix
Percy, Major the Hon Henry (1785–1825), xix, 119
Percy, Capt. & Lt. Col. the Hon Henry, VC, views on Lord Raglan, 7, 41, 106, 109, 120, 121, 167–168; at Alma, 15–20, 40; on Duke of Cambridge, 27, 41, 77; on Balaklava, 44–6, at Inkerman, 57–66, 81–84; 2nd arrival in the Crimea, 155; at General Hospital, Scutari, 136–138; commands B.I.L., 175–183; 3rd arrival in Crimea, 191; later years, 205–210

Percy, Isabel Greatheed-Bertie-, 7, 31, 90–92, 105–107, 138–141, 146
Percy, Vice Admiral the Hon Josceline, xix, 42, 126, 130, 153
Percy, Hon Josceline, MP, 122, 124–127, 129, 131–137, 141–145, 153
Percy, Lady Louisa, 31, 39, 42, 85, 87, 88, 117–119, 125, 138, 146, 152
Percy, Lady Margaret, 41, 118, 119, 152
Percy, Rear Admiral the Hon William, xix, 92, 126, 130, 153, 178
Petropaulovsk, 6, 87
Ponsonby, Lt. & Capt. Ashley, 105
Post Road, 53–55
Preziosi, Vittorio Amadeo, 5th Count, 127
Price, Admiral, 87
Prince, 99
Prince of Wales, xxv, 205
Purcell, L/Cpl., 62
Purchase System, xx–xxiv, 111, 206–209
Putrid Sea, 171

Quarry Ravine, 53
Queen of the South, 105

Raglan, Lady, 153
Raglan, Field Marshal Lord, xxvii, 4 ,7, 8, 10, 16, 25, 26, 33, 41, 42, 44, 78, 105–110, 133, 147, 162–164, 168–170
Ragni, Angelo, 133, 135, 136
Read, Lt. Col. C., 179, 180, 211–214
Redan, the Great, 34, 161–166, 170, 184–186, 188
Resolute, 99
Retribution, 30, 31, 33, 79, 99, 100, 125
Reynardson, Col. Edward

Birch-, xvi, 58, 73, 90, 112, 113, 118, 128
Ridley, Col. Charles W., 73, 113, 155
Ripon, 1
Roebuck, J. A., MP, 144
Rokeby, Maj. Gen., 6th Baron, 96, 113, 143, 155–158, 171, 172, 193, 195
Roll Call, The, painting by Elizabeth Thompson, later Lady Butler, 74
Rose, Mrs, 133, 135
Rowlands, Capt. Hugh, VC, 52
Rowley, Lt. & Capt. A. Evelyn, 34, 37
Royal Albert, 117, 133
Russell, Lt. & Capt. Sir Charles, Bt., VC, 3–5, 59–61, 65, 67, 70, 75, 77, 128, 140, 194, 200, 201
Russell, W. H., 22, 3, 98, 130, 170, 187, 195, 200

St Arnaud, Marshal A., 24
St Clement's Ravine, 62–64, 66, 72
St Jean d'Arc, 152
Salisbury, Marchioness of, 89
Sandbag Battery, ix, xvi, 54–67, 71, 74, 80, 110, 194, 198
Sanitary Commission, 144–145
Sapoune Heights, 32, 43, 53
Saxe-Weimar, Brevet Major HH Prince Edward of, 7, 37, 55, 78–80, 112, 128, 172
Scutari, 2, 3, 29, 92, 125, 130–138, 142–145, 148, 153
Sebastopol, possible *coup de main*, 25; First Bombardment, 34, 35, 43; Second Bombardment, 159; Third Bombardment, 161; Fourth Bombardment, 162;

assault of 18 June, 162–166; Fifth Bombardment, 183; Sixth Bombardment, 183; assault of 8 Sept., 184–188

Seacole, Mrs. Mary, 143

Selim Pasha, 189

Seymour, Col. Charles, 82

Seymour, Gaddy, 91

Shell Hill, 53, 72

Silistria, 3, 4, 53

Simferopol, 26

Simoom, 8, 9

Simpson, Gen. Sir James, 172, 180, 195

Simpson, William, xiv, 101, 128

Sinope, xxviii–xxix, 31

Smolensk, 45

Soimonoff, Gen., 72

Somerset, the Hon Charlotte, 39, 42

Stacey, Pte. Thomas, 118, 148, 149

Stanley, Miss Mary, 124, 132, 142

Star Fort, 25

Stratford de Redcliffe, Lady, 93, 137, 138, 155, 156

Stratford de Redcliffe, Viscount, 107, 125, 156, 189–191, 193

Sturt, Ensign & Lt. C. Napier, 56, 58, 75, 76, 96

Suvoroff, Field Marshal, 84

Tartars, xiv, 11, 160, 161, 192

Taylor, Frances, 143

Tchernaya, Battle of, 183

Tchernaya, River, 26, 32, 51, 54, 56, 75, 76, 78, 96, 101, 158, 159

Telegraph, electric, 36, 39, 40, 85, 90, 169, 172, 173

Thompson, Elizabeth, 74

Times, The, 28, 42, 88, 102, 115, 123, 127, 130, 147, 148, 150, 166, 195, 201, 203

Tipping, Lt. & Capt. Alfred, 3, 12–14

Todleben, Lt. Col. F., 26

Torrens, Brig. Gen., 82

Tower, Capt. Harvey, 25, 56

Tower, Thomas, 146, 147

Tribune, 136

Tudor, 215

Turkish Army, 43, 44, 53, 104, 189–191

Turner, Ensign & Lt. Charles H., 66

Varna, 3, 4, 6, 8–10, 30, 42, 100, 111, 122

Verschoyle, Ensign & Lt. Henry W., 56, 66, 128

Victoria, Queen, 7, 10, 78, 151, 153, 158, 172, 195–197, 199, 202–204

Victoria Cross, ix, x, xv, 17, 52, 55, 60, 110, 184, 210; origin, 194–200; first investiture, 200–205

Vladimir Regiment, 18

Vulcan, 28

Wallachia, xxviii, 3,6

Ward, Lord, xix, 156, 157

Waterloo, xxvii, 7, 8, 53, 119, 156, 162, 166

Wellington, Duke of, xix, 7, 8

Wellway, 55, 80

Williams, Brig. Gen. William Fenwick, 189–191, 208

Wilson, Lt. Col. C. T., 111

Windham, Col. Charles Ashe, 185

Wood, Col. Thomas, 73, 90, 112, 113, 197, 200

Woronzoff Palace, xv, 157

Woronzoff Road, 43, 44, 101

Wyndham-Quin, Lt. & Capt. the Hon Windham H., 155

Yalta, xiv, xv, 157

Yacht Committee & private yachts, 118, 126, 147

Yea, Col., 164, 165

Zouaves, xxvii, 68, 107, 141, 156